'Laws are like cobwebs, which may catch small flies, but let wasps and hornets break through.'

Jonathan Swift (1667–1745)

For Abolition: Essays on Prisons and Socialist Ethics
David Scott

ISBN 978-1-909976-82-5 (Paperback)
ISBN 978-1-909976-83-2 (Epub ebook)
ISBN 978-1-909976-84-9 (Adobe ebook)

Copyright © 2020 This work is the copyright of David Scott. All intellectual property and associated rights are hereby asserted and reserved by the author in full compliance with UK, European and international law. No part of this book may be copied, reproduced, stored in any retrieval system or transmitted in any form or by any means, including in hard copy or via the internet, without the prior written permission of the publishers to whom all such rights have been assigned worldwide.

Cover design © 2020 Waterside Press by www.gibgob.com

Main UK distributor Gardners Books, 1 Whittle Drive, Eastbourne, BN23 6QH. Tel: (+44) 01323 521777; sales@gardners.com; www.gardners.com

North American distribution Ingram Book Company, One Ingram Blvd, La Vergne, TN 37086, USA. Tel: (+1) 615 793 5000; inquiry@ingramcontent.com

Cataloguing In-Publication Data A catalogue record for this book can be obtained from the British Library.

Printed by Severn, Gloucester, UK.

Ebook *For Abolition* is available as an ebook including via library models.

Published 2020 by
Waterside Press Ltd
Sherfield Gables
Sherfield on Loddon, Hook
Hampshire RG27 0JG.

Telephone +44(0)1256 882250
Online catalogue WatersidePress.co.uk
Email enquiries@watersidepress.co.uk

For Abolition
Essays on Prisons and Socialist Ethics

David Scott

❅ WATERSIDE PRESS

Table of Contents

About the author *ix*
The author of the Foreword *ix*
Acknowledgements *x*
Dedication *xiii*
Publisher's note *xiv*
Table of Cases *xv*
Endorsements *17*

Foreword 21

Preface 25

1 **The Prison Puzzle and Socialist Ethics:
   Making the Case for Abolition** 33

   Prisons: the puzzle we cannot solve *34*

       Prison labour: enforced idleness or penal slavery? *36*

       Education: learning new crimes or reinforcing failure? *37*

       Relationships on the outside: intensifying pains or natal alienation? *37*

       Relationships on the inside: isolation or forced relationality? *38*

       Taking responsibility: coerced sense of duty or no moral choices? *39*

       Life and wellbeing: failed-treatments or undermining health? *39*

   A place of death: 'negative ethics' *41*

   The ethics of life: 'affirmative ethics' *45*

   Conclusion: socialist ethics, human rights and abolitionist activism *48*

2 Abolitionist Ethical Hermeneutics:
Hearing and Interpreting Voice 51

    Interpreting prisoner narratives in situational context *54*

    Negative consequentialism *56*

    Discourse ethics *58*

    Virtue ethics *61*

    Libertarian socialist liberation ethics *63*

    Abolitionist ethical hermeneutics *65*

    Critical judgement *67*

    When the estranged Other cannot speak *68*

    Six conditions of speaking *72*

    Conclusion: learning to learn *73*

3 Invisible Brutal Hands:
The Problem of Prison Officer Violence 75

    Legitimacy and visibility *77*

    Which voices are heard? *79*

    The prisoners' tale: prison officer violence in historical context *80*

    The prison officers' tale: recollections and justifications *92*

        Turning a blind eye 92

        Masking Violence 93

        Normalisation 95

        Payback 96

        Pathological prisoners 97

    Conclusion *97*

4 Phantom Faces at the Window:
Prisons, Dignity and Moral Exclusion 99

    Face and acknowledgement *100*

    Moral inclusion *102*

    Moral exclusion *105*

        Width of imprisonment 107

        The indignities of prison life 109

    Ethical questions *120*

5 **Prison is Not a Home:**
   Estrangement and the Prison Zone of Abandonment 121
   - There is no place like home *123*
   - Warehousing the unwanted *125*
   - Institutionally-structured violence *127*
   - Legitimate abandonment *129*
   - Solidarity with the unwanted *136*

6 **Falling Softly to Your Grave:**
   Time Consciousness and the Death-bound Subject............................ 139
   - Time and the death-bound subject *141*
   - Freedom, relationships, place and the lived experience of prison time *144*
   - Psychological survival — coping with prison time? *153*
   - Hurtling towards death consciousness *156*

7 **Abolitionism as a Philosophy of Hope:**
   System 'Inside-Outsiders', Freedom and the Reclaiming of Democracy..161
   - Pedagogy beyond the neo-liberal university *165*
   - Organic collective intellectuals *167*
   - Reclaiming democracy *171*
     - *We should hear diverse voices and write what we like* *172*
     - *Researching and platforming subjugated and marginalised voices* *173*
     - *Expert witness to the courts* *175*
     - *Testifying for freedom in official submissions to the state* *176*
     - *Contesting state-corporate power* *178*
     - *Selective engagement with the existing media and creating new forms of media* *179*
     - *Building communities and the production of insurgent knowledge* *181*
   - Freedom, hope, and praxis *182*

8 **Ordinary Rebels, Everyone:**
   Abolitionist Scholarship and the Struggle for Freedom 185
         Seven rules of engagement for activist scholars *188*
             Challenging privilege 189
             Recognition and the relational dimension 190
             Accountability to the community 191
             Levelling up and capacity-building 191
             Consciousness-raising among the populace 192
             Building new alliances and power bloc based on difference 192
             Community spaces and the agora 192
         The encounter: penal abolitionism beyond safe[r] spaces *193*
             Pies Not Prisons 195
             The encounter—Bickershaw social club 196
             Engaging in local politics 201
             Connecting with the local media 203
         An ethical encounter? *204*

9 **The Abolitionist Imagination:**
   Ethics of Empathy, Dignity and Life 207
         The motivational deficit and the pedagogy of freedom *210*
         Empathy *213*
         Dignity *216*
         The paradigm of life *223*

Afterword *231*
         A lost opportunity... *231*
         But a world to win... *233*

Bibliography *237*

Index *255*

About the author

Dr David Scott works at The Open University. He has published widely on prisons and punishment. His books include *Why Prison?* (2013, Cambridge University Press), *Against Imprisonment* (2018, Waterside Press) and the *International Handbook of Penal Abolition* (2020, Routledge).

The author of the Foreword

Joe Sim is Professor of Criminology and Co-Director of the Centre for the Study of Crime, Criminalisation and Social Exclusion at Liverpool John Moores University. His books include *Punishment and Prisons, Medical Power in Prisons* and *British Prisons* (with Mike Fitzgerald). He is a trustee of the charity INQUEST, which campaigns around contentious deaths inside and outside of state custody.

Acknowledgements

I would like to thank all of my excellent colleagues at The Open University for their encouragement and support over the last five years, especially Dan McCulloch, Deborah Drake, Adam Nightingale, Amanda Vaughan, Vickie Cooper, Carly Speed, Teresa Willis, Gerry Mooney, Lynne Copson, Lee Curley, Gabi Kent, Eleni Dimou, Sian Hamlett, Monika Zulauf, Kier-Irwin Rogers, Tony Murphy, Peter Redman, Alison Penn, Steve Tombs, Avi Bouki, Ross Ferguson, Julia Downes and Louise Westmarland. Thanks also for the support of my friends and colleagues at the University of Toronto, Canada, especially Mariana Valverde, Audrey Macklin, Ayobami Laniyonu and Ana Ballesteros, where in the fall of 2019 as Visiting Professor at the Centre for Criminology and Socio-Legal Studies I wrote and delivered papers on three chapters of this book. Thanks also to the kindness of Justin Piché, Kelly Struthers Montford, Chloe Taylor and Maeve McMahon who helped make my stay in Ontario a wonderful experience and for also inviting me to speak on topics and chapters included in this book. Friends, colleagues and students at the University of Padova, Italy, have on numerous occasions in the last six years greeted me with enormous hospitality; and a number of chapters in this book were first delivered as lectures on the MA Critical Criminology Programme. Thanks also to friends and colleagues at Manchester Metropolitan University, especially Kathryn Chadwick, Becky Clarke, Craig Fletcher, Sam Fletcher and Patrick Williams for all of their kindness and support and inviting me back again and again to discuss abolitionist ideas with students over the last eight years.

Enormous gratitude to Mary Cater and Nazir Ansari for being great friends and for sharing their home with me when I am in Stony Stratford. Many thanks are also due to my family and friends for their constant encouragement, especially John Roland Scott, Ben Scott and Ian Scott. Much appreciation should also go to Flossy 'Mercury' Scott (my dog) for keeping me constantly entertained and taking me on long and interesting walks in and around Ramsbottom, all of which proved ever so helpful for the writing process. Thanks also to Corina

Rogerson, Emma Bell and Joe Sim for reading through the full manuscript of the book before submission to the publishers; and to Bryan Gibson and all at Waterside Press for their encouragement and dedication in producing *For Abolition* (and the previous volume *Against Imprisonment*).

I would like to thank all the socialist inspired activists engaged in struggles against inequalities and the penal industrial complex in the United Kingdom with whom I have campaigned over the last few years — I salute you for your commitment, solidarity and direct engagement — and very much hope the arguments and evidence cited in this book are of assistance in the struggle for social justice. I would also like to acknowledge all my friends and colleagues in the European Group for the Study of Deviance and Social Control. In particular, thank you Chris Allen, Kym Atkinson, Anne Alvesalo-Kuusi, Giles Barrett Alana Barton, Anette Ballinger, Vanessa Barker, Andrea Beckmann, Emma Bell, Monish Bhatia, Michelle Brown, Tony Broxson, Jonny Burnett, Tony Bunyan, Victoria Canning, Bree Carlton, Eamonn Carrabine, Mick Cavadino, Kathryn Chadwick, Gilles Chantraine, Becky Clarke, Roy Coleman, Deborah Coles, Mary Corcoran, Michael Coyle, Janet Cunliffe, Tom Daems, Pamela Davies, James Deane, John Dennison, Andrew Douglas, Anne Egelund, Yarin Eski, Johannes Feest, Samantha Fletcher, Craig Fletcher, Billy Frank, Peter Francis, Stratos Georgoulas, Joanna Gilmore, Barry Goldson, Helena Gosling, Penny Green, Sarah Greenhow, Simon Hallsworth, Emily Luise Hart, Anne Hayes, Andrew Henley, Paddy Hillyard, Jim Hollinshead, Munira Hussain Patel, Will Jackson, Elton Kalica, Laura Margaret Kelly, Janet Jamieson, Andrew Jefferson, Robert Jones, Alessandro Maculan, Margaret Malloch, Anna Markina, Thomas Mathiesen, Simon Mackenzie, Maeve McMahon, Will McGowan, Helen Monk, Linda Moore, Wayne Morrison, Bepe Mosconi, Emma Murray, Gloria Morrison, Ida Nafstad, Christina Pantazis, Georgios Papanicolaou, Simon Pemberton, Justin Piche, Scott Poynting, Paddy Rawlinson, Rebecca Roberts, Vincenzo Ruggerio, Mick Ryan, Simone Santorso, Alvise Sbraccia, Holger Schmidt, Adam Scott, Sebastian Scheerer, Phil Scraton, Joe Sim, Paula Skidmore, Ragnhild Sollund, Faith Spear, Lizzy Stanley, Rene van Swaaningen, Sarah Tickle, Katherine Tucker, Waqas Tufail, David Tyrer, Francesca Vianello, Reece Walters, Steve Wakeman, Tony Ward, Lisa White, David Whyte, Patrick Williams, Tunde Zak-Williams and Per Jorgen Ystehede.

For Abolition

Despite the help of all of the above I take responsibility for any errors that lie within.

David Scott
September 2020

This book is dedicated to the memory of my mother, Joan Scott (1943–2011), who taught me the importance of empathy and being on the side of the underdog because they need our support the most.

Publisher's note

The views and opinions in this book are those of the author and not necessarily shared by the publisher. Readers should draw their own conclusions concerning the possibility of alternative views, accounts, descriptions or explanations.

Table of Cases

United Kingdom:

R v Hull Prison Board of Visitors, ex parte St Germain and others (No. 2) [1979] 3 All ER

The Queen (oao Roy Davis) v Secretary of State for Justice EWHC 978 (Admin)

European Commission and Court of Human Rights:

Golder v United Kingdom 1 EHRR 542

For Abolition

'This collection of essays constitutes a thoroughly engaging and passionate challenge to dominant understandings of crime and punishment. Taking a broad, historical perspective, David Scott shows the futility of efforts to reform deeply flawed penal systems that fail to provide adequate responses to harmful behaviour, instead generating yet more harm and suffering. Prisons are revealed as sites of mental and physical brutality, utterly incapable of providing constructive transformative regimes. Drawing on the socialist ethics of liberation, Scott forcefully demonstrates that nothing short of penal abolition can open the door to new, innovative ways of addressing harm and conflict that seek to further, rather than constrain, human freedom. By encouraging dialogue, critical consciousness and enhanced popular participation in the public agora within and beyond the academy, the politics of penal abolitionism go far beyond the penal question, promising to rejuvenate democracy and foster safe, socially-just societies in which liberty can thrive.'

Professor Emma Bell
University of Savoie
July 2020

'In this collection of nine essays, David Scott provides a timely and urgent reminder of the need for Abolition. He questions the legitimacy and accountability of contemporary penal policy and practice revealing the harmful negative consequences and acute pains of imprisonment. Using the voices of prisoners, Scott excellently exposes prisons as institutions of domination, repression and power. Significantly, though he also reminds us of our moral and ethical responsibilities to act now and engage in abolitionist activism. This timely collection is unique in linking together abolitionism, socialist ethics and human rights in the struggle to achieve social justice and democratic accountability. A must read for all concerned with the state of prisons.'

Dr Kathryn Chadwick
Principal Lecturer in Criminology
Manchester Metropolitan University
August 2020

David Scott

'*For Abolition* is a book that should be cherished by scholars, students, practitioners and activists alike. Written at a timely moment (for we currently live in very cold times) this compilation of essays presents the case for prison abolition through the lens of a socialist ethics of freedom, reflecting Scott's own scholarly dedication and activist commitment to this cause. Imprisonment generates a range of serious harms including death, be that physical (the premature ending of life due to violence, suicide or the reduced life expectancy that prisoners and even prison staff can expect); civil (the denial of rights) or social (the destructive impact on human relationships with those inside and outside the prison). Scott meticulously unpacks the plethora of ways in which prison reformers have attempted to tackle these harmful consequences, and thus solve the 'moral puzzle' of the prison over the last 200 years, but have ultimately failed because the puzzle is unsolvable. The prison cannot be morally justified. Whilst it is not uncommon for academic texts to be rigorously researched and robustly argued, as this book is, it is rarer to find a text so sensitively and empathically composed. Through these essays, Scott reminds us all of the moral and ethical obligations we have to each other, to those who are 'othered' and, ultimately, to the safeguarding of socialist ethics and the preservation of human dignity'.

Dr Alana Barton
Reader in Criminology
Edge Hill University
August 2020

For Abolition

Foreword

Joe Sim

For Paul Simon, the American songwriter, 'the thought that life could be better is woven indelibly into our hearts and our brains.' Simon's sentiments reflect the tenor and tone of David Scott's book. In the best sense, it is unashamedly idealistic in that it emphasises the inherent worth of all human beings and, in particular, prisoners. Nobody is beyond redemption.

As Scott argues, for two centuries the prison has been defended as an institution that protects the wider society from conventional criminality. However, it does not achieve this, or any other goal. And it certainly does not protect the wider society from the harms the powerful cause. Samuel Beckett's words could have been written about the prison: *'Try again. Fail again. Better again. Or better worse. Fail worse again.'* The book is an unapologetic critique not only of this abject failure but also of the unadulterated hypocrisy of the powerful and their remorseless focus on crimes committed by the powerless and the dispossessed while their corrosive crimes and misdemeanours, often euphemistically labelled as honest mistakes, are effectively ignored. Their rampant criminality—from the violent exercise of male power in the home through to corporate and state criminality—lurks menacingly behind a curtain of obfuscation and denial. The shameless response to the financial crisis in 2008 provides a powerful example of their hypocrisy. Blame the poor and ignore the criminal behaviour of the bankers and financiers at the centre of the crisis. Since then, as ever, they, alongside the other fractions of the capitalist class, have been left unhindered to continue with the predatory decimation of individual lives and the ecological destruction of the planet.

Allied to this, there is another misleading, hypocritical discourse articulated by the state, media and politicians which maintains that books such as this, and the ethical abolitionism on which it rests, ignores victims. However, it is *they* who, in 2020, still ignore victims particularly if they fall outside of the narrow stereotype of what constitutes a 'respectable' victim. The appalling levels of violence against women, and the state's often-abhorrent response towards those women who have suffered such violence, is a prime example of the philistine nature of their position.

The spine of the book is built on prisoners' accounts of life inside which Scott marshals into a poignant and powerful narrative. These testimonies challenge the hierarchy of 'truth' about prisons and prisoners. Individually and collectively, the confined exist as a spectral presence at the bottom of the ladder of power and are socially constructed as untruthful, deceitful and mendacious. This position is constantly and robotically articulated by politicians, of whatever political party, the state and the media. It is based on the fallacious discourse that politicians never lie (a word that is not even allowed to be voiced in Parliament), deceive or dissemble, the media never print fabrications or engage in illegalities, and that state agents never lie or dissemble. Hillsborough and Grenfell; the phone-hacking and expenses scandals; the claim that prisons are safe; and the state's calumny that women, black and minority ethnic groups and LGBT plus people lie about the daily violence committed against them, are only some examples which directly challenge the claims by the powerful that they always tell the truth.

The prisoners' accounts Scott utilises provide eloquent testimonies about the sheer pain the prison has engendered over centuries. It is a pain which is not only overtly physical in terms of state-legitimated violence inflicted on the body but is also psychological and, therefore, hidden. The prison dismembers prisoners, hollowing out their capacity to be human, creating bereft husks and further fragmenting their subjectivities as the brutal, discretionary power that is exercised within the institution further traumatises the already traumatised. The harrowing testimonies by women prisoners underline this point. Prisoners' accounts have been ignored and smothered by a fog of mystification and self-righteousness articulated by politicians, the media and the Prison Officers Association all of whom have done very little, if anything, to safeguard the confined from the ravages of the discretionary, formal and informal exercise of state power on the desolate landings and wings.

This is also one of the first books which systematically and comprehensively utilises the autobiographical accounts of state agents, in this case prison officers. One of the perennial complaints from prison staff is that they are never listened to. However, Scott *has* listened to them. And what does he find? Prisoners' accounts are *supported* by prison officers' testimonies. The majority of staff socially construct those inside as less eligible subjects, a discourse built on pejorative, dehumanising labels which are always underpinned by the threat and use of violence. The discretionary exercise of power, and the culture of immunity and impunity that has seeped into the bones of staff culture, means that institutions operate as autonomous fiefdoms outside of democratic scrutiny and control. These official accounts *confirm* what prisoners have been saying for decades. Prisons twist and break the already broken and lay waste to their lives. In Freud's terms, this results in 'scarring in the mental structure[s]' of prisoners. And prison staff, despite those honourable exceptions who exhibit empathy and compassion for prisoners which often results in them having a hard time from other staff, have been integral to the daily imposition of punishment and pain.

Scott rightly calls for academics to think critically about their role in challenging, to borrow Pankaj Mishra's phrase about the British ruling class, the 'malign incompetence' of the prison and the wider criminal justice system. The book is clear. Academics should self-reflect on their political role as intellectuals and the numbing conformity of the often-cosy, careerist-orientated, collusive relationship many have with the state which denies the eviscerating harms the prison generates. This would mean transcending the soul-sapping, marketised discourses which dominate universities, avoid state co-optation and connect with grassroots organizations who are involved in the struggle against the expansion of prisons.

What is to be done at this pivotal conjunctural moment? Scott argues that liberal reform has no answer to the prison crisis which has lasted for 200 years. Liberal reform is not part of the problem, it *is* the problem. Furthermore, even when politicians were presented with an ideal opportunity for radical decarceration, such as during the Covid-19 pandemic, they could not step outside of the ideological straightjacket within which, ironically they are imprisoned, an ideology built on the discredited idea that 'prison works.' It was, and is, a pitiless position to take and has had a searing impact on the mental health of prisoners who have remained locked down since March.

For Scott, the prison, and the criminal justice system's pathological obsession with vilification, pain and retribution needs to be radically transformed, indeed abolished, and replaced with policies based on a socialist ethics of care, compassion and empathy thereby ensuring safety and protection for all. This means making links with local communities. This is not easy, as the book acknowledges. Challenging the common sense that surrounds prisons is extraordinarily difficult. At the same time, making these links — in a Gramscian sense creating an anti-prison bloc based on 'good sense' — needs to be approached in a non-condescending, sensitive and empathic manner. Abolitionists should be self-reflective and recognise that they do not necessarily have a monopoly on preordained penal truth, despite what some of them might claim. Political interventions should be based on the wisdom of self-critique while constructing an interventionist strategy which recognises the contradictions and contingencies within the state and public consciousness. Failing to do so inevitably leads to abolitionist academics *and* activists descending into the political and personal hell of patronising sloganeering, sectarian negativity and irrelevant posturing.

In the end, this book is about the interlocking relationship between morality, ethics and politics. Radical social change requires recognising this key point. To build an alternative, compassionate social order, where confinement becomes a policy of very last resort, remains the key goal for abolitionists. To focus on anything less, and, as a society, to bury our collective heads in the punitive sand, simply legitimates the immoral and amoral decadence and cruelty of the current social order and the prison system which legitimates this order.

James Baldwin, the great American writer and political activist, maintained that 'you write in order to change the world … if you alter, even by a millimetre, the way people look at reality, then you can change it.' In these regressive, authoritarian times, books like this reflect Baldwin's inspirational intervention that a better world is possible. When the doors of penal perception are opened then radical political, ethical and spiritual change is possible. That is David Scott's message in this profoundly humane book.

Liverpool, September 2020

Preface

Uniting the following nine chapters is the argument 'for abolition'. This book is a collection of papers providing an analytical resource to be used by those wishing to survey, scrutinise or adopt the interpretive framework of penal abolitionism. Specifically, this text has been brought together for socialists actively engaged in struggles against imprisonment. Rather than being a straightforward monograph, however, the following chapters are a compilation of fragmented writings, which are part of this author's ongoing activist-scholarship arguing for abolition through the lens of socialist ethics.[1] In this sense, the book has more in common with the ethical and socialist writings of Antonio Gamsci, Stuart Hall and Peter Kropotkin than just their libertarian socialist ideas. Gramsci (1971), Hall (1988) and Kropotkin (1924) also at times wrote in fragments and whilst the chapters in this book can stand in isolation, they have been edited together so that they also read as one narrative.

The arguments in *For Abolition* may also be situated alongside those in my previous book, *Against Imprisonment*. That book questioned the extensive use of prison sentences and deconstructed claims that penal institutions are a success in terms of meeting their stated goals. It argued that common sense justifications of the prison place are based on the unreflective assumption that because prisons exist, somehow, they must 'work'. The chapters in *For Abolition* continue this process of deconstruction by further highlighting inconsistencies and contradictions in penal policy and practice. It does so by drawing upon the reading of more than 100 autobiographical accounts by prisoners or prison officers as well as direct experience of engagement in abolitionist struggles and prison research. In many ways this book is about voice. In particular, it is concerned with ensuring that the voices of various different informed people — prisoners,

---

1. This book consolidates some of my publications from 2016 to 2020. Some of the chapters are an amalgamation of previously published work as either short articles, journalistic writings or blog posts. Three of the chapters are based on previously published book chapters but these have been substantially edited and re-written for this work. The previous writings drawn upon for this book are cited in the associated chapters and bibliography.

prison officers, activists, and penal abolitionists — are heard and empathetically listened to in rational democratic dialogue about the ethical limitations of the prison place.

It is essential from the outset to recognise that the ethics explored in *For Abolition* are underscored by a commitment to solidarity with all people who have been victims of social harm and/or subjected to unnecessary suffering. Solidarity with victims is a central concern of contemporary socialist politics and ethics (Bauman, 1990; Cohen, 2001; Dussel, 2013) and the starting point of abolitionism is acknowledgement of victimhood across the social structure; irrespective of who the victims or perpetrators are. This includes calls for empathy, dignity and the meeting of the necessary needs of victims of 'criminal harm' (that is, the social harms prohibited by criminal law) and their hurt and injuries which, rightly so, are of considerable concern in public, media, policy and academic forums (though it should be noted that some criminal harms, like rape and violence against women, are still not taken as seriously as they should be). But victimhood today is not restricted to only those who have experienced harms codified in the criminal law. There are many other harms, which for various reasons are given much less attention. The focus of this book is on harms and injuries that are less talked about; are often denied political legitimacy; and where there is currently limited public sympathy, empathy or recognition.

Whist those people found by a criminal process to have broken the law cannot easily be defined as 'ideal victims', they may still be subjected to social harms. Discussing the harms and injustices experienced by those processed by the criminal law should in no way detract attention away from people who are victims of criminal harms. In fact, they are often the same people. Socialists should work together to recognise the myriad of social injustices that plague us; offer solidarity to victims of social injustice; and advocate interventions that can appropriately redress or repair the collateral consequences of the social harms that are deeply embedded in advanced capitalist, patriarchal and neo-colonial social relations. Indeed, it is logical that those calling for harm minimisation more broadly should question all forms of harm, including those generated by state institutions.

Historically, the police and other crime control agencies have failed to deal with most serious social harms, including those by states and corporations. Most harms perpetrated by people with power avoid the sanctions of the criminal process. Yet it is state-corporate generated harms that ravage the earth, propelling the planet towards a climate catastrophe that threats the very existence of humanity and most other forms of life too. In such circumstances, the criminal law seems a woefully inadequate response to the most serious social harms. This book should then be considered as part of a wider critical literature recognising the harm, injury and victimisation that lie outside the boundaries of the criminal law; in this instance through questioning the harms and useless suffering generated by the punitive rationale. It has often been noted by socialists that prisons can act like cobwebs that are able to capture the small flies whilst at the same time allowing the larger bumble bees to break through at ease.

A key theme in *For Abolition* is the critique of imprisonment through a consideration of socialist ethics. One of the most significant socialist ethics underscoring penal abolitionism is human freedom. There are three broad ways on conceiving human freedom: personal freedom; political freedom and the ethics of freedom (Svendsen, 2014). Personal freedoms refer to individual lived experiences and whether someone is directly experiencing coercion or not; political freedoms refer to both individuals and groups and refers to the ability (or not) to participate in democratic dialogue and processes of norm creation in a given society; and the ethics of freedom refer to how well people (individually and collectively) use freedom to generate human solidarity, build relationships with others and meet human need (Svendsen, 2014). Transcending these broader categories are two further ways of defining human freedom: negative freedom and positive freedom (Dixon, 1986). 'Negative freedoms' refers to calls for the removal of constraints placed upon freedoms through (state) coercion; whereas 'positive freedoms' imply that a person is 'free only to the extent that one has effectively determined oneself and the shape of one's life' (Dixon, 1986: 15) and thus require socialist inspired social policies and institutions.

Socialists, however, have largely come to understand human freedom through their direct participation in struggles against coercive state power (Davis, 2012). For Orlando Patterson (1991) freedom is a 'value, learned in struggle, fear and hope' (Patterson, 1991: 2). He persuasively argues that freedom is something that is defined through the removal of oppression and domination (such as historical systems of slavery). For penal abolitionists inspired by socialism, freedom means the ending of all forms of subjugation, domination and exploitation and the creation of a world which facilitates human wellbeing and opportunities for all people to realise their full potential. Penal abolition is a 'pedagogy of freedom' (Friere, 2001) that calls for democratic participation in current struggles for freedom. It implies an ethical responsibility to question the penal apparatus of the capitalist state and influence the moral formation of individuals and groups through emancipatory politics and praxis.

Penal abolitionists question the legitimacy of legal coercion, arguing that penal laws forcing people to undertake actions they do not wish to perform raise profound moral questions. The legal coercion of penal confinement inevitably involves the deliberate infliction of pain. Without doubt, prisons undermine autonomy, restrict choices and violate free will in an attempt to induce conformity. Imprisoning people therefore raises questions regarding 'negative freedoms' (Dixon, 1986: 11), for it results in significant restrictions on human interactions, hearing voice and other opportunities to engage in democratic dialogue. Yet depriving people of their liberty also raises concerns regarding 'positive freedoms' (Ibid: 15), as imprisonment removes the ability/opportunity to make voluntary agreements with others and/or undermines life-affirming relationships. Prisons present a clear and present danger to human flourishing and self-realisation.

Socialist ethics of freedom inevitably also highlight its relational dimension. As humans are intersubjective beings, human freedom cannot be limitless, but rather must always be bound within human relationships and encounters with others (Friere, 2001). Human freedom can only be exercised by living life with others in a given place/space and time and through recognition of our ethical responsibilities for those we encounter. The ethics of freedom considered in this book range then from the 'negative' critique of how the deprivation of freedom undermines our lived experience of time through to an autobiographical account of the ethical encounters emerging in the struggles against the mega prisons in England and Wales.

When it comes to the denial of positive freedoms, there have long been concerns that prison sentences fundamentally undermine the health and life expectancy of prisoners and prison staff (Scott, 2018a). It has though proved difficult to isolate the ways in which the specific harms of imprisonment result in avoidable and premature deaths because most people who are incarcerated are from low status impoverished social backgrounds that are known to impact on life expectancy (Drake and Scott, 2019a). However there is some research, such as the recent longitudinal study of the health of child prisoners by Barnet, Abrams and Dudovitz, et al (2018) which evidence what many have feared for some time (see for example discussion in Sim, 1990; Scott and Codd, 2010); that the pains of imprisonment systematically undermine health and slowly kill both the keepers and the kept. Places of high stress certainly can undermine the immune system and if we focus on self-harm, suicidal ideation and self-inflicted deaths in prison, there is no shortage of evidence. In early 2020 there was a reported incident of self-harm in prisons in England and Wales every eight minutes whilst data from INQUEST (2020) shows that from January 2010 to May 2020 there were 2,698 deaths. Of this number, 830 were self-inflicted deaths and this number may still rise as there were still 106 deaths awaiting clarification at the time of writing. It should perhaps then come as little surprise that prisons have been consistently critiqued as places immersed in violence, suffering and death (Scott, 2018a).

Socialists have long advocated the abolition of prisons. For libertarian socialists, such as Peter Kropotkin (1924), it is only through non-coercive and voluntarily chosen human associations that humanity can reach its highest form of development and thus ensure that the fundamental principle of 'from each according to their ability, to each according to their need', can become a reality. The following nine chapters are primarily concerned with the application of socialist ethics to the prison place. The call in *For Abolition* is ultimately for a critique of the penal apparatus of the capitalist state drawing upon a combination of both 'negative' and 'affirmative' socialist ethics. Alongside an underscoring emphasis on the socialist commitment to freedom, there is also considerable focus upon three further core socialist principles: the paradigm of life; innate human dignity; and empathy. Let us briefly explore these three principles.

The *paradigm of life* has been principally promoted by the great Argentinian socialist philosopher Enrique Dussel (2013). The paradigm of life forms the bedrock of a life-affirming socialist ethics, placing human wellbeing and the protection of life at the centre of the organisation of a non-coercive state. This ethical principle is committed to ensuring that *all people* have access to the appropriate material resources they *need* to live, rather than just survive. The paradigm of life also informs the negative ethical critique of civil death, corporeal death and social death (Scott, 2018a). Civil death, death in the law, refers to the manner in which the voice of prisoners has been largely absent in legal rulings (for discussion see Scott, 2013a, 2016a). Corporeal death, the death of the body, is literal death and negative socialist ethics critique any state policies and institutional practices which lead to avoidable deaths of its citizens. 'Social death' is a concept introduced by Patterson (1982) to describe living death under the dehumanising conditions of slavery; and may indeed precede corporeal death. For Patterson (1982) social death had three dimensions: 'natal alienation' (estrangement from family and friends); the systematic violation of dignity (which may be structured in state institutional daily practices); and violence (including both physical violence and the injuries accrued through institutionally-structured violence). This book, however, adds a fourth dimension to the concept of social death in the prison place: 'death consciousness', where the prisoner is consumed by thoughts of death because of the absence of hope for the future.

Innate human dignity has long been central to socialist ethics (Kropotkin, 1924). A good life is a dignified life. Whilst human dignity cannot be removed, it can be violated by degrading and inhuman treatment. Dignity is relational and its respect or violation are ultimately determined through human relationships. Prisons can be hostile and antagonistic environments that result in prisoners (and sometimes prison staff) feeling vulnerable and powerless. Prison relationships are also shaped by the exercise of penal power and unfortunately, all too often, the abuse of such power. This can result in feelings of humiliation and inferiority that damage wellbeing. For abolitionists, violations of dignity are structured within the workings of the penal machine, though protection of dignity is also important when thinking about alternative ethical ways of handling conflicts and ameliorating social harms.

One further key socialist principle acting as a leitmotif is *empathy*. An ethics of compassion and care; hearing subjugated voices; and acknowledgement of the pain and suffering of others are all central to ethico-political judgements. Empathy is important because it points to the significance of 'putting oneself in the shoes' of those who have directly experienced social harms and injustice, which means privileging the meeting of need and equity over equal opportunities and desert (Hudson, 1993; Cohen, 2001; Scott, 2006a). It also highlights the importance of meeting the needs of victims of social injustice and showing 'sympathy for the devil' (Scott, 2012); a crucial opening point for an abolitionist imagination. Such empathetic understandings stand in direct contrast to what Zygmunt Bauman (1989) calls the 'social production of moral indifference'; and both empathy and indifference are highlighted in a number of the following chapters.

The aims of the opening chapter are threefold. First, it explores the limitations of penal reform. Utilising a jigsaw puzzle metaphor, six ethical dilemmas generated in the prison place are considered, concluding that despite more than 200 years of reform, this moral puzzle remains unsolved. The chapter then discusses what Dussel (2013) calls 'negative ethics' and how 'negativity' informs much of the ethical critique in this book. The chapter then provides an overview of what Dussel (2013) calls 'affirmative ethics', linking together socialist ethics, abolitionism and human rights. *Chapter 2* goes on to provide a building block for the remainder of the book, primarily focussing on the empathetic hearing of voice and abolitionist ethical hermeneutics. The chapter draws upon the insights of three different ethical frameworks — negative consequentialism; discourse ethics; and virtue ethics — before finally focusing on the ethics of libertarian socialism. It is argued that whilst it is important to 'learn to learn' from the voices of prisoners and appropriately respond to such voice, an ethical interpretation requires normative critical judgement; taking into account biographical and institutional contexts. As a result, the chapter explores the criteria upon which voice can be ethically evaluated and follows the guidance of Dussel (2013) that the 'mission of the *critical theorist* is to reduce the discrepancy between [their] comprehension and that of *oppressed* humanity for which [s]he thinks' (Dussel, 2013: 239).

Chapter 3 focuses on prison officer physical violence and provides detailed evidence of their invisible brutal hands. Citing harrowing testimonies, the chapter situates prison violence within the wider context of social death. As well as providing a detailed historical context through the writings of prisoners and official discourse, the chapter also considers five interconnected themes ascertained from prison officer autobiographies. *Chapter 4* further explores social death and details how prison life is inevitably underscored by deprivations of need; systematic violations of dignity; and failure to recognise shared humanity. Pointing to the importance of acknowledging 'face' when meeting our ethical responsibilities, the chapter argues that prisoners have 'phantom faces' and that their sufferings are largely met by moral indifference. It is argued that the structured obstacles to fulfilling ethical responsibilities in the prison place ultimately questions its moral basis.

Chapter 5 maintains that prisons are steeped in social death because they result in coerced 'natal alienation' (Patterson, 1982) and the creation of estranged

Others. The chapter draws attention to how 'institutionally-structured violence' (Scott, 2015a), is insipid within the daily rules, norms and legal procedures of penal institutions, thus undermining the ability of prisons to secure the place characteristics of a home. *Chapter 6* makes connections between corporeal and social death; giving particular focus to prisoners struggling to cope with the passing of prison time. This chapter highlights the differences between what socialist philosopher Henri Lefebvre (1991) called physical, mental and social 'space-time', noting that 'prison time' can be excruciatingly painful and open a window to re-experiencing past trauma. The chapter concludes with a discussion of death consciousness as a fourth dimension of social death and how, when hope for the future is extinguished, prisons systematically produce 'death-bound subjects' (JanMohamed, 2005).

In contrast to the spectre of death haunting the prison place, *Chapter 7* argues that penal abolitionism offers a philosophy of hope. Abolitionist activist-scholars, it is argued, should engage in radically alternative ways of promoting socialist ethics and reclaim democracy through counter-hegemonic knowledge production and the pedagogy of freedom. *Chapter 8* embellishes on these insights and returns to abolitionist ethical hermeneutics and hearing voice, though this time socialist activists are of central focus. *Chapter 8* is also informed by autobiographical reflections of this author regarding the 2017 campaign to challenge the building of a new mega prison near Wigan, Lancashire.

Chapter 9 brings the substantive arguments of the book to a close by contemplating ways in which empathy, dignity and the paradigm of life can enlighten an abolitionist imagination and address the 'moral deficit' plaguing advanced capitalist societies (Critchley, 2012). Drawing upon both negative and affirmative socialist ethics and utilising the case studies of sexual violence and avoidable and premature deaths, this final chapter explores how a non-coercive mediator state (Cole, 1920) can attain legitimacy by delivering life-affirming public services focused on *repair, equity and answerability*.

The book then concludes with a short *Afterword* considering some of the key issues and debates around the legitimacy of the penal apparatus of the capitalist as this book has gone to press; notably, UK Government penal policy in the context of the coronavirus; and the mass grassroots movements springing up all around the world calling for the defunding of the state police in the aftermath of the killing of George Floyd in Minneapolis, USA in May 2020.

CHAPTER 1

The Prison Puzzle and Socialist Ethics:
Making the Case for Abolition

> All ethical critique emerges from the recognition of the suffering of the other. This suffering, however, is always material and bodily. The condition of possibility of all critique is the recognition of the dignity of the other subject, the core subject, but from the perspective of them being seen and experienced, above all, as a human living being. (Dussel, 2013: 13)

In his final book, *Ethics*, the great libertarian socialist Peter Kropotkin (1924) argued that cooperation, mutual support and empathy are natural human dispositions. For Kropotkin (1924: 14), as social beings, our 'social instinct' is to create caring and mutually reciprocating relations with others in an inclusionary moral society. People are considered to have a natural 'mutual sympathy' for fellow humans resulting in a tendency to help each other meet our necessary needs. Thus, it is important to create life-sustaining socialist institutions, which can achieve this goal. Throughout his writings, Kropotkin emphasised the necessity of building a society facilitating human connectedness committed to supporting the right to human wellbeing. He believed that such interventions would respect dignity—a moral property inherent to all humans. Respecting dignity is of such salient importance because the recognition of one's own dignity is intimately tied to respect for the dignity of others; or put the other way round, to deny the dignity of others is also to deny dignity of the self.

Kropotkin (1887) argued for the abolition of social institutions, which systematically violated human dignity and/or undermined the right to life. Included in his call for abolition was the prison. For abolitionists inspired by Kropotkin (1887) and other libertarian socialists, the prison place, in one form or another, is suffused by death—corporeal death (the literal ending of human life); civil death (the denial of full legal rights and citizenship); and social death (the removal of safety, hope and dignified human relationships) (Scott, 2016b). Prisons are nothing but soul-destroying pits of human misery that can lead to atrophy, stasis and suicidal thoughts and actions. The prison place is so inherently destructive to human life because it *steals time* from people; estranging them, day after day, from friends, families and loved ones; destroying hope and leaving prisoners vulnerable to violence and petty humiliations on a daily basis.

Drawing upon libertarian socialist ethics, the chapter has three main parts. The first part argues that despite the best of intentions of penal reformers, the prison is a moral puzzle that cannot be solved. The ethics of empathy, dignity and life are constantly undermined or violated. Six different attempts to make 'prisons work' are discussed, but each is found to have only created new problems just as bad or even worse than what existed before. Quite simply, the removal of human freedom inevitably creates a situation that lurches from one form of indignity to another. The chapter then establishes the ethical framework underscoring subsequent chapters of the book. The second part of the chapter explores what Enrique Dussel (2008) describes as 'negativity' and suggests that imprisonment is a form of social death utilised at the behest of the sovereign state. The third part then discusses what Dussel (2013) calls 'affirmativity' and the importance of real utopian policies and practices enshrining the ethics of empathy, dignity and life. The chapter concludes by making a connection between socialist ethics and the language of human rights and their role in critiquing the prison place in our historical conjuncture.

Prisons: the puzzle we cannot solve

Let me now, if I may, ask you to think metaphorically and conjure up in your mind a complex jigsaw puzzle.

> The jigsaw puzzle box cover provides people who like solving puzzles ('puzzle solvers') with a noble and beautiful image of what the completed jigsaw picture will look like. Puzzle solvers all approach this jigsaw in a similar and logical way; starting by focusing on the picture on the box and then trying to put the jigsaw together piece by piece so that their pattern

and ordering matches this image perfectly. Puzzle solvers soon find however that this is a rather complicated and perplexing jigsaw—for each piece is double sided—and it is not always clear which is right side up. Puzzle solvers generally have very good reasoning skills and over a period time keep on turning over the pieces again and again to see which best matches the puzzle box picture. These changes to the ordering and visible side of the pieces continue for more than 200 years and yet this intriguing puzzle is no nearer to being solved. Time and time again, no matter what changes are made, puzzle solvers constantly create a hideously ugly picture that defies all logic. Yet despite this continued failure, there is no shortage of puzzle solvers from one generation to the next wishing to test their ingenuity and knowledge by trying to solve this puzzle. But what if this is a jigsaw puzzle that cannot be solved? What if the image on the box is fake and unrealistic? What if the pieces at the disposal of problem solvers, no matter which side is visible, are unable to match the image on the box? What if the only way forward is to think 'outside of the box' and find new and different ways of creating the beautiful image that it shows?

Let us now translate this 'jigsaw puzzle metaphor' into a reflection on the limitations of reforming the prison place. Penal reformers and those who advocate punishment through the criminal law (*puzzle solvers*) are often motivated by the noble aim (*the image on the jigsaw box*) of trying to find ways to protect society, deliver justice and rehabilitate people. Following the logic of 'crime' (that is, the focus on criminal harm and criminal blame), they attempt to achieve their goals by calling for prisons to be turned into healthy and humane institutions. Yet despite more than 200 years of reform (*changing the side of the puzzle pieces over and over again to see if they match*), this noble goal is still no closer to being realised. Deadly harms and injuries remain and the picture we see before us today is the *hideously ugly* reality of the prison. Of course, in certain ways things are different to when reformed prisons began in the early 1800s, but in others—notably the ethical problems it raises regarding violations of dignity, avoidable and premature deaths and use of physical violence—it remains all too much the same. For penal abolitionists, the time has come to think outside the box and find a different way of creating a beautiful society where there is justice for all (BBC, 2020).

Penal reformers continue to attempt to solve a complex moral puzzle that we just do not know how to solve. Various reforms have been put forward, which claim to answer *the puzzles of imprisonment*, but it seems that every time new policies are initiated a different set of moral problems emerge. Let us now very briefly consider *six* policies where attempts to solve basic ethical dilemmas of imprisonment connect with our metaphor of *turning over the jigsaw puzzle pieces*.

Prison labour: enforced idleness or penal slavery?

The prison place is often criticised because it results in enforced inactivity. Prisoners are denied normal working practices and are damaged by coerced idleness (Kropotkin, 1887). Leaving aside concerns around mental health problems and high levels of unemployment prior to incarceration, one widely advocated policy is to make prisons sites of work and training. Yet an immediate problem is encountered: the opposite of coerced idleness is not voluntarily chosen work, but exploitation and 'slave' labour. Even if appropriate skills among prisoners existed; wages were paid at a decent level to prisoners; and appropriate technological/industrial infrastructure were on site; *penal slavery* is an inevitable side effect because prison work symbolically connects with historical punishments of the body through manual labour (Sellin, 1976). For Esposito and Wood (1982), imprisonment meets all of the basic attributes of slavery: 'ownership, possession or control of a person; denial of citizenship rights; and denial of labour rights (the rights to sell one's own labour)' (Esposito and Wood, 1982: 2).

Penal slavery is coerced and involuntary labour grounded in economic 'super-exploitation' and is the legacy of legal punishments that evolved through a race-and-class-based system of domination and exploitation, where the punished occupied 'a status below the bottom of the social order' (Sellin, 1976: 177). There remains considerable evidence of super-exploitation of prison labour, both in terms of internal prison markets (such as food, laundry and cleaning) and also external jobs (such as doing the laundry and other services for businesses on the outside) (Scott, 2018b). The kind of work that is available in the prison place is often mundane and low skilled; and this work is also often antiquated and reflects a gendered division of labour (Scott and Codd, 2010). Prisoner sabotage, inadequate industrial infrastructure and hostility from local communities for undercutting wage labour are also likely negative outcomes of escalating and intensifying work in prisons (Parenti, 1999). This ethical dilemma, focusing primarily on the problem of enforced idleness, is returned to in *Chapter 6*.

Education: learning new crimes or reinforcing failure?

Prisons have also been heavily criticised for being 'schools for scoundrels' (Kropotkin, 1887), where people learn new skills and networks for performing criminal behaviour. Through the prison code, prisons have long been known to 'educate' in skulduggery and 'crime'. Penal reformers, however, have consistently argued that prisons can do the exact opposite and be a conduit for educating prisoners in pro-social skills. The prison place, though, is an eminently unsuitable environment for pedagogy and personal and intellectual growth. The educational focus in prisons has largely been on either the very basics of numeracy and literacy — adults in prisons in England and Wales have the learning and writing skills of that expected of an eleven-year-old child (Scott, 2008)–or the funnelling of support to a very small number of prisoners who grasp educational opportunities (Scott and Codd, 2010). Whilst there are exceptions, inadequate educational provision simply reinforces failure, as coercive and hostile penal environments are much more likely to lead to educational disappointment and resistance; rather than facilitate educational achievement. In a nutshell, you cannot train a man or woman for freedom under conditions of captivity (Paterson, 1951). The unsuitability of the prison place as an environment conducive to personal growth is discussed in more detail in *Chapter 5*.

Relationships on the outside: intensifying pains or natal alienation?

Prisons sever bonds with the wider community. Sometimes to psychologically survive the prison place it is essential for a prisoner to detach themselves from the outside world (Cohen and Taylor, 1972). Prisoners may also be abandoned by former associates and family. By default, prisons are places of physical separation and estrangement; or to use the language of Orlando Patterson (1982) 'natal alienation'. Enforced separation is painful and creates long-term damage to relationships outside of the prison place (Scott and Codd, 2010). Maintaining family networks can have a positive impact on desistance post-release, yet ironically such relations may intensify the pains of confinement — prisoners will now have greater knowledge of troubles in a family or local community, whilst at the same time are unable to help or participate in dealing with such problems and thus further reinforcing the prisoners' sense of powerlessness in such situations. Prisons seem to be stuck between breaking life-affirming bonds or generating even more difficulties for prisoners in trying to cope with their estrangement. These issues are discussed in greater depth in *Chapter 5* and *Chapter 6*.

Relationships on the inside: isolation or forced relationality?

The human need for intimacy, friendship, safety, security and mutual respect are extremely difficult to achieve in a coercive environment that leads to the social production of moral indifference. Irrespective of the physical conditions of prisons—which are often dilapidated, dirty and inhumane—the lived experience of the prison place is shaped by the quality of relationships within the context of the deprivation of basic freedoms. A number of structural problems in the prison place undercut healthy and positive human relationships (Scott and Codd, 2010). The inevitably polarised and deeply entrenched divisions between captors and captives, 'us' and 'them' mentalities and the antagonism and hierarchies they reproduce, constantly undermine feelings of security and safety (Fitzgerald and Sim, 1979). Further, the lack of voluntary and free association and movement in prison can generate the problem of 'forced relationality' (Guenther, 2013). In other words, relationships and the amount of time people spend with others are not chosen, but coercively imposed. The loss of basic freedoms has profound implications for the daily penal regime.

Prison wings are public spaces where there is no privacy or opportunity to retreat into private spaces. Cell inspections and searches by prison officers also undermine privacy and violate human dignity. When situated within restrictive and sometimes highly repressive physical surroundings, that may well be crowded, life-affirming human relations are undermined and conflict is likely to ensue, including sometimes violent confrontations. Given security and resource considerations, the provision of alternative forms of living space is often restricted to smaller units or prisoners are placed into isolation. Smaller units often become 'prisons within prisons' and may be no more effective at securing privacy (Drake, 2012). They may also be places where prison officer power can operate almost with impunity. Isolation through solitary confinement, such as in the prison segregation unit, can remove relationships almost entirely and be incredibly detrimental to long-term mental health. These issues are explored in more depth in *Chapters 3, 4, 5* and *6*.

Taking responsibility: coerced sense of duty or no moral choices?
Prisoners have no control over their environment or daily timetable. There are very few *real choices* and freedoms in the prison place. They do things because they are coerced into doing so. Calls for facilitating 'responsible prisoners' and giving prisoners choices flounder because it is exceptionally hard to give prisoners responsibility in any meaningful sense (Scott and Codd, 2010). Consequently, whilst prisoners are sent to prison to learn to become responsible for their lawbreaking, in reality prisons largely take away any sense of responsibility. Further, any sense of moral duty is inevitably coercively imposed rather than consensually and freely agreed. But worse, prisons have historically been grounded in deprivations — deprivations of liberty, goods and services, autonomy, feelings of security and heterosexual sex (Sykes, 1958)–where prisoners are conceived as less eligible subjects. The punitive deprivations, especially when policies focus on penal austerity, also generate enormous unmet human need; whilst at the same time preventing prisoners (and also many prison officers) from making appropriate moral choices to address such needs. Ethical responsibilities to help those in pain and suffering cannot be undertaken in the prison place. Rather than facilitate the taking of responsibility for what has gone wrong or trying to make things right, prisons take away moral responsibility and the freedom to choose a moral pathway. Thus, instead of leading to better future outcomes that benefit both the victim and the perpetrator, prisons create a blockage to taking responsibility (Scott, 2018a). This concern is central to discussion in *Chapter 4* and *Chapter 9*.

Life and wellbeing: failed-treatments or undermining health?
Whilst the language of rehabilitation creates a veneer of legitimacy for the prison place, there is very little evidence that prisons have ever been places of rehabilitation or health promotion in England and Wales (Sim, 1990). Despite long standing claims of penal reformers, prisons cannot address individual needs through rehabilitative and treatment programmes (Scott and Codd, 2010). The opposite approach, humane containment, is also problematic because prisons systematically deny the shared humanity and dignity of those they contain

(Scott, 2018a). In fact, prisons are institutions characterised by the ill-treatment of prisoners, where the humiliating, disrespectful, degrading and dehumanising atmosphere of the coercive prison place is more likely to generate mental health problems than wellbeing (Scott and Codd, 2010). Rather than being places which promote health, they may well be places that are conduits for disease. Historically prisons have spread diseases like typhus, TB (tuberculosis) and HIV and there are fears they could also be a bridgehead for new diseases, like COVID-19 (see *Afterword*). Ever-present coercion, denials of freedom and security can also undermine efforts for effective treatment. The very 'place characteristics' of a prison (Medlicott, 2001) are profoundly damaging to human life and wellbeing; and rather than build dignity, vitality and life the prison place is much more likely to create the exact opposite. These issues are explored in more detail in *Chapter 5* and *Chapter 6*.

Although there have been times when the prison has facilitated positive human transformations, such instances are exceptions that prove the rule. One early notable critique of the failure of prisons to meet their stated goals came from Sir Godfrey Lushington (cited in Gladstone Report, 1895), who was Permanent Secretary of State for the Home Office[1] in the UK from the mid-1880s to 1895. In his evidence to the House of Commons *Report from the Departmental Committee on Prisons* (the Gladstone Report) of 1895, Lushington famously stated:

> I regard as unfavourable to reformation the status of a prisoner throughout his whole career; the crushing, of self-respect, the starving of all moral instinct he may possess, the absence of all opportunity to do or receive a kindness, the continual association with none but criminals, and that only as a separate item amongst other items also separate; the forced labour, and the denial of all liberty. I believe the true mode of reforming a man or restoring him to society is exactly in the opposite direction of all these; but, of course, this is a mere idea. It is quite impracticable in a prison. In fact, the unfavourable features I have mentioned are inseparable from prison life. (Ibid: 8)

---

1. The prison function now attaches to the Ministry of Justice and Justice Secretary.

Prisons are shackled to conditions that undermine any attempts to rehabilitate. Even well-intended progressive reforms can have unforeseen negative consequences. This does not mean nothing can be done in the here and now, but it does indicate that great care and consideration needs to be given to how the prison subverts and claws back progressive reforms. The *prison puzzle* remains unsolved (if not unsolvable) and now is the time to recognise this and try something new. This is not just because of the failings of the prison puzzle, but because there is an ethical demand that we find new and better ways of dealing with troubled and troublesome people. We shall consider the ethico-political commitments of penal abolitionists and other socialist 'collective organic intellectuals' in *Chapters 7, 8* and *9*. Let us now though consider the libertarian socialist ethics of 'negativity' and 'affirmativity' (Dussel, 2013) that inform this book.

A place of death: 'negative ethics'

Penal abolitionism as informed by libertarian socialism, is undoubtedly closely aligned with negative ethics. Negative ethics explores the meanings and content of human dignity, life and wellbeing through a focus on its violation (Kauffmann, Kuch, Neuhauser and Webster, 2011; Dussel, 2013). By drawing attention to what happens in environments characterised by degradation, humiliation, shame and disrespect, penal abolitionists can help to shine a light upon what is most essential in human life; and learn about what underscores our common humanity through a focus on its denial (Cohen, 2001). Indeed, the very term 'abolish' indicates that penal abolitionism is an approach aiming to end a given state of affairs and is grounded in the principles of 'negativity' (Dussel, 2013); in other words, critique and *saying NO* to a given state of affairs. The negative ethics of penal abolitionism delegitimate coercive institutions, such as the prison place, which systematically violate dignity and generate death consciousness. For the Polish abolitionist Michal Porowski (1991) the prison place systematically undermines our 'inborn human dignity'. Consequently:

> …dignity will always be liable to suffer a certain damage as a result of deprivation of physical liberty, the overall humiliating atmosphere of prison, and

the impossibility of eliminating coercion, supervision, lack of privacy, and the fact and symbols of subjugation. (Porowski, 1991: 100)

Prisons can desecrate the identity and sense of worth of prisoners and are steeped in morally questionable actions that violate dignity: isolation; lack of recognition; monotonous daily routines; restrictions of liberty and movement; and unwarranted physical force and violence. As such, prisons structurally deprive prisoners of even the most elementary of human needs and undermine any sense of solidarity or 'brotherhood' (Ibid). The prison is 'a space and situation where violence reigns indivisibly' (Ibid: 94). Drawing parallels with Johan Galtung's (1994) conception of 'structural violence', Porowski (1991) highlights the insidious and largely invisible nature of prison violence, which he defines as 'something which could be avoided but which hinders human self-realisation' (Ibid). For abolitionists, prisons are hierarchical and authoritarian spaces of exploitation, domination and harm; and this 'institutionally-structured violence' (Scott, 2015a) can break the human spirit.

To claim that prisons are places of institutionally-structured violence is to argue that they are places that thoroughly deny human need and generate injury, harm and death in the daily workings of the penal regime (Scott, 2018a — see also *Chapter 5*). They systematically infringe human dignity and lead to abandonment and estrangement. As such, prisons fundamentally undermine identity and may even engender death consciousness. Humans are intersubjective beings where self is formed within a social world; shared with other people and dependent upon the love, fellowship and support of others. The prison impacts upon human identity formation because it undermines 'mutually constitutive' relationships; and in practice, many prisons are rooted in mutual suspicion and mistrust (Guenther, 2013).

The prison is also a state institution that systematically generates death. For Geoffrey Adelsberg (2015)[2] penal abolitionists should make principled opposition to all life-and-death decisions by the capitalist state. He argues that the capitalist state, a bloc of alliances ultimately grounded in maintaining structural and material inequalities, defines itself through its power to determine the life

---

2. Arguments that penal abolitionism is 'a matter of life and death' were made previously to Adelsberg (2015) by philosophers such as Michel Foucault and Jacques Derrida. See Adelsberg (2015) for discussion.

and death of its subjects; and indeed, its sovereignty is dependent upon the continual operation of the power of death. The state must be able to take life to demonstrate its continued potency and power. As the sentence of imprisonment condemns an individual to violence where there is an abdication of state protection, it is tantamount to a form of 'social death' (Patterson, 1982; see also *Chapters 3* to *6*). For Adelsberg (2015), penal abolitionists should therefore challenge the violence of incarceration by calling for the 'unconditional abstinence' (Ibid: 85) of all decisions by the state, which extinguish human life. Adelsberg (2015) argues that penal abolitionism can only challenge the capacity of the sovereign to decide on life-and-death issues if it makes a stand in 'opposition against all instances of the sovereign decision over life and death' (Ibid: 85). If it does so, Adelsberg (2015) maintains, the arguments of penal abolitionism can present a fundamental challenge to the continued existence of the penal apparatus of the capitalist state and its sovereign law. In this sense, abolitionist ethics and political and intellectual interventions revolve around questions of life and death rather than the justification of punishment and the prison place. It means conceiving of the debate in terms of violence, social death and state power and proposing non-coercive alternatives that promote the paradigm of life.

Adelsberg (2015) is not alone in arguing that penal abolitionist ethical discourses should be saturated in the language of life and death. The historical darkness of the deadly penal abyss is well illustrated in the beautifully composed writings of Caleb Smith (2009). For Smith (2009), prisons deliberately reduce those confined to an empty life and a 'living death' (Smith, 2009: 40) within a carceral tomb of 'material dehumanisation' (Ibid). He argues that this living death goes to the 'very heart of the birth of the penitentiary'.

> The creation of prisoners as the living dead—encoded in law and in the rhetoric of the reform movement, violently enacted in the rituals of prison initiation and discipline—drew from an old and complex punitive tradition…Again, the prison is a scene of dehumanisation, and the processes of initiation into its discipline invokes the symbolism of death. (Ibid: 40)

The long history of corporeal death in prisons in England has been charted in writings of Joe Sim (1990); and the prisoner autobiographies cited in *Chapters*

2 to *6* also provide a further source of evidence of social death. Of course, to say that prisons are a place of (social) death is to argue that penal incarceration is a *social relationship* shaped by human encounters and power relations (Patterson, 1982; Guenther, 2013; Price, 2015). The power to morally exclude and construct someone as outside normal ethical codes is key here, as imprisonment secures status and maintains social inequalities through Othering and as such, perpetuates a social relationship rooted in the denial of human dignity (Esposito and Wood, 1982).

To draw upon the concept of social death leads us to the inspirational work of the anti-slavery thinker Orlando Patterson (1982). For Patterson (1982) social death entails '*the permanent, violent domination of nataly alienated and generally dishonoured persons*' (Patterson, 1982: 13, emphasis in original). To explore the language of social death with regards to imprisonment is not the same as saying that all prisoners are enslaved. What it does is indicate, however, is that prisons are dehumanising institutions that (re)produce social relationships that alienate or extinguish human life. Social death then is a form of 'symbolic death', where the former self is consciously extinguished as a worthy moral subject (Patterson, 1982; Cacho, 2012; Guenther, 2013; Price, 2015; Scott, 2018b). It is about the 'death' of human relationships, status and moral standing and at its extreme refers to the non-recognition of the prisoner as a fellow human. Social death is also characterised by an absence of hope in the future and a withering of commitment to continued living (death consciousness). Whilst in prison the prisoner is treated like an outcast, a less eligible subject whose views, opinions and voice can be refused or ignored; and ultimately someone who is ontologised as an outsider—the 'estranged Other' (Scott, 2018b).

Prison life can lead to the deterioration of the body and ruination of the mind. Prisoners can become ghosts of their former selves. The longer people spend, either as prisoners or staff, within these toxic and hostile penal environments, the more likely they are to experience long-term harms. For penal abolitionists there are no easy simple solutions to the humanitarian disaster facing prisons all around the world today. The problems confronting the prison are so deeply entrenched within its very structures and daily workings that any progressive way forward must stretch beyond simply changing penal policy and practice. It requires ethical critique and political transformation.³ The long-term harmful consequences of imprisonment come from the literal severing of the prisoner from previous relationships in the wider community. An individual's self-identity is shaped through relations with other people and a person can only recognise themselves through engagement with fellow humans. Prisons remove previous positive foundations of personhood (Sofsky, 1993). The removal of relationships can result in the demolition of the former personality. Imprisonment inevitably takes away mechanisms of support and mutual aid; undermines family life and damages the ability to live in human society on the outside, thus preventing re-socialisation. Living relationships become dead ones. The long-term harmful consequences wrought by social death are thus further evidenced by high recidivism rates and the difficulties in successful resettlement (Scott and Codd, 2010).

For the penal abolitionist, it is essential that prisons are named as *institutions that create death*. But that is not enough. For penal abolitionists legitimate state interventions should build institutions that can generate life; protect human beings; and result in people fulfilling their potential, instead of that potential being destroyed. It is to this discussion, regarding 'affirmative ethics' and the 'ethics of life' (Dussel, 2013), that we now turn.

The ethics of life: 'affirmative ethics'

The socialist ethics informing penal abolitionism have been explored in two ways — as either negative ethics or affirmative ethics (Dussel, 2013). Life-affirming socialist ethics clearly have an important place in penal abolitionist traditions. Affirmative ethics are a positive approach deducing the basis of human rights, freedoms and dignity from moral principles and values. It is argued throughout this book that penal abolitionism raises fundamental ethical questions about both *life and death*. When looking forward with regards to how we should deal with individual troubles and social problems, it is important for abolitionists to frame their thoughts through what Dussel (2013) calls the paradigm of life.

---

3. This means that rather than focus on 'non-reformist reforms', the latter parts of the book (*Chapter 7* to *Chapter 9*) focus on activism and the broader application of socialist ethics.

The *paradigm of life* (Dussel, 2013) is a socialist ethical doctrine privileging human fulfilment and ensuring that resources and opportunities that create and sustain human life are available for all people. To propose the paradigm of life is to emphasise the material and emotional aspects of social existence that actually generate life, vitality and wellbeing. Without first ensuring that there are appropriate material conditions for human flourishing nothing else can be achieved. For Dussel (2013), justice is predicated on 'an ethics of life' (Ibid: 108); a 'community of living beings' (Ibid: 217) where the 'ethical duty [is] to reproduce and develop the life of the human subject' (Ibid). Dussel (2013) maintains that there is an ethical responsibility to ensure that those with the least power and resources are treated with dignity and that their basic needs are met. Abolitionist scholars, such as Barbara Hudson (2003), have also argued that our responsibilities to other humans stretch way beyond our close family, friends and community to also include the 'stranger', 'outcast' and others not known to us directly or sharing similar characteristics or social backgrounds.

This is all underscored by an affirmative commitment to a dignified human life (Dussel, 2008). Dignity cannot be earned; nor can it ever be lost, although it can be violated. All humans have equal moral worth and are deserving of corresponding respect and recognition. Everyone, by virtue of being human, has equivalent status and value and should be treated as an end in themselves. To meet the requirements of dignity, basic human needs and material necessities should be adequately addressed for all people. The material conditions underscoring existence must allow full participation in community life and be favourable to the realisation of positive freedoms and human potential.

Dussel (2013: 207) empathetically refers to people, who are excluded, marginalised, denied dignity and 'affected by a situation akin to death' as 'victims'. Victims are often silenced, or their voice cannot be heard and Dussel (2013) demands that we challenge the validity of such denials from the perspective of the victim themselves. This means, as discussed in *Chapter 2*, listening and learning to learn from victims. It also means having empathy and showing solidarity with the suffering of victims:

> …the victims of any system will always appear illegitimate from the standpoint of that system…to that extent [ethical] critique turns into delegitimating…the legitimacy of the status quo. (Ibid:13)

This socialist focus on delegitimated voices of those who are 'akin to death' and positioned outside the 'system' has obvious relevance to penal abolition. The mere presence of the estranged Other (the prisoner) is sufficient for an ethical dialogue to begin. Their voice must not be delegitimated from democratic dialogue, but heard as the cry of oppressed creatures demanding recognition.

To achieve any such connection to victims almost certainly means empathising and stretching our moral universe beyond our close kin and friendship networks and offering solidarity, respect and dignity to those unknown to us. Acknowledgement of shared humanity includes standing alongside those who may have very different ways of thinking and behaving to ourselves (Bauman, 1990; Cohen, 2001). Offering solidarity to victims and recognising the inherent dignity of the Other also means attempting to see things from their point of view. To do so requires us to engage empathetically in direct human engagement with the broader community of victims of injustice. For Dussel (2013) the only way to understand the Other is through the experience of ethical encounter; and that means facilitating either physical or psychic proximity. From this perspective, ethics is grounded in the sustaining of human life and to be ethical is to engage directly in the protection of those whose life is under threat of extinction. This includes offering solidarity to all people under threat of death from the sovereign power of the capitalist state and engaging in political and counter-hegemonic struggles for social justice. This does not mean adopting a 'zero-sum mentality' and ignoring victims of criminal harm. Rather it implies the importance of adopting a much wider definition of victimhood than that bounded by the criminal law. To liberate those from the clutches of death and facilitate the generation of human necessities in order to fulfil the doctrine of the paradigm of life is for Dussel (2008, 2013), to liberate the whole of humanity. Freedom is not true freedom unless all are genuinely free. Dussel (2008) puts it this way:

> The victim is a victim because he or she cannot live...But the victim of the imperfect system, which is inevitably unjust in some moments and intolerably unsustainable during its terminal crises (when injustice multiplies the suffering of the exploited and the excluded), are those who suffer most, like open wounds, the sickness of the social body. They show the *location* of the system's pathology, the injustices that we need to know how

to repair...The affirmation of the life of the victim is at the same time the historical improvement of the entire community. (Dussel, 2008: 85)

For Dussel (2013), the ethical relationship, that is, the relationship between ourselves and those to whom we owe responsibility, arises through a face-to-face encounter with the 'exterior being' of another person. In the encounter, the face of the other speaks to us through words, expressions or actions and we then choose whether to engage in a 'non-violent' dialogue with them. The strongest moral claims upon us often arise from encounters with the stranger, or who has been forcefully estranged. The stranger/estranged is a relatively powerless (enforced) outsider beyond our normal social circle. They are someone with enormous unmet needs; and the greater the asymmetry in our relationship to the Other, the greater our responsibility. This does not mean that we will adhere to the demand of the 'face of the other'; we may ignore this as though they have 'phantom faces' whose suffering is invisible to us, as discussed in *Chapter 4*.

However, to fulfil our ethical obligations, we must freely attempt to meet the needs of the less powerful Other. Significantly, as this means helping the powerless, this moral discourse cannot be easily appropriated by the powerful for their own interests. Prisons are profoundly hierarchical institutions that set asymmetrical relations in stone and are immersed in human suffering, structural denials of needs and violations of dignity. Consequently, as discussed in *Chapter 4*, whilst the ethical demand for responsibility in the prison place is immense, at the same time, prisons structurally deny the possibility of an ethical encounter with the 'estranged Other' (the prisoner). Neither fellow prisoners nor members of staff are in a position to affirm their responsibilities *for* the estranged Other as the prison place undermines empathy, care, kindness and other actions derived from our moral conscience.

Conclusion: socialist ethics, human rights and abolitionist activism

For penal abolitionists talk of freedom, empathy, dignity and the paradigm of life are not just restricted to the language of ethics—they can also be conceived as a political language—notably through motivating social protests directed against domination, authoritarianism and violence and the development of a pedagogy of freedom (see *Chapter 7* and *Chapter 8*). Socialist ethico-political doctrines should highlight both the present excesses of capitalist accumulation and the ever-growing reach of the punitive rationale. For the latter, socialist ethics can be conveyed in certain ways as human rights. Human rights provide a language that common people understand. They can be a medium for articulating resistance, critique and dissent; and whilst this is not the only language through which the principles of dignity, empathy and the paradigm of life can be expressed, human rights are perhaps the ethico-political language of our times. This is not to approach current understandings of human rights without caution — human rights discourses have hidden and obscured social harms in the past often as frequently as they have shed light on those which are, or have been, marginalised or ignored — but irrespective of their limitations, abolitionists should promote human rights as part of their ethico-political counter-hegemonic strategy and pedagogy of freedom.

Drawing upon the 1948 *Universal Declaration of Human Rights*, Lech Falandsyz (1991) believes that abolitionism is 'a particular version of [the] human rights movement and philosophy' (Falandsyz, 1991: 18). For Falandsyz (1991), abolitionism is part of 'a long struggle for human rights in the history of mankind' with the never-ending goal of 'abolishing the restrictions on human freedom, equality and dignity' (Ibid; 18). This ethico-political struggle must result in abolitionists combining their intellectual insights with emancipatory politics and praxis, something that is explored in detail in *Chapter 7* and *Chapter 8* of this volume.

The ethics of life are all about organising society so that it meets human need (Kropotkin, 1924). For Dussel (2013), the 'moral formal principle' (Dussel, 2013: 55) of rational intersubjective dialogue is directly connected with the 'material principle' of ensuring that the needs of the Other are met. The demands of the Other ultimately require social welfare or other forms of collective provision to meet their needs, rather than individual philanthropy. Socialist ethics then must always lead to socialist politics. For Dussel (Ibid), the face of the (estranged) Other enjoins us to actively partake in an emancipatory struggle against injustice, domination and asymmetrical power. Dussel rightly acknowledges that asymmetrical relationships are inevitable given human diversity; equality cannot mean treating all the same and the boundaries of justice must be informed by an 'ethical openness' that can accommodate difference in all its variety (Hudson, 2003). Such an approach by libertarian socialists to human rights is underscored by a transformative political agenda from below seeking to promote human freedom and abolish social and economic inequalities and structural violence. Thus, whilst we should acknowledge difference, we must also assert the common humanity of the Other, irrespective of a person's actions and social background.

An abolitionist human rights agenda inspired by socialist ethics will always be 'unfinished' (Mathiesen, 1974; Friere, 2001; Dussel, 2013) for it should be forged through emancipatory struggle and acts of defiance. Abolitionist approaches to human rights will of course continuously evolve but one pressing and immediate priority should be to focus on making more visible the physical violence of prison staff and the 'institutionally-structured violence' insipid with the daily regimes of penal incarceration. Abolitionist human rights have to move beyond a merely humanitarian approach reflecting the content of international covenants and grounded in the amelioration of suffering. Theirs should be a human rights agenda that reflects the struggles of the powerless and contributes towards an emancipatory and transformative abolitionist praxis. Genuine human freedom can come through their direct participation in struggles against coercive state power. The aspiration should be for positive freedoms that create life; and for negative freedoms protecting humanity from domination, exploitation and useless and unnecessary suffering. These objectives can only be achieved through abolitionist activism from below and so it is to the socialist ethics of the 'view from below' that we now turn.

CHAPTER 2

Abolitionist Ethical Hermeneutics:
Hearing and Interpreting Voice

> The point of departure is the 'experience' of the victim…[Yet] the situation of the [victim] is not a guarantee of understanding either. Even if the [victim] experiences itself in the absurdity of *the persistence and increase of misery and injustice*…For the [victim] as well as the world has a surface appearance which is different. This is why it is necessary to accept that the victims themselves, alone, cannot carry out a sufficiently analytical and explanatory criticism against the system: The theoretician, whose activity consists of accelerating developments that might lead to a society without injustice, may find [her] himself in opposition to opinions that prevail, precisely, of the [victim]. If such a possibility of conflict did not exist, theoretical work would be unnecessary…The mission of the *critical theorist* is to reduce the discrepancy between [her] his comprehension and that of *oppressed* humanity for which [s]he thinks. (Dussel, 2013: 239)

Voice entails the *act* of speaking and the *art* of listening. As an expression of our distinctive place in the world, the acknowledgement of voice is essential for human wellbeing and the respect of human dignity (Couldry, 2010). Acknowledgement of voice occurs when a person's self-narrative is heard and receives an appropriate response. Everyone, irrespective of their background, should have the opportunity to speak and engage in open dialogue without violence. Doing so can sometimes visibilise hidden human suffering, for acknowledgement entails empathetically hearing the voice of *all* people, including those who are considered radically different or repulsive (Cohen, 2001). The aim of this chapter is to highlight the importance of empathetically hearing the voice of prisoners by providing an interpretation and context for the citation of prisoner autobiographical reflections in the following four chapters on social death in the prison place.

When voice is silenced, speech is disqualified or words invalidated, such refusal can be painful and damaging. The voice; lived experiences; and most notably, the pain and suffering of people in prison, are often ignored or neglected (Scott, 2008b). There are numerous examples in penological literature of the de-legitimating of the prisoners' voice. Gordon Rose (1961, cited in Caird, 1970: 200), for example, argued that 'unfortunately, most (books by ex-prisoners) are so obviously exaggerated that they are worthless', effectively disqualifying them from consideration in penal debates. This critique does not go unnoticed by Rod Caird (1974) who, in his own prisoner autobiography, gave a 'tongue in cheek' response to Rose (1961) when he wrote:

> After all, everyone knows that criminals (and ex-criminals) are a deceitful, unreliable lot, and ill-educated to boot—certainly not trained in the best standards of aloof fair play. It is very easy to devalue the opinions of ex-prisoners, who appear to have a vested interest in attacking the institutions which have incarcerated them. Ex-prisoners must be among the least credible groups in society. (Caird, 1974: 200)

This being said, there is extensive penological literature emphasising the centrality of the voice of people in prison for understanding the prison place (Goffman, 1963; Cohen and Taylor, 1972; Sim, 1990; Pratt, 2002; O'Donnell, 2014). The insights of the great French philosopher Michel Foucault (1980) on the subjugation of prisoner knowledge remain hugely influential and the *political* grounds for acknowledging the world-view of the prisoner are now well established (Sim 1990, 2003). Over the last four decades a number of penal abolitionists, such as Joe Sim (1994), have also pointed to the denial of prisoner voice and championed what is commonly referred to as the 'view from below' (Sim, Scraton and Gordon, 1987). In this literature it is clear that the words and writings of the prisoner can (and sometimes should) be questioned, but they must never be dismissed out of hand.

For penal abolitionists the prisoner is an enforced stranger—the *estranged Other*—a person who is Othered and forcefully separated from family, friends and loved ones through penal confinement. Estrangement (or natal alienation) is one aspect of social death. It is argued throughout this book that the estranged Other is held in an institutionally-structured violent context characterised by indignity, relational distance, the evaporation of hope and need deprivation. In the prison place the 'voice from the inside' can be manipulated, distorted beyond recognition or silenced (Scott, 2015a, 2016c). Penal abolitionists have drawn upon the view from below to highlight contradictions and inconsistencies between the rhetoric of penal policy and actual practice; to visibilise the inherent harms and violence of incarceration; and to illustrate the limitations of penal reform (Sim, et al, 1987; Sim, 1994). Accounts from both prisoners and prison staff can illustrate how power really operates within the penal machine. This chapter explores the careful and selective adoption of the prisoner's worldview on *ethical grounds* and, in so doing, it considers a number of different ethical approaches to voice.

The chapter starts by locating the interpretation and understandings of prisoner narratives within the situational pains and harms of the prison place. It then positions this discussion within the context of socialist ethics, focusing on the harmful negative consequences of imprisonment before moving on to consider whether discourse ethics can effectively safeguard the voice of the prisoner. This is followed by a brief discussion of the insights of virtue ethics and the idea of habituating a sensitivity to the voice of others. The discussion next turns to insights of socialist libertarian ethics of liberation and how this provides the basis for an abolitionist ethical hermeneutic (Dussel, 2013). Taking into account the multi-layered ideologies and discourses shaping prisoner voice, this section postulates that an abolitionist ethical hermeneutic can contribute towards an emancipatory politics and praxis, albeit that the actual interpretation of prisoner voice is complicated.

Whilst it is important to listen with empathy, *to learn to learn* from prisoners (and appropriately respond to their voice), an ethical interpretation also requires normative critical judgement taking into account biographical and institutional contexts. As a result, the chapter explores the criteria upon which prisoner voice should be ethically evaluated. The chapter then contemplates some of the principles that can guide penal abolitionists when the prisoner is prevented from speaking.

Interpreting prisoner narratives in situational context

We never get a 'pure' unadulterated voice that stands objectively outside situational contexts, but rather a culturally mediated representation (Denzin, 1989). Voice and the meanings expressed, derives from biographical experiences in combination with human encounters in immediate social settings (Schmidt, 2016). Rather than providing an unmediated account of the 'real', voice inevitably draws upon available 'cultural scripts' in a given time and place (Smith and Watson, 2010: 56). Yet, whilst the voice of people in prison is shaped through culture and language, it still refers to *real* circumstances, events and experiences (Leiblich, Tuval-Mashiach and Zibler, 1998; Roberts, 2002). Therefore, when ethically interpreting the voice of the estranged Other, we must recognise that prisoner narratives are always positioned within the very *real* context of an institution designed to morally condemn and inflict pain.[1]

Imprisonment is experienced by many prisoners as a lonely, isolating and brutalising environment, where dull and monotonous routines systematically deprive basic human needs (Sykes, 1958; Crewe, 2009; Scott, 2015a, 2016b). Prisons create situational contexts denying privacy, intimacy or sufficient living space alongside the daily indignity of eating and sleeping in what is in effect a lavatory (Guenther, 2013; Scott, 2015a). Acute pains are also formed through an awareness of 'time consciousness' and the resulting sense of wasting life (Medlicott, 2001; Scott and Codd, 2010). The prison place is shaped by a distinct morality, which generates scenarios where prisoners are considered *morally unworthy* of narrating their lived experiences. Distanced and perceived as morally inferior, prisoners, by their *very status as prisoner*, can be denied membership of our common humanity (Scott, 2008b); and through such *categorical dehumanisation* prison officers sometimes conceive prisoners as lesser beings who are no longer deserving of human rights.

The prisoner label constructs the incarcerated self as a 'bad person' who is now defined primarily by their 'crime' and subsequent punishment. It is likely then that a salient factor motivating the voice of people in prison will be the wish to present a more positive construction of the self (Mills, 1940; Presser, 2004). Pointing to the dehumanising nature and 'badness' of the penal machine

---

1. In similar vein, when considering the voice of the prison officer, it is important to consider his or her role within this system of 'pain delivery' (Christie, 1981). See also the following chapter.

does allow for the assertion of a 'good', or at least less obviously spoiled, identity as well as articulating the pains of confinement. Yet interpreting prisoner voice is by no means simple. The 'symbolic violence' of the prison place (i.e. its categorical dehumanisation) can sometimes erase the possibility of constructing a 'good person' narrative; the prisoner may be so broken by the structural and material relations of penal power and the daily degradations of prison life that an alternative positive narrative no longer seems possible (Davies, 1990). Alternatively, prisoners may come to accept the pain and suffering of the prison place without question as a means of accommodating to their circumstances (Schinkel, 2014) or even start to 'parrot' the dominant language of the penal regime (Lacombe, 2008).

Penal institutions are conceived to not only constrain the freedom of movement of prisoners, but also as machines that can write over previous identities and create a new self. At a micro—level, institutional practices aim to foster an 'internalisation of ideology and hegemony' (Moore and Scraton, 2014: 33) as a means of 'incorporating' or 'eliminating' opposition to penal regimes. Prisoners are sometimes coached to 'tell their stories properly' (Polletta, Chen, Gardner, and Motes, 2011: 15) and teaching prisoners to reproduce 'hegemonic scripts' goes back centuries. Some of the first voices to emerge from the convict prisons in England were mediated by prison chaplains. For example, in 1853 Chester Castle chaplain, H S Joseph (1853), published an anthology of prisoner narratives entitled *Memoirs of Convicted Prisoners*.[2] The prisoner narratives, all extolling the virtues of prisons, were carefully selected to tell a story of successful prisoner reformation. Subsequent exposure of the manipulation of prisoner voice; the proliferation of counter-narratives challenging tales of rehabilitation; and the generally catastrophic failures of prisons to meet such a goal, has done little to extinguish rehabilitative myths.

The historical evidence of prisoner acquiescence and incorporation of voice to support existing Prison Service practice fits all the hallmarks of a hegemonic project. Penal power, it would seem, 'is at its most effective when least observable' (Lukes, 2005: 1) and can exclude certain ways of thinking, speaking or acting. This can lead to prisoner voice being used to advocate interpretations of prison life, which undermine their wellbeing. Contemporary studies of violent

---

2. The anthology of Joseph (1853) is considered one of the first publications of prisoner autobiographies in the UK following the introduction of 'reformed prisons' earlier in the 1800s.

offenders (Fox, 1999) and prisoners on sex offender treatment programmes (Lacombe, 2008) highlight how prison treatment professionals attempt to 'penetrate the mind' of prisoners and reconstruct prisoner narratives through the logic of cognitive behavioural treatment programmes. The end product is a reassertion of the prisoner identity grounded in a 'pathological self', but this time created by the internalisation of psycho-medical discourses (Scott and Codd, 2010).

Through speaking psycho-medical language, prisoner voice provides a new cloak of penal legitimacy. Yet while prisoner voice may well be easily manipulated, even prisoners expressing 'hegemonic scripts' challenge moral assumptions that their world-view is irrelevant as well as giving them some control over the representation of their identity. It is correct to recognise that the voice of people in prison cannot always be taken at face value, but this in a way indicates that prisoner voices should never be disqualified just because of *who they are*. Whatever the difficulties of interpretation, prisoner voice can be a means of expressing human spirit, inspiring struggles against dehumanisation and giving 'witness to oppression' (Spivak, 1988; Gilmore, 2001; Roberts, 2002; Smith and Watson, 2010).

The important thing is to judge not the speaker, but *what is said*. It is also important to locate the voice of prisoners (and also prison officers) within the situational harms of the prison place and reflect upon their testimonies with care and attention. Prisoner narratives can be challenged, but that must be done in a respectful manner based on transparent and inclusionary criteria. In other words, it must be *ethical*. To this purpose it is first helpful to consider the insights of three normative ethical approaches to voice within the situational context of the prison place: *negative consequentialism*; *discourse* ethics; and *virtue* ethics. This is followed by a discussion of the socialist libertarian *ethics of liberation,* which inform this book.

Negative consequentialism

There are two key principles of negative consequentialist ethics: *ends justify means* and *no future harm*. The first principle—ends justify means—indicates that facilitating prisoner voice should be judged on results, not on how it is heard. Given the inevitable silencing of the prisoner voice through physical security measures and the very fact of penal confinement, voices that are heard via illegal means (i.e. contacting media or activists through use of prohibited mobile phones) or sending messages to penal authorities about unacceptable prison conditions or authoritarian regimes through prisoner disturbances, are considered legitimate. The political utility of hearing prisoner concerns that may not be accessible in any other way, are considered as the most significant ethical factors. If it is a choice between the prisoner voice being heard through illegal or unconventional means, or no voice being heard at all, then it seems like a very strong case can be made for justifying this end.

For 'negative consequentialist' moral philosopher Jamie Mayerfeld (1999), ethical considerations should focus on alleviating everyday experiences of human suffering, however mundane it may at first appear. For Mayerfeld (Ibid) it is our ethical duty to facilitate voice expressing the feelings of people who are suffering humiliation, despair, powerlessness and vulnerability. In other words, to 'relieve suffering' (Ibid: 118) created through violations of dignity. For Mayerfeld, this ethical duty should be of a consequentialist character, as this is the only ethical framework which is always firmly grounded in the promotion of human good and the elimination of badness.

> The duty to relieve suffering arrives and arises from the badness of suffering, requiring us to behave in whatever manner will lead to the circumvention of the worst forms of suffering. (Ibid: 118)

For negative consequentialism the ontological badness of the prison place means there is an ethical demand to help facilitate voice from inside that can evidence, interpret and explain the kind of everyday suffering permeating the prison place. This means recognising the inherent (institutionally-structured) violence of the prison place and then, on *negative ethical* grounds, taking action to prevent future useless and unnecessary suffering.

But moral dilemmas when facilitating voice can arise when the second principle of negative consequentialism—do not generate foreseeable future harm—is considered alongside the first—*ends justify means*. The problems of grounding the ethics of voice exclusively on *ends justify means* is well illustrated in the infamous Stanford Prison Experiment, undertaken in the basement of Stanford

University's Jordan Hall in the summer of 1971, which split volunteer students into groups of 'prisoners' and 'guards'. Overly influenced by cultural representations of prisons and prison officers in films such as *Cool Hand Luke* (released in 1967) a number of students undertaking the role of guards became aggressive and abusive. Treatment of students in the prisoner role (especially those who rebelled) included being stripped naked; denial of sleep; solitary confinement; deprivation of meals and blankets; and being forced to do push ups and other meaningless activities. Whilst this experiment shines light on the impact of the prison place upon human mentalities, it is hardly ethical. The Stanford Prison Experiment was terminated after six days because of serious concerns for the safety and wellbeing for all of those participating; and it was later documented that some students suffered trauma following it (Haney, Banks and Zimbardo, 1973).[3] Therefore, whilst the situational harms of the prison place should never be ignored, it is important that the hearing of voice is sensitive and responsive to the emotional feelings of people in prison and does not result in foreseeable future harm.

Discourse ethics

Discourse ethics provides an approach to hearing voice grounded in 'deontological' ethical traditions, which privileges moral duties and rule-based obligations. For those advocating discourse ethics, *all* people should be allowed to engage in open reciprocal and meaningful dialogue, no matter whom they are or what they may have done. The plausibility of voice should be determined through the 'forceless force' of rational discussion (Habermas, 1994; Benhabib, 2004) where the better argument wins the debate. In the discourse ethics of Karl Otto Apel (2001) and Jurgen Habermas (1994), respect for, and protection of, *inviolable human dignity* underscore formal processes through which voice is heard. For Apel (2001) discourse ethics are universal principles aiming to provide practical procedures for how to act in 'everyday situations'. To speak is to have an opinion heard, to count as a fellow and unique human being (Benhabib, 2011). In these

---

3. A small number of studies similar to this have been conducted. One example is the BBC prison study *The Experiment* in 2002, which was much more ethically attuned to the potential harms of the prison situational context to its participants (although this experiment also was called to an end early due to concerns over wellbeing of participants).

'special argumentation situations' (Ibid: 13) all people capable of the speech act should be allowed to participate in moral conversations. All participants are equal conversational partners and each participant in the dialogue is allowed to ask questions and initiate new discussions, as well as contribute answers.

The emphasis on protecting human dignity in discourse ethics indicates compatibility with penal abolitionism. Rene van Swaaningen (1997), for example, has argued that in a period dominated by 'authoritarian populism' and hence a time when state policies and institutional practice have scant regard for dignity, penal abolitionists must look first to ensure that 'dignity and integrity of the individual' (Ibid: 46) are 'procedurally guaranteed' (Ibid). In a more affirmative sense, 'discourse ethics' may also provide a normative ethical framework for regulating conflicts through meaningful and reciprocal dialogue and reaching a decision acceptable to all who participate, such as through restorative justice (Hudson, 2003). For Barbara Hudson (2003), discourse ethics make it easier for people to be comprehensible to each other and facilitates a greater understanding of difference and diversity. There seems little doubt that in ideal social circumstances discourse ethics have a great deal to offer. The problem is that prisons are not ideal circumstances.

Whereas negative consequentialist ethics justifies the circumvention of process in the facilitation of prisoner voice, discourse ethics emphasises adherence to legal rules and procedures. Procedural justice, due process and fairness in prisons are emphasised in a number of liberal penological studies as the best way to facilitate prisoner voice. Prisoners are to be treated with respect and their voice heard in an impartial manner (Sparks, Bottoms, and Hay, 1996; Liebling, 2004), with one of the most influential proponents being Lord Justice Harry Woolf (1991). In his report into prison disturbances in England and Wales in April 1990,[4] Woolf made numerous recommendations grounded in principles of procedural fairness that initially appear to follow the principles of discourse ethics. Yet, his is actually a consequentialist rather than deontological (duty based) approach to hearing voice. Whereas Woolf was prepared to promote change following the prisoner disturbances (and hence hear voice outside the 'hegemonic idiom'), problematically, he sought procedural justice not 'for prisoners for their own sakes. To think that would be to fundamentally misconceive the

---

4. The prison disturbances in April 1990 were the largest and most prolonged uprisings among prisoners in the UK in the last 70 years.

argument' (Woolf, 1991: para 14.5). Processes facilitating hearing voice were a *means to an end;* with the end being prisoner rehabilitation. Further, rather than promoting an unprejudiced listening, Woolf maintained that the procedural safeguards for hearing voice were predicated on responsible prisoner behaviour. Ultimately Woolf fails to value prisoner voice in and of itself.[5]

It is also important to note how fairness and procedural justice can be undermined by the daily workings of prison life (Scraton, Sim and Skidmore, 1991; Sim 1994) Having procedures in place is one thing, but problems continue if genuine access is obstructed. This is especially the case if an authoritarian staff culture is deeply structured within penal practices and power relations are exercised through discretion and personal authority rather than due process (Scraton, et al, 1991; Scott, 2006b). Further, there is a tendency for liberal penologies to place too much faith in fair procedures alone (Schmidt, 2016). Emphasis on 'procedural justice' has meant that alternative conceptualisations of justice and 'just outcomes' have been inadequately considered in the prison place (Ibid). This is particularly well-evidenced in both prisoner and prison officer autobiographies, which highlight how the prison rules and discipline procedures can be invoked to legitimate the actions of prison officers and disadvantage prisoners.

Discourse ethics are confronted with several serious challenges when considering prisoner voice. Given the nature of prisons, it is almost inevitable that the prisoner will be physically and/or structurally prevented from participation in conversations with members of the general public and there may be no, or only limited, access to spaces for dialogue with debating partners within the prison place. Further, given their socially excluded backgrounds, many of those behind bars have found it difficult to perform the 'language games' of 'normal society' (Ibid), which is unlikely to be addressed in prison society. Neither would discourse ethics automatically raise concerns if the estranged Other is only invited to speak through the 'hegemonic idiom', which refers to dominant ways of speaking and communicating, even though this may result in silencing. Alternative means of communication, such as collective prisoner protests

---

5. See further discussion of Woolf (1991) on prisoner voice and prison officer violence in *Chapter 3*.

and individualised forms of resistance and contestation, often fail to be interpreted as speech acts under the rules of discourse ethics (Scraton et al, 1991).[6]

Through harnessing the principles of mutual respect and cooperation, discourse ethics attempts to arrive at a valid, mutually-recognised consensus. Yet its predication on equal co-responsibility for dialogue means discourse ethics will collapse without reciprocation (Apel, 2001). Discourse ethics also reduce ethics to mutuality alone. As Kropotkin (1924) has argued, whilst a political system based upon mutual aid and reciprocation may be the preferred option, it is the non-reciprocated act of self-sacrifice for another person that signifies true ethics. For Enrique Dussel (1985, 2013) our ethical responsibility exists irrespective of the question of reciprocation. In other words, even if the prisoner is disrespectful and fails to engage with us, we should still patiently listen and respond when they speak (Hudson, 2003). Reciprocation can lead to unjust compromises where the interests of the powerless are erased in appeasement of claims of the powerful. Ultimately, we must be prepared to surpass reciprocity and procedural fairness in the pursuit of hearing prisoner voice, but this aspect of libertarian socialist ethics is something which is also important for engagement with community activists, as explored in *Chapter 7* and *Chapter 8*.

Virtue ethics

For virtue ethicists like Miranda Fricker (2007), attempts to facilitate the voice of those on the margins of society should be underscored by a commitment to the *search for truth*. Accepting that there can be no objective or value free approach to hearing voice, for Fricker problems arise when epistemology (the nature of knowledge) is either compromised by a bias or prejudice against the credibility of the voice of participants (Becker, 1963), or when people do not have appropriate social or cultural resources to understand a given participants voice. As such, the best guide to acknowledging prisoner voice is for it to be habituated into culture and practice sensitised to hearing the voice of others. By this Fricker (2007) means instilling virtues around unprejudiced listening, ethical trust, respect, honesty, sensitivity and scholarship so we can collectively

---

6. See discussion of Woolf (1991) as an example where the communication of prisoners through disturbances was to a certain extent heard.

develop our own 'ethical consciousness' (Fricker, 2007: 74) and a 'virtuous perception' (Ibid) of the world (Ibid: 74). In so doing we can develop wise and virtuous judgements and become reflexive enough to recognise our own privileged position and personal prejudices (Scott, 2015c).

The notion of the virtuous listener is clearly an important and significant approach with much to its merit. Whereas many prisoner testimonies and autobiographies are excellent in articulating why prisons are so painful and generate so much suffering for those they hold—with perhaps Peter Kropotkin (1887) and Victor Serge (1929) providing the best early examples of this—it is clear that members of the general public and even some of those working in the prison place, such as prison officers, are currently *not* virtuous listeners. In both ethnographic studies (see for example Scott, 2008b; Crewe, 2009) and in a number of prison officer autobiographies cited in later chapters, it is clear that there is only limited understanding of the harms and institutionally-structured violence inflicted on a daily basis on prisoners. There appears to be problems in interpretations that could be described as a form of 'penological illiteracy' (Drake and Scott, 2019b) among prison officers, which goes to the very heart of the application of virtue ethics in the prison place. In direct contrast to the kind of listening advocated by Fricker (2007), relationships and dialogue in prison are characterised by an absence of respect for human dignity and complete lack of virtue. Whilst prison officers seem able to recognise the inappropriateness of prisons for prisoners with extreme or highly noticeable mental health problems, empathy does not extend to all prisoners (Scott, 2006b, 2008b).

There may then be collective (societal) failures of interpretation (how we understand). The prison experience may be 'obscured' from our collective understanding. If we cannot understand or frame an issue/harm appropriately the actual reality of the prison experience is unable to be communicated effectively to others. On the surface the daily prison regime seems mundane. Some have even gone as far as to claim that it is easy—a 'holiday camp' (Barrett, 2015). Yet one of the most insidious aspects of imprisonment is the manner in which the enforced boredom of prison life leads to an increased sense of time consciousness (Cohen and Taylor, 1972; Medlicott, 2001). Fricker's (2007) suggestion is that what we need is a new common sense—a new shared interpretation—of the lived realities of the marginalised and excluded and a commitment to become a responsible and 'virtuous hearer' (Ibid: 5): that is, prepared to listen carefully, empathetically and without prejudice to not only what is said, but also *what is not said,* thus identifying structural denials of voice (Cohen, 2001). By carefully reading the accounts of prisoners in their autobiographies (such as Serge, 1929, whose writings are cited at length in *Chapter 6*), we may yet though be able to facilitate such a shared understanding and meaning.

Libertarian socialist liberation ethics

Dussel (2013), in his meta-ethical framework, indicates that the estranged Other (the prisoner) must not be forced to suffer in silence. In fact, recognition of voice is 'the first constitutive moment of the ethical process' (Dussel, 2013: 52). His engagement with consequentialist, deontological and virtue ethics discussed above, however, is both critical and selective. For example, whereas discourse ethics represent the 'linguistic turn' in philosophy, libertarian socialist ethics prioritise meeting the corporeal and material need of what Dussel (1998) calls the 'paradigm of life' (Dussel 1998: 13). The intention is not to uncover universal, transcendental or abstract principles of dialogue, but to understand human existence here and now within its historical, social, political, temporal and spatial contexts. For Dussel (2013: 55), whilst the 'moral formal principle' of rational intersubjective dialogue as developed in 'discourse ethics' is necessary, we must first ensure that all possible conversational partners have life conditions conducive to human flourishing. In other words, human voice is embodied and has corporeal and material needs that must be met before the speech act can be performed. Life must always come before language, for the dead cannot speak. Dussel (1998; 2013) refers to this as the 'material principle'.

For Dussel (2013), socialist ethics have an inevitable social dimension and each person's individual morality is connected with the lives of others. Responsibility for the Other emerges through an asymmetrical relationship; that is, an encounter with someone who is less powerful than us. We cannot in good conscience turn away from those in need, those who are suffering, those facing trouble, trauma or torment. In this power/responsibility axis, responsibility is not reciprocal or mutually reinforcing, but an obligation that is owed. The voice of the estranged Other demands our attention because we are 'impelled by an *ethical duty*' (Ibid: 285, *emphasis in original*) through a 'co-responsibility' (Ibid) for their life and wellbeing. Indeed, a transformative logic lies at the heart of the ethical relationship; there is an ethical responsibility to work towards the emancipation of the Other who is excluded, marginalised and exploited, whoever they may be. There is then an ethico-political responsibility to liberate the Other from authoritarian domination, violence and false hierarchies of power. For a clean 'ethical conscience' (Dussel, 1985: 59), we must demand an end to injustice, directly participate in activist struggles and work towards rebuilding destroyed human lives. This means challenging institutionally-structured practices of violence, social death and abandonment (Stauffer, 2015; Scott, 2015a). For Dussel (2013), we should recognise and respond to the pain and suffering of those without power or when control over their lives is greatly diminished. This means then, not just having processes in place to facilitate prisoner voice but acknowledging and responding appropriately to that voice.

The ethical responsibilities placed upon us are also much more than simply calculations of harm and utility, for *means are also ends* in terms of respecting dignity. It also means more than just developing virtuous value judgements and being virtuous hearers. For Dussel (Ibid) and situational ethicists like Donna McCormack (2014), we have an ethical responsibility to ensure that *all* are heard, even when words are not spoken. This means having empathy and looking at the world through the eyes of the Other, adopting or translating their language, meanings and understandings and/or trying to read unexpected forms of communication.

> When words cannot be heard, the body becomes the only means of communication. Hunger strikes, silent marches and destruction or harm to the self can be political actions that make manifest the extreme violence and inequality of the ruling system, and thus the impossibility of communication and justice under the existing institutional parameters. (McCormack, 2014: 184)

Self-harm, self-inflicted deaths (SIDs) and para-suicide (attempted self-inflicted deaths) in prison may be ways of trying to communicate the unspeakable and ungraspable pain and suffering generated by institutionally-structured violence (Scott, 2016b). SIDs may well be a tragically sad way of expressing a prisoner's ontology (reality) of prison life as well as being overwhelmed by death consciousness. Therefore, it is imperative then that we learn to understand the experience and feelings of otherness; to excavate silences; acknowledge that which is normally denied and attempt to translate into narrative currently unarticulated stories of human life (McCormack, 2014).

Like in virtue ethics, solidarity with sufferers entails patient, respectful and careful listening (Bauman, 1990; Dussel, 1998). But for libertarian socialists, ethical dialogue should begin with the voice of the estranged Other and listeners have a responsibility to both acknowledge what is said and to learn to learn (and thus hear with empathy) from this voice (Dussel, 1998). The voice of the estranged Other must be heard, even if they cannot speak the language of the system or know the conversational nuances of the hegemonic idiom. There is an ethical responsibility to move beyond existing ways of interpreting the world (ontologies) and to *embrace the world view* of estranged Others—that is people who are now considered outsiders and no longer belong to our sense of moral community (see *Chapter 4*). When the estranged Other does speak—for the very appearance of the face of the estranged Other automatically starts a dialogue—we must listen patiently with great care.

Abolitionist ethical hermeneutics

Negative consequentialism helps understandings of institutionally-structured violence; discourse ethics highlight the absence of a genuine consensus when some people are excluded from participating in democratic dialogue; and virtue ethics can lead to the searching out and acknowledgement of denied, silenced or ignored voices. Dussel's (1985) 'ethical hermeneutics' (the ethical interpretation) consolidates and deepens these ethical priorities by calling for us to *interpret the world* from the perspective of the view from below (Dussel, 1985; Sim et al, 1987; Barber, 1998). For Dussel (Ibid, 2013), assuming the voice least likely to be heard is the only way that we can rationally guarantee all views are considered in a dialogue between conversational partners. As a result, ethical interpretation should be attuned to the domination, exploitation, repression and silencing the Other.

'Abolitionist ethical hermeneutics' requires activist-scholars to undertake a 'pedagogic apprenticeship' (Barber, 1998: 53) with the estranged Other and slowly but surely develop new understandings of their and our world. This means having sensitivity and appreciation not only of how penal power shapes prisoner voice, but also recognition of how prisoners can subvert existing power relations (Scraton et al, 1991). Such a commitment is essential for an abolitionist *pedagogy of freedom* (Friere, 2001 and see also *Chapter 8*). Developing this kind of awareness is key for such an apprenticeship. Our ears must become habituated to the language of the Other and our eyes must learn to see what they see so we can be educated by them (Dussel, 1985). What was previously hidden or invisible may be revealed through their words:

> One who lives out this ethos...locates herself in the 'hermeneutic position' of the oppressed and takes on their interests, thereby discovering previously unnoticed values and emphases and opening the horizon of the possible constitution of objects of knowledge often invisible to those ensconced within the Totality. (Barber, 1998: 69)

Through attuning our ears in such a way means being prepared to hear stories and accounts that may challenge our pre-existing understandings of the world (Stauffer, 2015). Hearing prisoner voice must always be rooted in empathy, genuine openness and engagement with negative ethical critiques of what is said about the harmful situational contexts of the prison place and exercise of penal power.

Despite its merits though, there can then be no unmodified translation of Dussel's (1998) call to assume the worldview of the least powerful in the prison place.[7] Ethical interpretation is especially challenging in an institution designed to manipulate voice through the logic of rehabilitative programmes and/or the moral discourse of less eligibility (Sim ,1990; Scott, 2006b; Lacombe, 2008). Prisoner worldviews, including those in autobiographical accounts, may also be profoundly conservative or discriminatory. The potential though of a modified 'abolitionist ethical hermeneutic' is undoubted; through a careful and selective adoption of the prisoner worldview sight will never be lost of the (currently often unacknowledged) suffering of prisoners (Cohen, 2001; Scott, 2015b). But always sitting alongside silencing and denial is the institutionalised manipulation

---

7. This point is anticipated by Dussel (2013: 239).

of prisoner voice. Consequently, what is said in prisoner autobiographies must always be open to critical evaluation. Let us consider this point further.

Critical judgement

The ethical relationship between the self and the Other is a dialogue rather than a monologue (Dussel, 2013). The call of the estranged Other should initiate a response, but there remains a requirement for critical judgement. An abolitionist ethical hermeneutics (Scott, 2016c) champions the emancipation of the powerless, dominated and repressed and attempts to understand the world from their marginalised perspective. But there is no guarantee that listening to the prisoner voice will automatically lead to greater enlightenment; the estranged Other may endorse or exaggerate discriminatory ideologies such as racism, sexism and homophobia (Sim, 2003). Prisoner voice must also be understood within the multi-layered discourse and ideologies that permeate the prison place. Penal power is expressed through rehabilitative programmes and moral discourses that have the explicit purpose to transform the self. Such hegemonic practices and ideologies can manipulate and transform prisoner voice into the service of penal authorities. Abolitionist ethical hermeneutics must always then evaluate prisoner voice (and the voice of the prison officer) with consideration of its consistency with the normative principles of human rights, social justice and democratic accountability (Scott, 2013b).

Critical judgement should be made in the interests of the Other rather than the self. This means two things for an abolitionist ethical hermeneutic. First, that we should be prepared for self-critique in response to the voice of the estranged Other and second, if we do criticise their voice, we should do so *for* them. We are called to engage in a dialogue with the Other; and a reluctant, but critical, appraisal of their words, actions and beliefs is part of that ethical responsibility. The ethical demand arising through an encounter with the face of the estranged Other is the start of a rational dialogue. We should listen and learn; but may also be compelled to disagree. When the estranged Other espouses views that perpetuate or would create injustice they should be challenged (Sim, 2003). There must then be a careful and selective approach to prisoner voice, one that is sensitive to the way in which voice is situated within the ideologies and discourses of the prison place.

Abolitionist ethical hermeneutics require only that the voice of the estranged Other is heard, not that it dominates proceedings or is considered unproblematic. The ethical responsibility is to facilitate a rational dialogue, not create 'epistemic privilege'. The difficulty with 'epistemic privilege' is that in privileging a particular person or group at the expense of all others, any statement by them is impervious of critique. It cannot be challenged as nobody else is qualified to comment. 'Unwelcome knowledge' (Cohen, 2001) about the inherent harms and violence of imprisonment can come from many different sources. Those who have knowledge should be given the opportunity to speak, whoever they are. The responsibility is to ensure the inclusion of the voice of the estranged Other at the start of the communication process, not to thoughtlessly follow their views.

We should constantly question our right and competency to judge and be open to amending our decisions (Scott, 2018a). Judgements should arise alongside, together and with others, but perhaps most significantly of all *we must primarily judge to prevent injustice*. Equally importantly, an *ethical judgement should never in itself lead to further manifestations of injustice* (Dussel, 2013). We should be angered by unjust practices which dehumanise, threaten dignity and destroy world. This means judging social structures and institutions, which result in the ruination of a person's body, mind and soul. A just judgement acknowledges the Other's common humanity (Bauman, 1990; Gaita, 2002). If we have to judge voice it should not be the speaker, but the strength and rationality of *what is said* (Apel, 2001). Critical judgement should be linked with interventions promoting the 'paradigm of life' (Dussel, 2013) and be in the service of an emancipatory politics aspiring to deliver justice for all (Alcoff, 1995; Dussel, 1998; Gaita, 2002; Scott, 2016b).

When the estranged Other cannot speak

But what should penal abolitionists do in situations when the estranged Other cannot speak? Can it *ever* be appropriate *to speak for the prisoner*? Hegemonic forms of cultural and political representation (idioms) can directly exclude the

Abolitionist Ethical Hermeneutics

prisoner from speaking; manipulate voice so that it reflects hegemonic penal constructions of reality; or morally condemn them as unworthy of being heard (Foucault, 1980; Spivak, 1988; Scott, 2008b). The way the prisoner communicates may not be understood by the hegemonic 'master discourse' (Dussel, 1985). The prisoner may not know or adhere to the dominant idiom of the speech act. They may communicate in a different idiom; prisoners may speak, but not be able to be widely understood (Spivak, 1988). The problem is that speaking on behalf of the marginalised and excluded could, paradoxically, facilitate the silencing of voice (Ibid; Hooks, 1991). The estranged Other may be 'ventriloquized' by a more privileged speaker, which does nothing to disrupt existing hierarchies of power (Spivak, 1988; Hooks, 1991; Alcoff, 1995), and as such, speaking for others 'is arrogant, vain, unethical and politically illegitimate' (Alcoff, 1995: 97–8). Therefore, the question of whether the abolitionist (certainly as a political activist-scholar) should speak *for* the Other must always be a 'second order question' (Ibid), as first the abolitionist must help the prisoner give their own account, something that may be a necessary part of the healing process (Scarry, 1985).

Deliberately ignoring prisoner voice is linked to the exercise of penal power. As we discussed earlier, the views and opinions of prisoners, whether in autobiographies or otherwise, can be deemed as invalid or illegitimate. Those in positions of penal power define and set parameters on what can be said and who can speak (Foucault, 1980). For knowledge to be utilised the 'knower' must establish a right to speak, for acceptance of any given statement is often linked to the status of the speaker. In the view from above (official discourse) prisoner voice can be reduced to a subjugated knowledge that is either entirely neglected or discredited. We shall discuss this in some depth in the next chapter, but a notorious example can be found in the Keith Report investigating the death of Zahid Mubarek.[8] Lord Justice Brian Keith (2006) declared that '[i]nvariably what the prisoner says is not reliable ... There is no reason to suppose that prisoners always tell the truth when asked' (Ibid: 500). Sadly, echoing many before him, Keith disqualifies prisoner voice unreservedly. The moral condemnation associated with the prisoner label systematically undervalues voice and

---

8. Zahid Mubarek was a young Asian prisoner who was killed in Feltham Young Offender Institution by known racist Robert Stewart on 21 March 2000. Following a long legal battle by the Mubarek family a public inquiry into his death was ordered, which was headed up by Mr Justice Keith.

blocks self-narratives, denying the estranged Other a platform from which to speak (Foucault, 1980; Couldry, 2010). The prisoner is thus silenced because they cannot register as a sovereign speech act or are unable to denote who they are in the existing structures of representation (Spivak, 1988).

But this is not the whole story, for prisons are world destroying places. Prisons create not the 'paradigm of life' but pain, suffering and *civil, social and corporeal death* (Scott, 2015a, 2016b, 2018a). Human life is largely about building meaningful and fulfilling relations with other humans, but the prison place individualises and undermines our inter-subjectivity, not only by removing people from previous relationships, but by creating a type of social death that prevents the formation of new life-affirming relationships (Kropotkin, 1924). Voice is 'co-authored' and only reveals its true meaning and importance in conversation with other people (Stauffer, 2015). To have voice is to be part of a wider community, to engender feelings of belonging, trust and security. Prisons silence voice and unmake the life-world; that is, the concrete social relationships and interpersonal connections with other human beings that provide the foundations for our identity and being-in-the-world start to unravel and such unravelling can lead to the collapse of self. The denial of voice combined with *social death* results in a new and profound sense of anguish, existential crisis and 'ethical loneliness' (Ibid: 1). Not hearing the voice of the estranged Other, failing to respond to a cry of pain, matters enormously to those who are not heard because the sense of abandonment impacts upon how the past resonates in the present and how they face the future. To feel intense pain is to be overwhelmed in the present and to experience the past as alien and 'unfathomable' (Scarry, 1985).

Yet, whilst the voice of the Other can be interpreted as a cry of pain, or as a means of diminishing pain, it is pain and suffering which present some of the greatest threats to voice. Suffering destroys our capacity to speak and the ability to relate to others. For the American literary scholar Elaine Scarry (1985):

> Physical pain does not simply resist language but actively destroys it, bringing about an immediate reversion to a state anterior to language, to the sounds and cries a human being makes before language is learned (Scarry, 1985: 4).

The pain and suffering generated through penal incarceration can destroy the capacity to speak (Stauffer, 2015). At times human suffering is 'unsharable' (op cit:4) and cannot be spoken. The sufferer, who no longer has the words to express what they are feeling is silenced, made invisible and denied full participation in the human community (Ibid). An abolitionist ethical hermeneutic therefore also entails virtuously listening to what remains unsaid (Stauffer, 2015). Some things cannot be said without revealing weakness; and sometimes the truth is so horrible that it is best left unsaid (Ibid). But at other times denial of voice only exacerbates injustice.

Talking about suffering may also be so disturbing that it silences others. Listeners may become illiterate and unable to understand or acknowledge what the prisoner has told them because they do not understand the extent or meaning of the pain described (Ibid). The Other is muted. There does not necessarily have to be the intention to deliberately silence the estranged Other. It is that *we just do not always know how to hear the voice of the Other.* The hegemonic idiom does not understand when the estranged Other speaks (Spivak, 1988). It needs educating.

None of this means that penal abolitionists should *never* speak on behalf of the estranged Other. What it does suggest though is that the prisoners should not be forced to follow the language rules of the hegemonic discourse. Nor should they be silenced (Dussel, 1998). If the prisoner does not know the hegemonic idiom, or the hegemonic idiom does not understand the prisoner, the abolitionist should act as interpreter. Those who have served their 'pedagogic apprenticeship' have a responsibility to understand, placing even greater emphasis on careful and patient listening and interpretation of voice within a complicated prison situational context. Sometimes what is being said is not clear. Sometimes nothing can be said. Sometimes no-one can speak. Who then hears the voice of prisoners with serious mental health problems; the dead or dying; the deaf; the foreigner who does not speak the national language of the country in which they are imprisoned; or those in solitary confinement denied contact with another person? Who will speak *for* them? How can their voice be heard?

Six conditions of speaking

For Gayatri Chakravorty Spivak (1988) intellectuals must find a balance between listening and responding to the voice and participating in a dialogue that does not result in the *paralysis* of the Other's ability to speak or be heard. Though abolitionists should be reluctant speakers, there are certain 'conditions of dialogue' (Alcoff, 1995: 110) that when all else fails allows speech on behalf of prisoners. Detailed below are six such conditions drawing explicitly on the insights of Linda Alcoff (1995: 110–113):

1. *Fight against the impetus to speak.* The first priority always must be to *hear* voice. The speech act is legitimate only if prisoners have been prevented from speaking or are struggling to articulate their own experiences, such as the largely invisible harms of institutionally-structured violence.

2. *Not silencing the Other.* Abolitionists should ensure their speech act does not silence voice. Their narrative should draw either implicitly or explicitly upon the experience, actions or words of the estranged Other. Questions should be raised about the absence of the actual prisoner voice and their presence championed. Speaking *for* must be an act of last resort.

3. *Acknowledge privileged speaking position.* Abolitionists should make their privileged identity and subject position clear from the outset. It should be made obvious that the speech act is from *their* speaking position, not that of the estranged Other. The abolitionist should speak with great care, utilise rigorous scholarship and draw upon the words of prisoners as faithfully as possible.

4. *Take responsibility for the Other.* The abolitionist should speak *on behalf* and *for* the estranged Other. The speech act of the abolitionist is in place of silence. Speaking is an act of responsibility *for* the estranged Other. Abolitionists should speak only when nobody else can or will speak with such ethical responsibility.

5. *The emancipatory objective of speaking.* Abolitionism is a form of emancipatory knowledge challenging injustice, need deprivation and the state manufacture of suffering and death. The speech act should stimulate a counter-hegemonic narrative visibilising the pain and suffering of the prisoner. It should aim to facilitate emancipatory politics *for* the estranged Other and to promote broader values and principles of social justice.

6. *Self-silencing.* Abolitionists cannot bring closure to dialogue about the estranged Other. As reluctant contributors, they should always be open to critique and a counter-narrative or 'counter-sentence' by the estranged Other.

The above conditions of speaking suggest an ethics of listening to and providing a platform for the voice of the prisoner whenever possible. A number of the following chapters attempt to do this by drawing upon prisoner (as well as prison officer) autobiographies. Hearing voice of people in prison does not though imply, as argued above, epistemic privilege of the prisoner voice or the denial of other voices in prison. Whereas the voice of the prisoner can be marginalised or silenced by others in the prison place—such as prison officers or in official reports—it can also be validated by such voices. Abolitionist ethical hermeneutics therefore aims to facilitate prisoner voice, carefully listen to what is said and (under certain conditions) engage in dialogue with and alongside the estranged Other about the realities of prison life.

Conclusion: learning to learn

Abolitionists inspired by libertarian socialist ethics should be both interpreters and legislators. As *interpreters,* abolitionists should help translate the idiom of prisoners for a wider audience, selectively platforming or assuming their interpretive stance. Alongside engineering a platform for the prisoner voice, abolitionists should help those who have limited criminological literacy understand the prison life-world and what it means to see the world through their eyes. This means acknowledging how prisoner voice can be manipulated as well as heard or silenced. There is an *art* to listening and interpreting prisoner voice. Further, it is as important for the hegemonic idiom to change its way of hearing and listening to the estranged Other, as it is for the estranged Other to engage in the hegemonic idiom of rational discourse. As Jill Stauffer has argued:

> It will be important for those who listen to reflect on the limits to what they already know and how that affects *what they are able to hear*. Perhaps then people and the institutions they design will be able to listen for their own failures—and thus begin to live up to what justice…or long-standing injustice demands (Stauffer, 2015: 8 *emphasis added)*.

We need more pedagogical apprentices 'learning to learn' from the voice of the estranged Other to aid the development of an abolitionist pedagogy of freedom. But abolitionists should also be *legislators*. Abolitionists should critique all unjust institutions of domination and repression. They should also challenge discriminatory stereotypes, including those expressed by prisoners. Interpreting prisoner voice can be difficult and so must be contextualised within a broader commitment to emancipatory politics and praxis. In times of great social injustice there must not be silence, nor only a small number of voices considered suitable to speak on injustices, but rather an open dialogue fostering transformative and emancipatory change, visualising real utopian 'life-affirming' alternatives to the penal rationale and promoting new visions of justice for all.

CHAPTER 3

Invisible Brutal Hands:
The Problem of Prison Officer Violence

> …a large number of people cling to the idea that warders [prison officers], as a class, are brutal bullies. This is ridiculous, and if I had not heard people pass the same opinion, I should not waste my time and yours replying to it. As I've said before, you may drop-across one now and then who has plenty of bark, and perhaps an occasional one who is inclined to be brutal, but they are the exception. (Triston, 1938: 242–3)

On 30 April 2020 the European Committee for the Prevention of Torture and Inhuman or Degrading Treatment or Punishment (CPT), published a report following inspections at HMP Liverpool, HMP Wormwood Scrubs and HMP Doncaster. The report was damning, highlighting a 'climate of fear' (CPT, 2020: 6) and a general absence of feelings of safety. The CPT (2020) investigated 13 cases of 'unprovoked and unjustified infliction of violence on prisoners by staff' (Ibid: 22) at HMP Liverpool. The report pointed to dismissal or suspension of prison officers at Liverpool Prison, for 'engaging in unprovoked physical attacks upon prisoners' (Ibid) and cited similar evidence from HMP Wormwood Scrubs. The unprovoked violence, which was recorded on CCTV, included one prison officer at HMP Liverpool punching a prisoner in the head 'without any prior warning or justification' (Ibid) and another striking a prisoner with eight punches after they had tried to take an extra chocolate biscuit. The CPT found that prison officers at HMP Liverpool had produced 'detailed, almost entirely fictional, accounts of their behaviour' after they claimed their violence had been provoked by a 'terrifying situation' (Ibid).

The CPT (2020) investigated other allegations at HMP Liverpool, including where a prisoner received extensive facial injuries after being assaulted by four prison officers (Ibid: 23). Alongside this the CPT (2020) described how a prisoner received back and neck injuries in HMP Wormwood Scrubs after, without provocation, a prison officer picked him up by his clothes and 'slammed his head down on the floor' (Ibid). The CPT (Ibid) continued that 'events of this nature [by officers] were not likely to be isolated incident[s]' (Ibid: 24) and

> …of utmost concern was the evolution of an informal practice of 'preventive strikes' (i.e., 'preventively' punching compliant prisoners whom staff perceived might, at some point in the future, become a threat). The CPT recommends that the United Kingdom authorities explicitly prohibit the reprehensible practice of 'preventive strikes' by prison officers on [prisoners] and, more generally, undertake a proper investigation into all allegations of ill-treatment and ensure that prison staff understand why ill-treatment is unlawful and will result in severe disciplinary sanctions or criminal prosecution. (Ibid: 6)[1]

Yet the evidence cited in the CPT is just one recent example of an enduring problem.[2] This chapter, drawing upon official discourse as well as autobiographical accounts of prisoners and prison officers, points towards historical continuities in prison officer violence. The first part of the chapter focuses on the legitimacy and 'visibility' of violence before moving on to reflect upon the potential and pitfalls of hearing prisoner and prison officer voice. The third and most substantive part of the chapter, considers historical evidence of prison officer violence since the 1850s as evidenced by prisoners and in official discourse; and the fourth part focuses on recollections and justifications of violence in prison officers' own words.

---

1. Prison Service guidance from 2015 indicated that prison officers did not have to wait to be assaulted to use physical violence themselves. The CPT (2020: 23) cited the 'Use of Force Coordinator' at Liverpool Prison who found unprovoked physical violence acceptable if an officer 'anticipated that [the prisoner] might pose a threat'.
2. The main recommendations of the CPT (2020: 24) were to call for changes to official guidance on the use of prison officer violence; more accurate monitoring of prisoner complaints; an increase in the number of prison officers; greater accountability for the actions of officers; and the development of violence prevention interventions. If implemented, the recommendations of the CPT may well improve the situation a little, but they are unlikely to address the root causes of the problem.

Legitimacy and visibility

Since the 1990s, there has been a significant increase in academic literature on prison officers. Much of this research has emphasised how prison officers *underuse* their powers by using discretion to maintain order and control and regimes with prisoners (Liebling and Price, 1998; Liebling 2004; Liebling and Price 2005). What is missing from this analysis is detailed consideration of the way prison officers *overuse* their power. Prison officers expect prisoners to adhere to an asymmetrical deference norm, where the prisoner must show deference and respect without reciprocation, at least in the first instance (Scott, 2006a). Conflict between officers and prisoners is inevitable because their different social roles create inherent antagonism in the penal machine, something which cannot be negated no matter what the quality of conditions. Coupled with this, prisoners are often regarded as less eligible subjects, undeserving of respect and dignified treatment. Indeed, the category of 'prisoner' is grounded in a set of moral claims, as someone is imprisoned because of flawed moral character.

Relationships in the distinct moral universe of the prison place operate by categorising people as 'good' or 'bad'. Johan Galtung (Corsen and Galtung, 2016), refers to this as the 'Self-Other gradient'. Following Galtung (Ibid), the badness, moral weakness and failings of the prisoner can be contrasted directly with the goodness of the prison officer. Indeed, the more untrustworthy, bad and problematic the prisoner, the more the goodness of the prison officer stands out. Collapsing these moral categories can be hugely threatening, for prison officer working personalities or the 'superior' prison officer identity is reliant upon a debased and 'inferior' estranged Other. Undoubtedly moral distinctions between prisoner and prison officer are important in terms of how prisons operate.

Prisons are always in a constant state of flux between coercion and 'consent' (if consent is truly possible within a prison). Indeed, coercion and violence underscore daily penal regimes. If prisoners do not conform to the rules of the prison, there is always the possibility that physical violence of some kind may manifest itself (Cover, 1986). In the words of imprisoned socialist activist Michael Davitt, writing in the 1880s:

> Good conduct in prison is partly the outcome of a resolve not to bring additional punishment upon themselves, or to prolong their imprisonment by insubordination, and partly the result of experience produced by former terms of imprisonment…(Davitt, 1885: 23)

Prisoner violence is largely considered an *illegitimate* form of violence. Prisoners involved in a disturbance, or who engage in physical violence, are widely condemned. The insidious, ever-presence of coercion; the structural violence underscoring prison life; plus, the violence of prison officers, however, are not *necessarily seen as illegitimate*. There are many instances where such violence is claimed to be simply not happening, or prisoner voice is seen as unreliable; disqualifying their testimony of violence. Physical violence perpetrated by prison officers, for example, is less likely to be reported and recorded in official data than violence by prisoners. In the main, accurate statistical records of prison officer violence do not exist, but there are other sources of evidence that visibilise it, such as autobiographies of prisoners and prison officers and official reports. There are testimonies from prisoners since the mid-1800s suggesting prison officer violence is a constant, if not daily, feature of prison life. Exposure to violence in such a way is consistent with what Orlando Patterson (1982) calls 'social death'.

All places where physical violence predominates are underscored by what Galtung (2013) calls 'cultural violence'. *Cultural violence* performs a key role in naturalising the 'way things are done round here', shaping how conflicts are handled and whether violence is celebrated, condoned or condemned. *Cultural violence* consists of cultural codes, norms and values adopted to define and legitimate violence in the prison place. Physical violence against prisoners is viewed by staff as not only necessary, but also morally justifiable. Violence used to control the less eligible prisoner is sometimes considered as 'righteous violence' (Edney, 1997: 291), because it is perpetrated for the greater good. Using violence against prisoners can also be a means of gaining respect and status as well as providing excitement in the otherwise bleak and monotonous routine (Scraton and McCulloch, 2009).

When thinking about prison violence it is important to consider if it is visible or invisible for public scrutiny and whether it is considered as legitimate or illegitimate. When it comes to most discussions about prison violence, it is *visible and illegitimate* violence that is the focus of attention. What this author is interested in discussing are *invisible* forms of violence, which may, at least for the perpetrators, be considered *legitimate*. Hence, this chapter focuses on the *legitimated violence* of the '*invisible* brutal hands' of prison officers.[3]

Which voices are heard?

This chapter recounts both the story of prisoners and prison officers, drawing extensively on autobiographical accounts. It first draws extensively upon prisoner autobiographies (see *Chapter 2* for discussion of prisoner voice) and official discourse. A number of official reports, inquiries and debates in the House of Commons considering prison officer violence, are cited in the following pages. Sometimes this official discourse hears the voice of prisoners, but at other times it either excludes their voice or presents prisoner voice as being less worthy of consideration than that of others. Official discourse has great authority and is largely not questioned, at least not in the same way as that of a prison officer (who may be construed as a sadistic or weak-minded brute) or a prisoner (who because of the wrongdoing might be considered as no longer having the right to speak).

Prison officer autobiographies, until the last decade or so, have been much less prevalent than autobiographical accounts by prisoners.[4] Harley Cronin claimed back in the 1960s that:

> Amid all the 'authoritative' voices—in print, and on the air—One voice has largely gone unheard. It is the voice of the prison officer, of the man in blue whose tyranny, stupidity, and lack of imagination usually figure so prominently in portrayals of prison life. (Cronin, 1967: ix)

Undoubtedly, there are concerns that should be raised about prison officer (and prisoner) autobiographies. Autobiographical accounts are often written many years after events have taken place. Further, autobiographies are written

---

3. Another form of 'invisible violence'—institutionally-structured violence—is discussed in *Chapter 5*.
4. Many of the below points are also relevant for prisoner autobiographies.

to be sold for profit and so there might be a tendency to focus on stories that can be easily sensationalised, rather than a re-telling of mundane, everyday prison experiences. Such writings are also inevitably subjective and could be inspired because the author has an axe to grind. This means that it may be hard to generalise from their evidence. Yet prison officer autobiographies, when considered collectively, do seem to indicate something is going fundamentally wrong within the prison regime.

All writings are in one way or another subjective and there is no guarantee than any will be genuinely neutral and objective. Also, time lapses between an event and written recollection do not necessarily undermine validity. Sometimes memories are frozen, like moments or pictures, where people can remember exact wordings because it is so important and can thus reflect back on those moments as if they were only yesterday. Claims made in prison officer autobiographies may also be checked against other historical records for accuracy. Prison officer autobiographies can then add to a chorus of voices about the realities of prison life, such as prison officer violence. They give us some indication of historical continuities in the prison experience; and some idea of how violence is part of their work. Despite the limitations, the voice arising from prisoner and prison officer autobiographies shines a light on invisible and legitimate forms of violence.

The prisoners' tale: prison officer violence in historical context

The brutal hands of prison officers have been ever-present since the introduction of 'reformed prisons' in the early-1800s. In an early warning, the intrepid observer of virtually all prisons and jails in England and Wales at that time, James Neild (1812/2012), noted that 'few men, or perhaps it will be better expressed, No Man is fit to be entrusted with uncontrolled power and yet by common gaolers is this mighty trust permitted to be exercised' (Neild, 1812/2012: 22). That such trust in prison staff was badly misplaced proved evident in the treatment and subsequent death of Edward Andrews, a 15-year-old boy sentenced to three months hard labour at Birmingham Prison in 1853. Andrews was deprived of sleep and required to turn the 'crank' 10,000 times a day, something almost beyond human capacity. In response to such intolerable circumstances the boy hanged himself. The subsequent Royal Commission on Birmingham Borough Prison, appointed 22 August 1853 heard evidence from both prisoners and prison warders (officers); and when it reported on 25 January 1845, it evidenced widespread use of illegal punishments, including repeated floggings and the hanging of a prisoner from landing railings in a straightjacket (Welsby, Williams, and Baly, 1854). The death of Andrews garnished further publicity through a 'fictionalised' account in the novel *It is Never too Late to Mend* by Charles Reade, which drew on the reported facts of the abuse:

> A lad about fifteen years of age was pinned against the wall in agony by a leather belt passed round his shoulders and drawn violently round two staples in the wall. His arms were jammed against his sides by a strait waistcoat fastened with straps behind, and those straps drawn with the utmost severity. But this was not all. A high leathern collar, a quarter of an inch thick, squeezed his throat in its iron grasp. His hair and his clothes were drenched with water, which had been thrown in bucket-full's over him, and now dripped from him on the floor. His face was white, his lips livid, his eyes were nearly glazed, and his teeth chattered with cold and pain. (Reade, 1856: 133)

A number of prison staff were dismissed and Birmingham Prison governor, William Austin, was jailed for three months for perpetrating ten assaults on Andrews. This brutality was not an isolated incident. The prisoner 'One who has endured it' (Anonymous, 1877) also testifies to the death of John Jones, a prisoner in HMP a few years later:

> While I was in Dartmoor, a case occurred of a man's death being caused by the harshness of the warden. John Jones, who has been under sentence of penal servitude, had been placed into the inevitable situation of being asked to lift heavy stones, heavier than what he actually could lift. And the strain and the nature of the strenuous lifting of the stones as part of his penal servitude, ultimately led to him being overworked. (Ibid: 169)

John Jones was officially recorded as dying of a disease of the heart, but actually the concern of one who has endured it was that he had been pushed to the very limits.

The institutionalised brutality, torture and nearly daily experience of violence by 'weak and mentally defective' prisoners in the 'convict prisons' of England and Wales was highlighted in numerous testimonies to the Royal Commission on Penal Servitude, which was led by the Earl of Kimberley and reported 14 July 1879. The Royal Commission explored accusations of prison officer violence at HMP Parkhurst but, as might well be anticipated, claims that prison officer violence took place were vigorously denied by prison authorities (Kimberley, Talbot, O'Conor, Whitbread, and Guy, 1879). Further evidence from the 1870s of the brutal hands of prison officers is given by Irish political prisoner, Jeremiah O'Donovan Rossa:

> The second next day at the dinner hour, my cell door opened and I was ordered before the governor, in order that I may hear him order, I was to get no dinner. I refused to go. Two, three, four, and five officers came. They dragged me outside the door. I laid hold of the iron railings. They could not unloosen me. The commander of the force cried out for the chain handcuffs. One of the officers ran downstairs and there was a cessation of hostilities till they came back up again. The handcuffs were put on. They pulled the long chain, but unless they pulled my arms off, they could not pull me away from the rails. In an imperative tone as I could command, I cried out, 'Hey, you man with that key, I order you to open these irons instantly.' He obeyed when I showed him that I had one of the iron bars in my embrace. I was tied again. The five or six of them laid hold of the long chain and pulled. I saw resistance was useless. I walked down the stairs, and then they led me in a monkey fashion in the presence of his majesty, the governor…a man in chains. (Cearnaigh, 1874/1967: 42)

This evidence from O'Donovan Rossa indicates an intense level of hostility between prisoners and prison officers and this impression is reinforced in the testimony of 'One who has tried them' (Anonymous, 1881) who noted, 'there are numerous and constant cases of gross cruelty and injustice in our prisons, and many prisoner's life is lost by the neglect and ill-treatment of brutal warders [officers]' (Ibid, 1881: 17).[5]

The testimony of imprisoned socialist agitator Michael Davitt on brutality at HMP Dartmoor to the Gladstone Report (House of Commons, 1895), further raised alarm about the frequency of prison officer violence within prisons. According to Davitt, at Dartmoor in the 1870s 'prisoners were frequently beaten underneath me in the punishment cells, in the night time, by the warders [officers]. The prisoners are being beaten up within particular segregation and punishment cells.' (cited in House of Commons, 1895: 384 (Gladstone Report)). Historically, prisoners housed in particular parts of the prison, such as segregation and punishment cells, are especially vulnerable to prison officer violence. Davitt (1885) also noted the futility of assaulting prison officers, as the system always makes sure the prisoner receives more violence than what they meet out:

> It is but the most stupid of lazy brutes who would act in this manner, as an attack upon a warder [prison officer] is always met by a defence in which the bruiser receives more than he bargains for, together with the additional punishment...(Davitt, 1885: 127)

There are many reasons why prisoners may not report prison officer violence. This could be, for example, because of fear of retribution from prison officers; or there could be concerns that the case would not be given appropriate credence. Responding to the concerns raised by Davitt, the Gladstone Report stipulated:

> It is only in human nature that there should be instances of unfair and unwise treatment of prisoners by warders in their constant daily personal relations with them...[S]o far as we have been able to find out, as a body they discharge their most difficult and responsible duties with forbearance

---

5. On 31st May, 1882, *The Times*, also reported that assaults on prisoners by prison warders (officers) were widespread, including detailed evidence on the death of a prisoner named Richards who had been virtually beaten to death in HMP Parkhurst. Only a few weeks later, on 1st July, 1882, the *Civil Service Gazette* published a letter from an assistant warder (prison officer), which claimed that prisoners were assaulted by prison warders on a daily basis. In 1890 a prisoner called Mr Gatcliffe died following a serious physical assault by a prison warder (officer) in HMP Manchester. The prison warder faced prosecution, but was acquitted, partly because evidence for the prosecution was reliant exclusively on prisoner testimonies (Radzinowicz and Hood, 1986: 565).

For Abolition

and kindness. On special inquiry, for example, at Dartmoor and Portland, we find that the following number of complaints were made by prisoners against warders

Table 1: Number of Complaints made against Officers by Convicts now at Dartmoor and Portland Convict Prisons respectively during the year 1894.

		Dartmoor	Portland
For violence		5	2
For abusive language		5	2
For unjust reports	{ for talking	-	7
	{ other offences	3	19
Total number of complaints		13	30
Total number of convicts in custody		1,028	1,066

No doubt, as Mr Davitt pointed out there may be many individual cases of hardship in which the prisoners, for obviously possible reasons, are afraid or unwilling to complain. But we consider this return, under the circumstances to be very satisfactory, bearing in mind that several times in every day of the year the warders were brought into personal relation with a total number of 2,094 convicts. (House of Commons, 1895: 17 (Gladstone Report))

The Gladstone Report, like many official reports and commissions prior and since, claimed that if there is prison officer violence, then it is down to a small number of problematic officers:

We have inquired into the allegations of brutal or harsh treatment by warders…We are satisfied that the cases of gross ill-treatment by warders which have occurred are very few in number, and that the harshness which is frequently imputed to the warders ought to be attributed rather to the compulsory enforcement of minute regulations than to any want of humanity on the part of the men themselves. [Those claiming prison officer violence was endemic were] unable to show that there was any ground for the charge other than the general à priori argument that in a large body of men there must be some black sheep. (Ibid: 35)

Despite evidence otherwise, claims of institutionalised violence by prison officers and the existence of a culture of violence, are denied. It is 'black sheep' and 'bad apples' that are responsible for any unwarranted violence.

There were reports from police officers of the brutal treatment of prisoners (though not just by prison officers) following the Dartmoor disturbances in 1932[6] and further evidence of violence against prisoners in the 1930s comes from Stuart Wood, who in a powerful account stated:

> I have seen men streaming with blood from blows with truncheons, and seen them thrown from the top of steel staircases to the bottom. I have seen men sustain broken limbs in resisting transfer to the punishment cells. I've heard them shrieking under the lash of the cat o' nine tails. And I've seen them thrust like beasts in straightjackets, lying helpless on the floors of padded cells. I have seen and worked with men in chains, with hideous sores on their ankles, and seen cells whose walls and floors were bespattered with blood after some poor devil had hacked his throat to escape the torture of solitary confinement or bullying. I have seen lots of things which nice people refuse to credit, or characterise as lies. (Wood, 1932: 190–1)

The testimony of the prisoner who calls himself Red Collar Man (1937), also published in the 1930s, gives further indication of how prisoners are vulnerable to prison officer violence and violations of dignity. Referring to the experience of a prisoner on hunger strike, he details how the physically weak prisoner is asked to take out his excrement and urine; is unable to do so; collapses; spills

---

6. According to the testimony of one police officer present that day, Steven Mansfield (cited in Greenwood, 2017), the suppression of the 1932 Dartmoor riot was led by chief constable Archibald Wilson, who said, 'in you go lads, it's them or us, so spare no mercy'. The prisoners were baton charged by the police and 23 prisoners received significant truncheon injuries. Seven prisoners were shot; one prisoner was shot in the neck by a prison warder. It is not the only example of brutal repression following prisoner disturbances. The violent suppression of prisoners after the disturbances at HMP Wormwood Scrubs 1907 also generated quite considerable concern. A number of prison warders (officers) were dismissed and prisoners given compensation.

his urine and excrement onto the floor of the wing; and then raised up by the prison officer and thrown headfirst into his own excrement and urine:

> Harrison was about halfway through this hunger strike, when I witnessed a disgusting act of perfectly unnecessary and revolting brutality towards him. At this time, it was obvious to anyone that he was too weak to stand, but one of the officers ordered him to get out of his bed and take his slops to the lavatory. He could not rise, so the warder took him out of the bed, wrapped a blanket around him, and then half carried, half pushed him along the corridor to the recess. When they reached it, the officer released his hold and Harrison immediately collapsed, spilling his slops all over the floor. The warder got a floor cloth and told Harrison to clean up the mess. He said that he could not do it. The warder seized him by the scruff of the neck, drags him onto his feet, and threw him down on his face into the mess. (Red Collar Man, 1937: 187)

Let us be clear here that slops are excrement, and at this time, there was what was known as slopping out, which is where prisoners would have to defecate within their cells, within effectively a bucket overnight, because there was no in-cell sanitation. And then, they would take their urine and excrement, and then they would slop it out[7] and throw it into effectively an entrance to the sewage system.

The wider circumstances surrounding the death of 20-year-old Arthur Clapworthy, who died of 'pernicious anaemia' (severe loss of blood) whilst serving in HMP Portland Borstal in September 1945 are also revealing. Clapworthy had served part of his sentence at HMP Wormwood Scrubs, where he experienced brutality at the hands of prison officers (House of Common Debate (HC Deb), December 19, 1945). His death led to questions in the House of Commons from his local MP:

> One day he punched him in his cell, and the exasperated lad hit back. The warder went out, locked the door, and came back with four or five other warders. Then the lad was punched, thrown to the ground, kicked and hit

---

7. Whilst slopping-out has long been replaced by in-cell sanitation virtually throughout the prison estate the notion of 'living and eating in a toilet' (*Chapter 5*) holds strong.

until the cell floor was a mass of blood. He was then lifted up, his hands were handcuffed behind his back, he was taken out of his cell, pushed down some steps, and given some further blows. (HC Deb, December 20, 1945)

This of course is not uncommon practice when it comes to responses to prisoners who are violent to prison officers. Where effectively 'my gang is bigger than your gang' and, if you fight back then you will be responded to with considerable violence. His mother shortly after he died went to visit the Prison Commissioners and was told, 'Oh, well, he may have had a hiding, and it may be that he was powerful and had to be restrained.' (HC Deb, December 20, 1945). It was discovered that a prison officer at Wormwood Scrubs had taken a strong dislike to Clapworthy and had punched him whenever the opportunity had arisen. The Wormwood Scrubs prison governor, drawing on official prison documentation of the incident, claimed only three (rather than five) prison officers had been involved; that the prisoner had not made an official complaint; and that he had not sought aid from the medical officer (Ibid). Chuter Ede, then Home Secretary, noted that in:

> …the prisons and Borstal institutions in this very difficult time, when every prison is understaffed, and when all sorts of additional difficulties beyond the normal have to be faced by prison officers, the highest possible standard shall be maintained, but, at the same time, I must protect my officers, if, in fact, they are in danger of assault or injury in the course of their duty. (Ibid)

More evidence of the invisible brutal hands of prisoner officers can be found in the inquiry into Liverpool Prison by Sir Godfrey Russell Vick QC (Vick, 1958). Concerns about prison officer violence were first raised by Labour MP Bessie Braddock, who stated that:

> [P]risoners [at Walton Prison, Liverpool] have been unable to find any way of making representations about the terrible screams and noises which go on in the punishment block [H.1. Block], not only on one day but on various days during the week. (HC Deb, 31 May 1956)

Braddock informed the House of Commons that on 25 April 1956, ten prisoners had raised concerns against such ill-treatment by petitioning the Home Secretary; and that each one was 'interviewed separately and threatened with disciplinary action' (Ibid). The resulting Vick Inquiry (1958), received testimony from 65 prisoners or ex-prisoners, who complained about the invisible brutal hands of 87 prison officers. The Vick Inquiry discredited the voices of a small number of prisoner testimonies (claiming some of the petitioners were mentally disturbed) whilst prison officers simply refused to give evidence. It also found there was evidence of assaults and grave personal violence; rough handling of prisoners; ill-conceived practical jokes (prisoners in the hospital were sprayed with water); deliberate actions by prison officers provoking prisoners; and the persistent use of foul language. Yet following the Vick Inquiry, only two prison officers were named for breaches of prison officer discipline. Neither were charged by the police and neither of the breaches were for ill treatment or violence towards prisoners.

In his alternative and unofficial inquiry into prisons, *Who Guards the Guards?*, Brian Stratton provides extensive testimony of prisoners who have been brutally dealt with by prison officers:

> Two screws grabbed me and dragged me away from the wall, still on the ground, when a third rushed at me like he was taking a penalty kick. His boot hit me somewhere around my left eye. It felt as though my head had been torn off. I remained conscious while he amused himself kicking the rest of me. All around I could hear agonising screams as this was being done. (Stratton,1970: 18–19)

> Your cell door is opened and two of them come in holding a mattress in front of them. So adept are they, that they will crowd you to the far end of the cell, allowing more screws to come in behind them. The latter screws wield riot sticks and just batter you to the floor. The mattress is dispensed with, and they really get to work on you with their boots. Your buttocks are the favourite target, as you roll up in a ball, and let them kick the rest of you to their hearts' content. When they are satisfied, they have lost all interest in the proceedings, they depart, closing the door behind them. You, who have been shrewdly lying there feigning unconsciousness (which is hard when

you are being kicked silly), think to yourself, it is over, and you start to move maybe a leg or arm. That's it. The door crashed open again and in they come. There is no mistake this time. When they do depart, you are not feigning unconsciousness. (Ibid: 37–8)

The following harrowing account from Jimmy Boyle also highlights merciless prison officer violence:

A short time later I heard the sound of heavy boots and the cell door opened. There stood the heavy mob all wearing coloured overalls and they told me to take off my clothes. I refused, saying that if they wanted to fight why didn't they get on with it. I was told that there would be no brutality, all they wanted was my clothes for the cops. I thought this over and accepted that they were telling the truth as there were enough of them to beat me up with my clothes on. No sooner had I stripped off than some of them moved in punching and kicking me. I tried to hit back, calling them cowardly lumps of shit. These were shouts of anger, but they beat me to the floor leaving me in a pool of blood. There is something totally humiliating about being brutalised when naked. Nakedness leaves a feeling of helplessness, and even though I was returning blows it felt as though they couldn't hurt the person they landed on. There was this feeling of impotence. I lay on the floor in an absolute rage, hating myself for being such a bloody fool as to trust them… (Boyle, 1977: 157)[8]

Mark Leech describes how he covered himself in his own excrement as a way of deterring prison officers from assaulting him:

I knew I was in for another beating, and I wasn't mistaken. So, I began shitting up. I look back now and wonder how on earth I could have sunk to

---

8. Violent assaults against prisoners from a multitude of prison officers have sometimes proved to be deadly. A notorious example is the violent death of Barry Prosser, at HMP Birmingham, 18th August 1980. His dead body was covered in bruises and he had a ruptured oesophagus (the food pipe from pharynx to the stomach). Although the inquest into his death in April 1981 found that Prosser had been *unlawfully* killed (Ibid: 39) and three prison officers were charged with the murder of Barry Prosser, the magistrates' court held in September 1981 found that there was 'no case to answer' (Coggan and Walker, 1983: 40). There was a further Crown Court trial in March 1982, where the jury returned verdicts that all three of the prison officers charged were not guilty.

such a level, but when you are treated like an animal, you invariably begin to act like one. I knew that if they came in for me, I'd have to do the only thing they couldn't abide, which was to hit them with shit. Ironically, they had to feed me, so it was a weapon that they could never remove. This notion of covering oneself in excrement as a way of actually trying to reduce the beatings, is something which again is a great infringement of an individual's human dignity. (Leech, 1992: 90)

Forcing prisoners into a situation of profound indignity indicates how endemic prison officer violence is. Indeed, by the early-1990s, harsh and brutal penal regimes, as well as inhumane and degrading living conditions—epitomised by 'slopping out', where prisoners were expected to take their buckets of urine and excrement and to place them into the prison sewage system by hand each morning—resulted in the penal system going into meltdown. Starting at HMP Manchester on 1 April 1990 (and continuing at this prison until 25 April), there were large scale disturbances across the penal estate in England and Wales for much of that month.

Lord Justice Harry Woolf (1991) was commissioned to investigate the disturbances at HMP Manchester and also at five further penal institutions: Glen Parva; Dartmoor; Cardiff; Bristol; and Pucklechurch. The report was heralded when published in February 1991 as, on the face of it, the methodology adopted appeared to facilitate prisoner voice. However, Woolf (1991) mirrored many previous reports by questioning the accuracy of that voice. The Woolf Report (1991) maintained that prisoner testimonies at HMP Pucklechurch were unreliable with regards to claims of prison officer retributive violence following the disturbance:

> …it is possible that the screams and the yells of pain which were allegedly heard, could be attributed to the use of control and restrain holders. Other screams and yells might have been deliberately misleading, put on by prisoners, who wanted to make out that they were being hurt. It is not possible for me to make any findings on these allegations. I am conscious, however, that my inability to do so will be unfair to staff, who are not in a position to rebut these and other allegations. (Woolf, 1991: para 8.142)[9]

---

9. Thanks to Joe Sim for highlighting this reference during the preparations of the chapter.

In other words, prisoner voice is not to be believed. Prisoners will give false impressions of being hurt. They will scream and yell, lie and deliberately mislead. There is a mismatch between evidence of prisoners regarding prison officer violence and its official recognition. The rather unpleasant reality did become a little more visible in April 1998, when evidence was published of 'torture'... 'systematic' and 'serious assaults'... 'inappropriate strip searches'... 'misapplication of control and restraint'... and 'illegal use of force' (Travis, 1999) by prison officers against more than 50 prisoners in the segregation unit at HMP Wormwood Scrubs. There was no official inquiry although eight prison officers were suspended and a police investigation was launched, but despite attracting media attention, no criminal prosecutions arose from this police probing.

The death of John Ahmed, a 42-year-old prisoner who died in the segregation unit HMP Manchester on 29 July 2015, also evidences prison officer violence. Ahmed died after a violent struggle with prison officers attempting to search him for allegedly concealing a package of drugs. He was violently restrained on three occasions. During the third restraint Ahmed 'began foaming at the mouth and made gurgling noises before becoming unresponsive' (Allison, 2017). No drugs were ever found. The coroner at his inquest highlighted the inconsistencies and contradictions in the evidence of the prison officers. When invited by the Prison and Probation Ombudsman (PPO) to give evidence regarding the circumstances of Ahmed's death, prison officers initially refused to respond, and interviews with the officers directly involved were not undertaken until December 2015, six months after the death. The PPO summed up the case as follows:

> Mr Ahmed became unresponsive while being restrained during a search after he had apparently concealed a contraband package in his mouth. While the restraint appeared necessary and the techniques employed by staff appeared to be in line with their training, the risks inherent in using them do not appear to have been fully understood or mitigated. In particular, Mr Ahmed was repeatedly kept in the prone position with his arms behind his back and even handcuffed while prone, without staff recognising his specific risk factors or, until it was too late, the distress he was in. (Newcomen, 2017: ii)

Whilst the post-mortem examination was unable to determine a definitive cause of death, Ahmed was held in a restraint hold that had high risk of positional asphyxia (self-suffocation). The inquest into his death heard that control and restraint (C&R) was being excessively deployed in the prison and found that Ahmed had been 'unlawfully restrained' by prison officers (Allison, 2017). There were no criminal prosecutions.[10]

The prison officers' tale: recollections and justifications

The above discussion shines a light on the neglect, brutality and violence of prison officers as charted in prisoner autobiographies and official discourse. Prison officer autobiographies also provide considerable historical evidence of violence (both physical and indeed psychological)[11] and this testimony is explored below through five key themes: *turning a blind eye; masking violence; normalisation; payback; and pathological prisoners*.

Turning a blind eye

Prison officers sometimes turn a blind eye to violence and allow prisoners to fight it out among themselves. One of the earliest published prison officer autobiographers—who described themselves as Warden—noted:

> It was customary in those days when a fight arose, to follow the same procedure, clear a ring and let them fight it out fairly, only interfering in the case of a foul. Then, after the fight, to discover and punish the aggressor, whether he was the victor or vanquished, and let off the other man. (Warden, 1929: 40)

Prison officers adhere to their own sense of justice. When prisoners start to fight, officers allow it to continue, only stepping in when a prisoner 'is seen to

---

10. Two prison officers were tried for the vicious assault of Nigel Halfacre, also in HMP Manchester. Mr Halfacre had been dragged into his cell (where there is no CCTV coverage) and then 'held down and repeatedly punched and kicked' (Bardsley, 2018) after he had thrown excrement and urine at prison officers on the prison landing. The accuracy of the evidence of Mr Halfacre was questioned as he was a substance user and both prison officers were cleared of assault in Manchester Crown Court in February 2018.
11. See the following three chapters for further discussion of psychological violence by prison officers.

be getting the worst of it' (Triston, 1938: 30). In a more recent prison officer autobiography, Robert Douglas (2008), put it this way:

> A general rule of thumb when two convicts start to fight is don't break it up too quickly. If it's between two guys who you think are hard cases and it starts off quite viciously, let them punch themselves out. Intervene too early, when their tempers are up and they're still fresh, then you're liable to get it clamped. It doesn't take long until they're knackered. Then they're only too pleased when you jump in and settle it. (Douglas, 2008: 41–2)

Masking violence

A second theme is the masking of violence. This is very vivid in the writings of Jim Dawkins (2006), a former prison officer, who paints a horrific picture of retributive, vengeful and brutal prison officer hands being directed towards prisoners on a regular basis. Dawkins indicates that officer violence arises in specific places and at particular times, all at the choosing of the prison officer. One example is the use of C & R:

> C & R [Control and Restraint]…[is] something that was designed to prevent injury and damage occurring to both staff and prisoners during incidents, but many staff abuse this knowledge and adapt their skills to inflict as much pain as possible to inmates [prisoners]. So, control and restraint, which appears to be a legitimate use of prison officer authority and power, is an opportunity to use greater physical pain than necessary. (Dawkins, 2006: 109–10)

On the face of it this is legal and legitimate violence and provides further ways of invisibilising the brutal hands of prison officers. Dawkins also had this to say:

> Each of the twelve inmates was then in turn dragged up from the floor and, still bent over double with an officer on each arm and one pushing his head down almost between his knees, he began the painful, slow walk to the segregation unit. The PO [principal officer] accompanied each move personally and kept the tension going with shouts to encourage the

escorting staff to tweak the wrist locks a bit if the inmate fell quiet for a moment. (Ibid: 14)

The 'screams of pain' of prisoners, so easily dismissed by Woolf (1991) at HMP Pucklechurch, are given here as direct evidence (albeit in a different prison at a different time). The testimony from Dawkins (2006) continues when the prisoners arrive in the segregation unit:

> Once in the strip cells of the seg [segregation] unit, the prisoners were subjected to a brutal disrobing of their clothes, which were literally torn from them, and they were left, many of them bleeding and complaining of injury, lying naked on the bare concrete floor of the cell. To relocate all twelve inmates took approximately forty-five minutes in total, and I watched in disbelief as they were manhandled down the stairs and at the ferocity and venomous way in which the staff took pleasure in causing as much pain as possible in order to look good, in front of the bearded wanker, a security PO [principal officer]. (Ibid:14)

There are also locations in prisons where there are no CCTV cameras working. Former prison officer Neil Samworth (2018) gives this important insight:

> The entrance to cell 17 in HMP Forest Bank, bottom of the landing on the right, was the only camera blind spot, and every prisoner down there knew that. There was another small area on the exercise yard outside, but that was it. You couldn't be filmed going into that cell. If you'd a badass on, you could threaten to put them in cell 17, and they'd fall straight into line. I'm not saying we gave them a kicking or anything, but disruptive prisoners drain resources from everyone, including their fellow prisoners. So, one spoken threat was enough. (Samworth, 2018: 26–7)

No cameras, no evidence. This may or may not have been a place of violence, but it certainly was used to control prisoners through the fear of physical violence. The very real possibility of physical violence, whether that be in terms of legitimated violence through the coercion of control and restraint, or the actual violence otherwise by prison officers beating up prisoners, underscore prisoner conformity.

Normalisation

There is evidence of cultures of violence among prison officers. Elizabeth Mawer (2006), a former prison officer in a prison for women, claims that the prison place is an institution where prison officers can, if they so wish, take vengeance at will against a prisoner. 'There was those that did enjoy it. They did enjoy inflicting pain. Why? Simply because they could' (Mawer, 2006: 28). *Screwed*, written by a prison officer who used the fake name of 'Ronnie Thompson', is a very sensationalised piece of literature, but nonetheless is also insightful. 'Thompson' (2008) noted the following:

> I will give you an example. A con is violent so he gets bent up. He's nicked, that is, he's placed on report and then seen by the Governor. The Governor's verdict? Three days' cell confinement. The con laughs at it; he does not see this as punishment at all. The result is he does not change his ways, or his violent behaviour. The screw, however, is resourceful and will find a way to make this con fall into line with everyone else. First of all, this piece of shit's daily newspaper keeps going missing. On top of that, he always manages to be the last to be let out for a shower and first to be banged up again. He never gets what he ordered for his dinner, and his mail constantly goes astray. Believe you me, this cunt will soon start to conform to the regime and what is expected of him. (Thompson, 2008: 80)

The normalisation of brutal and discriminatory treatment against a prisoner is one way of ensuring that an asymmetrical deference is established. It is just part of the job:

> If need be, a screw will go to a prisoner's cell to give him a personal lesson, so he knows exactly what the score is. I'm not talking about a load of screws going to a cell to give a scroat a good kicking. A decent screw is not a bully or an animal. I do stress the word 'decent'. Sometimes, if all else fails, a bit of man-to-man can sort it. I live in the real world. I don't say things to be politically correct. I say things that I think are right. If people don't like it, they can fuck off. Sometimes, if you take the piece of shit away from his audience, and you tell them how it is, when there are just the two of you, most of the time he will crumble like a cake. Sometimes he won't and there

will be a scrap in the cell. No alarm bell, no whistles, it gets sorted there and then between the two of you. The problem is then rectified, and he stops acting like a cunt. (Ibid: 81)

Physical violence is seen as a last resort perhaps, but it is something which is part of the prison officer armoury.

Payback

Then there is retaliation following prison disturbances. There is considerable evidence where prison officers 'get stuck into the cons' (Dawkins, 2006: 8) and get 'payback' (Ibid) on prisoners by inflicting pain for previous misdemeanours. Dawkins (2006:14), in his book, *Loose Screw*, describes it so:

> Then, the security PO [principal officer] took position in the middle of the spur and, with a sadistic grin on his face shouted, 'I can't hear much pain being inflicted'.
>
> No sooner had the words left his lips, than the spur erupted with ear-piercing screams of pain, as the officers heeded his words and tightened their hold on the prisoners' wrists and legs.
>
> 'That's better. Now that we have your attention, we're moving you to the segregation unit one at a time. I hope this has been a lesson that you do not fuck about in my jail'. (Ibid: 14)

Dawkins (2006) explains that prison disturbances are a way of settling scores and ensuring that prison officers in the long-term hold the upper hand:

> Some members of staff even seemed to look forward to a disturbance as it gave them the chance to get their hands on a prisoner. This was especially so if there was a particular prisoner who was not very well liked by the staff. It was common when a prisoner in this category received a visit for as many staff from his wing who could get away from their normal duties to congregate in the visits room in the hope that he would 'perform' and they could get a piece of the action. (Ibid: 82)

Prison officers were looking for ways and means of actually trying to get payback on prisoners. Now, this leads us to consider concerns around the justification of violence and the broader problem of violence of prisons.

Pathological prisoners

Prisoners are considered as morally tainted individuals. The prison officers are the 'good guys' and the prisoners are the 'bad guys'. Because prison officers are morally superior *their* violence is legitimate (Edney, 1997). L W Merrow Smith (1962) makes the point that prison officer violence has a more pragmatic basis — it is about trying to control those recalcitrant, disrespectful, pathological prisoners:

> Most screws are fair-minded men who are ready to give the moody prisoner a break but a determined challenge to authority can only be met by a firm hand if a working discipline is to be maintained. (Merrow Smith and Harris, 1962: 141)

It is implausible to argue prison officers *always underuse* their power to facilitate order and control. Considerable historical and contemporary evidence indicates that prison officers *overuse* their powers. They expect prisoners to operate within the notions of an asymmetrical deference norm, to be respectful and conform and prisoners who do not follow these 'unwritten rules' face violent reprisals; righteous violence against immoral people. This is something which seems to be normalised within the prison officer occupational culture. Alongside this, there is also the constant fear of violence and the discrete and masked use of violence by prison officers when undertaking their duties.

Conclusion

This chapter provides a historical context to the shocking revelations of the April 2020 European Committee for the Prevention of Torture and Inhuman or Degrading Treatment or Punishment (CPT) (2020) report on prison officer violence in the UK. Whilst in recent years there have been situational and technological interventions in the prison place (such as the introduction of CCTV and changes to prison designs) increasing the potential for the surveillance of both prisoners and prison officers, there has been no concerted challenge to the dominant prison officer occupational culture normalising violence against prisoners. What is remarkable, given the extent of prison officer violence detailed in the CPT (2020) report, is how the official bodies charged with holding prisons accountable, such as the Independent Monitoring Boards, Prison Ombudsmen and HM Chief Inspectorates, failed pick up on such systemic and widespread practices of violence earlier.

One reason for the of absence of any significant interventions tackling prison officer violence is that it remains shrouded in silence and 'literal denial' (Cohen, 2001). There has consistently been a failure to officially acknowledge that prison officer violence happens at all, and certainly not at a systemic level. The Prison Officers Association (POA) has for a number of years called for zero tolerance on physical violence in prison but their focus has been exclusively on the violence of prisoners. The POA have had virtually nothing to say about prison officer violence. The media also almost always focus on prisoner physical violence, and even a special issue of the usually well-informed *Prison Service Journal* on 'reducing prison violence' in 2015 concentrated mainly on prisoner violence (Prison Service Journal, 2015). Prisoners remain reluctant to report incidents of violence by prison officers for fear of retaliation whereas prison officers also appear unwilling to raise their voices as whistle-blowers, at least when still in the job. The literal denial of the brutal hands of prison officers is nothing new—it has been the dominant narrative since the first reformed prisons of the 1800s, albeit interspersed by regular revelations, often through auto-biographical reflections or submissions to official inquiries.

Whilst prison officer physical violence remains hidden to the outside world, the brutal hands of prison officers are certainly not invisible to prisoners. Prison violence should be understood within the wider context of legal coercion, repression and state violence. Violence is deeply embedded in penal confinement and hence, its very existence inevitably raises profound moral questions. Let us now though move on to consider some other ways in which social death manifests itself in the prison place.

CHAPTER 4

Phantom Faces at the Window:
Prisons, Dignity and Moral Exclusion

> Those who are morally excluded are perceived as undeserving, expendable, and therefore eligible for harm. Although both those inside and outside the moral community can experience wrongful harm, harm inflicted on insiders is more readily perceived as an injustice and activates guilt, remorse, outrage, demands for reparative response, self-blame, or contrition. When harm is inflicted on outsiders, it may not be perceived as a violation of their rights, and it can fail to engage bystanders' moral concern. (Opotow, 1990: 12)

Prisons submerge those they contain within a sea of hurt and suffering. Profoundly hierarchical institutions, prisons set deferential relationships in stone. It is only through face-to-face encounters rooted in empathy and compassion that obligations to respect the innate dignity of others are fully acknowledged (Bauman, 1989; Bauman and Donskis, 2013). Prisons steal ethical encounters, leaving prisoners with *phantom faces* and replacing recognition of necessary needs with insensitivity and moral exclusion. When it comes to empathising and showing solidarity with the suffering of victims of injustice, all too often it is not just about the extent of hurt inflicted, but also about *who* is harmed; *who* inflicted the harm; and if the victim is an insider or outsider in terms of the collective moral community (Opotow, 1990; Cohen, 2001; Scott, 2008b; Drake and Scott, 2019b). In other words, victimhood is shaped by whether the physically, emotionally or psychologically injured person is considered to be of value, worth and moral standing. It is also a question of empathy.

The focus of this chapter is on failures of recognition of prisoner suffering and innate dignity, as evidenced in prisoner and prison officer autobiographies. This is done in the following three ways. First, by considering dignified acknowledgement of *face*, empathy and our responsibilities for ameliorating the suffering of others. Second, by mulling over evidence of moral inclusion and respect of dignity; noting that whilst these exceptions prove the rule, prison life is never simply 'black and white' or locked in a total blanket of moral exclusion. And third, by exploring moral exclusion and the systematic violation of dignity in the prison place via discussion of 'less eligibility' and the 'width of imprisonment'. The chapter concludes by arguing that the prison place is morally blind because it is organisationally structured to produce moral indifference.

Face and acknowledgement

Humans are relational and intersubjective beings who need relationships with others for wellbeing. Stable human identities are dependent upon positive human interactions rooted in care, trust and respect. Humans also require certain freedoms (both positive and negative) and are more likely to prosper in non-coercive environments allowing voluntary human encounters. Consequently, deprivation of voluntary interactions, or experience of encounters with others grounded in hostility and/or violence are profoundly damaging. Enrique Dussel (2013) indicates that an ethical state institution is organised to facilitate life, wellbeing and respect of dignity; and such institutional arrangements should facilitate positive and negative freedoms and be as least coercive as possible. If we take these socialist principles of *freedom, dignity* and *right to life* (plus also *empathy*) as our starting point, then we should not only treat people, including strangers and the estranged, in a non-coercive or non-violent manner, but also with respect and regard to their wellbeing. If an institution is saturated in excessive coercion, whose daily workings threaten wellbeing and life and/or systematically violate dignity, it cannot be considered ethical.

Innate dignity can never be removed, but it can be violated. Dignity is threatened when encounters with others generate feelings of fear and pain (Luban, 2015). Violations of dignity include being humiliated or treated in a humiliating fashion; being exploited or being made to feel like a vulnerable and powerless person; and/or being subjected to physical, psychological, emotional or financial harm. Prisons are coercive institutions of social death and are often experienced as hostile, alienating and humiliating. The prison place deepens a sense of powerlessness and inevitably puts discipline and security above consideration of human rights or meeting needs. Prisoners are treated as devalued people, deprived not only of liberty, but also many taken for granted goods and services; heterosexual relationships; truly voluntary decision-making; independent choices and personal autonomy/freedoms; as well as a sense of safety and security (Sykes, 1958). Irrespective of prison conditions, which are clearly very poor in England and Wales (Scott and Sim, 2020a), prison regimes threaten to violate dignity.

Whether someone is included or excluded from our moral universe — and thus if we have empathy for their suffering — is also a profoundly ethical question. Dussel (2013) teaches that we have a non-reciprocal ethical responsibility to other people and that acknowledgement of this responsibility is prompted not by human connectedness or personal intimacy, but rather by the 'face' of the other — that is, their human existence. Knowledge of suffering, whether gleaned through an ethical encounter or other means, creates an ethical demand to do what we can to ameliorate it. There is undoubtedly then a profound asymmetry regarding responsibilities for others in socialist ethics. Power and responsibility are tied together with an umbilical cord; for the greater our powers in each social or situational context, the greater our responsibilities.

Meeting the demands of this asymmetrical responsibility, which contrasts directly with the 'asymmetrical deference norm' discussed in *Chapter 3*, requires an ability to *empathise* with people who are not similar to us. If there are blockages in acknowledgement a sufferer may be considered as having a 'phantom face', which invisibilises their suffering and innate dignity. There are times when prisoners are treated with humanity, empathy and dignity by prison officers (see Crawley, 2004; Liebling and Price, 1998; Scott, 2006a; and the section below) as well as occasions when prisoners are subjected to sadistic, cruel and potentially fatal physical violence (see previous chapter). Moral indifference may not characterise *all* relationships in prison, but it is perhaps the most likely emotional constellation.

Moral inclusion

To morally include someone means to situate that person within our moral universe and empathise with their lived experiences, including their pain and suffering. There is some evidence in prisoner and prison officer autobiographies of emotional literacy in the prison place and that some relationships between prisoners and prison officers have been grounded in mutual respect. Writing in the 1930s, William Holt (1934) notes that sometimes there were pleasant and supportive interactions between prisoners and prison officers. 'The prison officer was human and kindly, his face was pleasant, so long as we did our work he did not interfere, sometimes he talked and joked with us' (Holt, 1934: 3). Some years later Rupert Croft-Cooke gives further indication that some prisoners were treated, by at least some prison officers, well. Prison officers, he maintained were, 'decent men who interpret their duties with humour, sympathy and fellow feeling. They did not seek to take advantage of an unnatural situation…' (Croft-Cook, 1955: 96). This 'unnatural situation' may well be conducive to prisoner exploitation, humiliation and powerlessness, but it is *not always the case*. Rosie Johnston also found in her experience that prison officers recognise the common humanity of prisoners. Despite the moral condemnation which is attached to the category of prisoner, she felt that she and her fellow prisoners 'were not made to feel like a human sub-species because we were convicted criminals' (Johnston, 1989: 109). Prison officers have written about positive connections between prison officers and prisoners. Writing anonymously in the late 1920s, Warden gives testimony of genuine emotional bonds developing between prisoners and prison officers, something likely to ensure dignity is respected:

> I have known cases where really genuine friendships have sprung up between warders and convicts, where it seems quite natural a thing for the warder to talk to prisoners about all of his troubles and joys and where the warder has sincerely felt a sense of loss when the convict is gone. (Warden, 1929: 119)

Warden (1929), who also had recognition of the pains and harms of imprisonment, further powerfully states that:

Prison, the place where often souls are destroyed and bodies broken, is the only remedy that we attempt to apply in omnibus fashion to cover every anti-social activity. Manifestly there is something wrong here. (Ibid: 203–204)

Warden acknowledges that imprisonment results in the destruction of bodies and souls and fundamentally fails in regard to its overall objective of rehabilitating those who have broken the law. But he went even further, for a few pages later he wrote about how prisons are both brutal and deadly: '[I]t is the utter monotony of prison life which kills and with the monotony is coupled a system of calculated repression which is as stupid as it is cruel' (Ibid: 216).

In a more recent testimony, 'Ronnie Thompson' indicates that there can still be emotional connections and recognition of the shared humanity of prisons in the current day, albeit that his rationale is more instrumental; arguing for prisoners and prison officers to have decent relationships because it makes prison work more manageable:

Screws can have a close relationship with cons, at times. You spend more time with cons than you do with your wife or family. You want to get on with them because you want an easy life, and for the con it's the same. If you can have a laugh and get on with the prisoners while doing the job, great. (Thompson, 2008: 144)

Not only do prison officers sometimes have positive engagement with prisoners, but there is also some evidence of acts of kindness by prison officers. In his prisoner autobiography, George Dendrickson had this to say about one prison warder (officer) at HMP Dartmoor:

Acts of kindness which he performed, such as inviting a discharged prisoner to his house for breakfast before seeing him on to his train home, earned him the lasting gratitude of many prisoners and the disapproval of those less tender-hearted. (Dendrickson and Thomas, 1954: 81)

The 'less tender-hearted' (Ibid) Dendrickson is referring to are prison officers, indicating an absence of an occupational culture of kindness. Norman

Howarth Hignett writing at a similar time to Dendrickson, had this to say about the kindness of prison officers in HMP Wormwood Scrubs:

> He who would do good in prison may do so only by strength, while I do not forget many examples of roughness and brutality I am glad to express a real sense of gratitude to many officers at Wormwood Scrubs from whom I received kindness and helpfulness and who sought me out to wish me well when the end came. They are however not of the common breed and their like is rare to be found in other prisons. That they become part of an environment as dehumanising to themselves as it is to their charges and they are compelled to work in a world where kindness is possible only by subterfuge and where roughness is expected and brutality encouraged. (Hignett, 1956: 66)

Zeno acknowledges that there were a few traces 'of occasional compassion' among prison officers, but gives this powerful overall appraisal:

> These are the men who could change the whole prison service, for they have an empathetic understanding of what it feels like to be imprisoned. But they are a tiny minority. It is a constant surprise to me that they exist at all. It is hard to reconcile these men with their labour. (Zeno, 1970: 21)

These reflections indicate the *exceptional nature* of small acts of prison officer kindness: each small act is so significant because it is so rare. Noel 'Razor' Smith reinforces such a perception with the following moving account:

> I cleared my throat and engaged him in a pointless conversation about getting a clean blanket…He pulled out a packet of Embassy Number 10 cigarettes. I remember them because they had a bright red stripe on the packet, and it had been so long since I had seen a bright colour it really stood out in the gloom and drabness of the block. He looked out into the corridor to make sure that none of the other screws was about, and then handed me one of the cigarettes. I could barely believe it,…I was so surprised by this little act of kindness that tears prickled in the back of my eyes. (Smith, 2005: 152)

The strong emotional reaction of Smith (2005) to this small act of kindness is very telling; to receive a small gift (like a cigarette) from someone in most situations does not provoke tears. But this small act of kindness in the broader context of pain, cruelty and indifference is hugely significant. To use the words here of Smith in a slightly different way, any act of kindness or the showing of empathy in the prison place is a shining light against the overwhelming gloom and drabness of the daily penal regime. The backcloth is so dark and bleak that even the smallest glimmers of light and hope and kindness are remembered.

Ruth Wyner eloquently makes this very point in her testimony on prison life:

> In the evening we had: a visit from a screw, who whispered to Jules through the hatch; I'll bring you something later on, some cake if I can get it...Unfortunately, this officer, known throughout the prison for good heartedness, was one of a kind; an isolated harbinger of humanity, a faint beacon of hope in this landscape of desolation. (Wyner, 2003: 27–28)

Some prisoners do become part of the moral universe of some prison officers and there is also evidence of small acts of kindness and the showing of empathy, but they are rare and exceptional and not something that is nurtured in brutal penal environments. The opposite in fact is likely to be the case, with kindness perceived as weakness, thus constraining the impulse to show care and compassion. Life-affirming prisoner and prison officer relationships grounded in mutual empathy and respect occasionally exist, despite the daily workings of the morally exclusionary penal machinery, but they remain tenuous, contingent and easily torn apart.

Moral exclusion

Moral exclusion refers to failures to recognise the shared humanity of others. Susan Opotow (1990) argues that someone experiencing *mild moral exclusion* is constructed as less worthy of respect. This develops in a slow-but-sure way where 'over time harms and dissimilarities eclipse benefits and the similarities, gradually moving marginalised groups outside the scope of justice' (Opotow, 1990:6). Ironically, prisons are supposed to deliver 'justice', but in reality, are violent institutions grounded in the deprivation of liberty and moral condemnation. 'Reformed prisons' since the early-1800s are designed to separate out lawless and morally inferior people from the 'law-abiding majority'. Their indignities, deaths and injuries are not considered as significant as those befalling people on the outside because the socially dead prisoner is no longer eligible for our care and concern. This dehumanisation of prisoners does not seem to serve the interests of society or provide the kind of justice that victims are looking for. In this sense, imprisonment denies justice for victims of criminal harms as well as prisoners, indicating that a sense of justice for both victims and lawbreakers are not diametrically opposed.

An early statement on 'less eligibility' came from the Reverend Daniel Nihill, chaplain governor of the General Penitentiary in Millbank, London in the 1820s. Nihill believed that if prisons were tough and austere, they could be conduits for redemption. That is, that prisons could be places which could turn immoral people into moral ones. In his book, Nihill (1839) wrote that, 'Prison fare, *ex vi termini,* should be reduced far below that which falls within the reach of the honest and industrious' (Ibid: 18). In other words, Nihil argued that prison policy should ensure prisoners were treated worse than the common labourer. This was because the deprivations and denials of dignity characterising the prison place were not just about disciplining and controlling those confined within its walls; inhuman and degrading prison conditions were also meant to send a message to the rest of society encouraging them to conform to the rules. Nihill also had this to say:

> If it be found by the visits of strangers or the intimations made to friends that the food and clothing, the cheerfulness and warm, the medicine and diet and accommodations in times of sickness, the shelter and the bedding and various other comforts enjoyed by convicts present a luxurious contrast to the miseries of the honest labouring class, the effect must be to strip imprisonment of its awful character and give rise to many recommitments. (Ibid: 7)

Whilst having close physical daily contact with a person can lead to the fostering of empathy, prisoners are likely to be Othered through 'psychic distancing'; that is, they are psychologically placed outside of the moral universe and considered as less eligible for care and support (Bauman,1990; Sim, 1990; Scott, 2008b). Rather than acknowledgment, prisoner suffering is often denied by a mild form of moral exclusion, notably benign moral indifference (Cohen, 2001; Scott, 2006a, 2008b). The prison place invisibilises prisoner suffering and crushes empathy. Prisoners, become shadowy, ghost-like figures beyond the realms of shared humanity and this Othering is deeply embedded within the logic and structure of the daily operational practices of the prison place. The security, discipline and coercion of the prison place actively undermine attempts to mitigate pain, respect dignity and meet human need. Prisons prevent people from developing free relationships with others and thus fulfilment of potential. Instead there are deprivations of need; restrictions on interactions and choices; an almost complete absence of empathy; and the snuffing out of hope for the future, which ultimately can lead to the end of life.

Width of imprisonment

The width of imprisonment refers to the psychic Othering of prisoners and indicates that rather than a sense of closeness between prisoners and prison officers, there is a gap or emotional width between them. The width of imprisonment is perhaps inevitable given the antagonism generated by the different social roles of the keepers and kept. Each social role is likely to have a narrow and negative, if not downright hostile, stereotype of the other (Goffman 1963). The inherent antagonism and deeply embedded psychic distancing in prison indicate that close relationships between prisoners and prison officers will always be the exception (Scott, 2006a). Those defending the way prison officer and prisoner relationships currently operate argue there are differences between 'right'/'good' relationships and empathetic close relationships. Liebling and Price put it this way:

> The two most significant criteria used in relational thinking, 'closeness' and 'quality' (do two people like each other?)—cannot be directly translated into suitable criteria for the measurement of *prison* relationships. The Relationships Foundation try to measure relational 'proximity' (meaning empathy). Yet relationships between officers and prisoners are not straightforward, with complex power dynamics inherent within them—proximity

can have its dangers in such relationships, as well as its rewards. (Liebling and Price, 1998: 5)

Liebling and Price (Ibid) concede that it is virtually impossible for close and mutually empathetic relationships between prisoners and prison officers to be sustained in the prison place. The best that can be aspired to are 'good'/'right' relationships, yet such relationships are not grounded in an empathetic recognition of the face. The approach of Liebling and Price (1998) to prisoner-prison officer relationships rather conveniently sidesteps the problems of 'phantom faces', moral indifference and the denial of suffering. Socialist ethics require empathy and a dignified recognition of face, but such commitments are missing from the limited approach to human connectedness in 'good'/'right' relationships.

Drawing upon the insight of Alvin Gouldner (1973) prison officers can be considered as local 'caretaking officials'. That is, they are low-level bureaucrats who must operate within the daily constraints of their working conditions and dictates of managers. Their role is basically to ensure that penal regimes function from the morning to evening; there are no escapes; and prisons continue as disciplinary and punitive institutions. A moral problem raised in the daily functions of these 'caretakers of punishment' (Scott 2006b) is their inability to fully acknowledge the suffering of those below them in an organisational structure. Whereas prison officers are bureaucrats able to recognise their own suffering and some of the deeply entrenched problems of the prison place, they are unable to stretch out and broaden their moral universe to encapsulate the profound pain and suffering that prisoners encounter (Scott, 2008b).

That prison officers have systematically denied the pains of prisoners and violated human dignity through everyday working practices and procedures is well-established in the penological literature (Scott, 2006a. 2008b, 2018b; Sim 2008). Deborah Drake argues that the negative and hostile stereotype of prisoners held by many prison officers makes it difficult to build on a commitment to treating prisoners as 'fellow human beings' (Drake, 2011: 378). In an institution, which privileges security, discipline and control above all else, it is very difficult to deliver a caring custody approach. The width of imprisonment is deeply embedded and perhaps inevitable for detention justified not only by deprivation of freedom, but also moral condemnation and punishment.

The indignities of prison life

There is extensive evidence of the violation of dignity in the writings of prisoners. Walter Probyn gives us the following illustration of powerlessness, vulnerability and humiliation in prison:

> The screws had started one of their frequent campaigns of petty niggling in order to deprive cons of part of their visiting time. To humiliate them in front of their families, the screws stop cons who were just about to sit down with their visitors and order them to go and change into their greys. The con had often just come from work and was dressed in overalls and it would take 15 minutes or so for him to go back to his ward and change. It was not enough for the screw to assert their authority, there was no satisfaction in them unless their victims felt humiliated. (Probyn, 1988: 218)

Given such testimony, it should come as no surprise to learn that prisoners consider prison officers as people who at times deliberately dehumanise them and operate through mentalities of 'us versus them'. Trevor Hercules in his autobiography *Labelled a Black Villain*[1] notes that:

> Any defect you had, they would use against you: 'Hey, you fatso,' or 'You with the rubber lips, get up here.' They were conditioning you to accept that you were nobody, with no-one to help you, and any feelings of pride you had were now strictly taboo. (Hercules, 1989: 33)

Zeno put it this way:

> On the faces of some of the screws an animal brutality, a shallow-eyed insensitivity that is hard to imagine as being wholly human; on the faces of the majority of them a look of complete indifference born of an apathetic acceptance of narrow limitations of the job they do, and of their surroundings. (Zeno, 1970: 20)

---

1. A new and expanded edition of this book was published by Waterside Press in 2020.

Both testimonies indicate the presence of phantom faces and moral indifference; where the prisoner is someone who is treated without empathy. They also indicate the presence of 'dividing practices' where prisoners are categorised as either deserving or underserving, worthy or unworthy, eligible or less eligible for care, support and humane treatment.

There are of course two sides to the story. Prisoners use language to describe prison officers, which indicate antagonism and hostility underlying the prisoner/prison officer relationship. Therefore, let us consider some examples cited in prisoner autobiographies to describe prison officers:

- Dragon (Peckham, 1985: 211);

- Mugsie, who has face like a shoebox (Collins, 1998: 39);

- Chewing Gum Charlie (Ibid: 40);

- Goebbels (Parker, 1998: 23);

- Hitler (Smith, 2005: 109)

- Vinegar Tits, Mighty Mouse, and The Vulture (Kirby, 2002: 248);

- Pigs (Stratton: 1970: 16);

- Piggy Face (Ibid: 18);

- Tomato Necks (Ibid: 25);

- Stuffed Penguins (Wyner, 2003: 152); and

- Bastards (Ibid:159).

Christopher Burney (1962), gives a vivid account of this sense of antagonism and enmity as he talks about a prison officer who he called 'the toad':

[whose]...transmutation had been arrested half-way and had left the two sets of features into one diminutive body: bulging eyes, vast down-turned mouth, crapulousness wrinkles, and a sub-human peevish cunning which ever drove him to spy on us silently from behind our shoulders. He had a deep hoarse croak, and if there were no warts visible on the exposed portion of the skin, they were not lacking in his spirit. (Burney, 1962: 99)

This language seems to provide evidence of how prison officers are sometimes no longer considered fellow humans by prisoners. However, prisoners do not exercise power and authority over prison officers, nor are they likely to be able to humiliate or generate a sense of vulnerability and powerlessness among the staff cohort. In fact, the above re-naming of prison officers could also be interpreted as a form of resistance outside the hegemonic idiom contesting the abuse of power by prison officers and structured indignities of the prison place.

One way of violating innate human dignity—and something which is indicative to the social death of prisoners—is un-naming (Scott, 2011, 2018). It has long been common practice for prison officers to no longer use a prisoner's real name, but simply refer to them as a number through derogatory language. In so doing it is much easier to objectify prisoners and deny shared humanity. The derogatory language used by some prison officers in their autobiographies leaves a strong impression that prisoners are not widely recognised as fellow human beings.

L W Merrow Smith (1962), puts it this way when describing some prisoners: 'every prison population has a hard core of the worst type of cheats, liars and swindlers' (Merrow Smith, 1962: 152), implying that prisoners are immoral. Harley Cronin (1967) also gives us some indication of his perceptions and constructions of prisoners. He describes them, for example, as 'savages and persistent thugs' (Cronin, 1967: 13), as 'uncouth deadbeats' (Ibid: 24) and 'louts' (Ibid: 54). These are both accounts from the 1960s, but they do show how deeply engrained this notion is of the prisoner as lesser. The prisoner is an immoral ill-bred, uncouth, savage, liar and swindler. The language to describe prisoners in lesser terms can also be found in some more recent prison officer autobiographies. Let us consider just four—Jim Dawkins (2006), Robert Douglas (2008), Ronnie Thompson (2008) and Neil Samworth (2018). The language they used to refer to prisoners includes:

> ...twat, cock, scumbag, gobshite, scrote, dickhead, filthy bastard, wanker, cunt, toe rag, muppet, fraggle, weasel, con, fuck pig, ratbag, nonce, smackhead, shitbag and knobhead. (Dawkins, 2006; Douglas, 2008; Thompson, 2008; Samworth, 2018)

But there are other examples of where prison officers have shown disrespect and violated the dignity of prisoners. This ranges from things like the tone of voice right the way through to little tricks and psychological games played on prisoners by prison officers.

Hubert Pee, writing during the Great War, notes the manner in which prison warders (officers) spoke to him:

> The tone of voice used by some officers has a very depressing effect. Their speech was too often a mere shout, the voice in which one would herd cattle. I have many a time been cheered up for the whole afternoon just by one word from a genial curious officer. (Pee, 1917: 46)

What is interesting from Pee's account is the connection between the way prisoners are being spoken to and subsequent dehumanisation: the tone of address made prisoners feel they were being treated like animals. Probyn, describing Wormwood Scrubs in the 1940s, similarly states:

> The screws were like snarling animals shouting invective at the top of their voices. Almost everything they said was couched in the form of a threat. To intimidate anyone who they knew was new to the prison they would say, we tame lions here. (Probyn, 1977: 36)

Croft-Crooke (1955) illustrates the asymmetry in terms of prisoners and prison officers addressing each other, and argues that:

> The screw is a despot whether he wants to be or not by the very nature of his calling. The prisoner's awareness of this is in itself a degradation; he may be a man who has spent his life in a position of authority and to find that some impudent youth in blue uniform can order him and expect to be called sir

can be insulting and is a sufficient outrage to any sense of human dignity which may have been left to him. (Croft-Crooke, 1955: 93)

Prisoners may be referred to via all sorts of abusive words and be shouted at. But prison officers must be referred to by the title of 'Sir' or 'Mr' (Scott, 2011). In a further illustration, Judith Ward, describes the petty humiliations and sense of powerlessness deeply engrained within prisoner and prison officer relationships:

There were other officers that I despised and wouldn't pass the time of day with. They saw their role of one of power and authority and appeared to be lacking in even the basic psychological skills that some officers acquired after being in the job for a while. Many abused their power and showed an ignorance which made one wonder how they had got the job. They saw any [prisoner] who had even a smattering of education as a threat and tried in little ways to undermine us, but only succeeded in revealing their own insecurities. (Ward, 1993: 75)

Rather than *underuse* their power through discretion, prison officers clearly have often *overused and abused* their power and authority. Mark Leech (1992) also describes an experience of abuse of power by one prison officer, who one evening he found:

…outside my cell with a suspicious grin on his face. As he closed the door he winked and bade me goodnight as he went on his way; the alarm bells were ringing in my head before he'd gone three steps. I searched the cell convinced that he'd planted something and was on his way back to 'spin' me (to search my cell) at any moment. I eventually discovered his handiwork at 10 pm. As I went to climb into bed, I found he'd emptied the contents of a piss-pot into it. (Leech, 1992: 54)

There is then considerable evidence of prisoners being regarded as unworthy of being called by their first names, or even their surnames. Instead, they are shouted at; referred to by abusive and disrespectful terms; and made to feel the sense of powerlessness and vulnerability through petty humiliations.

Imprisoned socialist activist Des Warren gives us a further indication of the hostile and undignified treatment of prisoners, pointing to one prison officer:

> who made as much noise as possible, opening the doors and gates, rattling the keys and bolts, and stamping in hobnail boots to each cell. He left the lights on all night long, and when he looked through the spy hole in each cell door he would rattle the bolts. The purpose of this was to make sure we got no sleep through the night. (Warren, 1982: 119)

Again and again prisoner autobiographies point to prison officers subtly abusing their power to intimidate, humiliate and make prisoners feel vulnerable and powerless. Through mild moral exclusion the prisoner is forced to wear a phantom face via which their dignity, shared humanity and suffering is negated. Moral indifference, emotional detachment and an absence of empathy seem to be deeply engrained in the prison officer role. Rather than an aberration or something that can be explained by the immorality of individual prison officers, moral indifference is something which is essential to how the prison machine works.

Back in the 1890s, Frederick Brocklehurst reflected upon moral indifference and psychic distancing as follows:

> The mechanism of their routine duties and the severity of discipline have robbed prison officers of most of the attributes of humanity. They are machines not men, I never saw one of them smile. Their faces were continuously covered with an impenetrable mask, cold, hard, chilling, almost dismal. (Brocklehurst, 1898: 83)

Brocklehurst suggests that prison warders (officers) are cold, hardened machines who wear a mask. Witnessing the relentless suffering of others in the prison place must surely play its part here, as prisons generate enormous amounts of useless and unnecessary suffering—some of which is felt by staff—but mostly by prisoners. Prison officers have a physical proximity to this sea of hurt and suffering that drowns prisoners in degradation and the slow destruction of their sense of self. As Brocklehurst (Ibid) describes, perhaps to psychologically survive in the penal machine low-level bureaucrats must also become machine-like; mere automatons who are morally indifferent to the suffering of others. Lady Constance Lytton also writes of her observation of how prison officers appear to be wearing a 'mask' in order to conceal and protect their emotions:

> As a prisoner it was almost impossible to look in the eyes of my keepers, they seemed to fear that direct means of communication. It was as if the wardresses wore a mask and withdrew as much as possible all expression of their own personality or recognition of it in the prisoner. (Lytton, 1914: 75)

Moral indifference—the construction of prisoners as people with phantom faces to whom we owe no moral obligation—may then be a means of self-protection generated by the situational moral context of the prison place (Scott, 2008b). It is as if prison creates an emotional dam where human kindness had stopped flowing. Let us consider five further illustrations from prisoner autobiographies, ranging over several years, which emphasise this deeply-embedded nature of prison officer moral indifference and the general absence of empathy, care and kindness in the prison place. Norman Howarth Hignett put it this way:

> Such is the regime, a regime of futility and indifference where coarseness is the norm and uncaring inefficiency is the keystone. A regime in which men are clad in grey to become the sport of other men clad in blue uniforms, a regime of power without responsibility of authority without ability, of discipline without training. (Hignett, 1956: 55)

For Peter Wildeblood, (1957), 'prison officers become glass eyed automatons thinking only of overtime and retirement pension' (Wildeblood, 1957: 55), whereas Hercules when talking about Wormwood Scrubs prison officers, maintained:

> They appeared cold and distant and didn't attempt any form of conversation; there was a barrier between them and us. And the way they talked to the trustees left us in no doubt as to their attitude to us as prisoners.

> They had that cold, blank-eyed stare of zombies; that stare you usually associate with a complete lack of interest or sympathy, and a hardness that came with the dealing with hard men. I thought how easy it would have been for them to reverse roles and become prisoners. By now the screws at the desk had begun to call us up one by one to be stripped of our own clothes. (Hercules, 1989: 32)

Norman Parker put it this way:

> Perhaps, long ago, the milk of Human kindness had flowed in some of them. But no more. Long years of watching the most abject human suffering had inured them to the daily misery that they were part of. If there was such a thing as a bedside manner here, it was characterized by indifference and downright cruelty. (Parker, 1998: 5)

Ruth Wyner, eloquently as ever, writes:

> The screws (and I will call them screws) seem discomforted by any emotion other than anger. And yet they are surrounded by a sea of pain, pain that they are directly causing by incarcerating us like this. Perhaps to acknowledge that would be overwhelming: how could they get on with their work? So they josh and tease the few of us beneath them, and anyone who questions their authority gets clamped down upon hard. All to protect themselves from this excess of emotion, which threatens to engulf them unless they keep iron control. (Wyner, 2003: 70)

The sea of hurt and suffering overwhelms all and rather than facilitate an ethics of responsibility for those in need, it hardens emotions, producing either anger, shouting, violence and aggression on the one hand; or numbness, moral blindness, neglect and indifference of human suffering on the other. The iron coffins containing the socially dead provide an insurmountable obstacle to the fulfilment of the ethical obligations of empathy, respect of dignity and promotion of the paradigm of life. Evidence is not just restricted to the accounts of prisoners but is also abundant in the writings of prison officers.

H U Triston describes a situation where a prison officer went to tell a prisoner that his child had recently died:

> Callous to the last degree, I never knew him to possess the least spark of feeling. Off he went to the cell, thrust open the door, and said: 'Your little girl is dead!' then apart from giving the explanation that the man's wife had just sent the news, he turned around, shut and slammed the door and walked away.
>
> After an hour I had occasion to go to the man's cell and I found him in a terrible state of distress. (Triston, 1938: 200)

Another example by Thompson is the way prison officers reflect on prisoner resistance and protests, including dirty protests:

> … Get a needle and thread and sew your eyes shut so you can't see and, for good measure, do your mouth so you can't talk or tell anyone your problems. I can't put into words how fucking ridiculously stupid and idiotic I find it. As far as I'm concerned, put them in a fucking great hall together with a huge amount of thread and needles, and let them sew each other to the curtains. It's like shitting up. 'I know I cover myself in shit to protest!' Where is the bloody logic of these people? (Thompson, 2008: 234)

There is no empathy or understanding here of why prisoners might engage in what might appear to be self-harming and disturbing and undignified behaviours. But prison officer insensitivity and moral indifference to the phantom-faced prisoner goes beyond this; it is also present in life and death issues (such as suicidal ideation or attempting to take their own lives). Michael O'Brien in his prisoner autobiography describes his own suicidal thoughts and how at least one prison officer responded to his distress:

> Things got worse when a prison officer who I believe was a qualified nurse told me to pull myself together and then shockingly told me the best way to kill myself was to make sure I cut my arm in certain ways and demonstrated

how to do it. How many other suicidal prisoners has this officer said this to? (O'Brien, 2012: 89)

Prison officer testimonies add further evidence of how prisoners are sometimes not discouraged from cutting and harming themselves:

…there was one particular officer, who when threatened by the prisoner that she would 'cut up' if she didn't get what ever it was that she wanted, would turn around and say 'go on then, do it, it's not my body' and not bat an eyelid. (Mawer, 2006:27)

'People in prison are always going to want to kill themselves whether in prison or on the road', writes Thompson (2008: 228), who also maintained that:

There are those who cry wolf about suicidal thoughts, though. They use their status as self-harmers to manipulate the system. Fucking cunts: While they are crying wolf, some poor sod could be swinging in his cell. (Ibid: 146)

There is no sense of the internalising of pain and suffering, but rather a presumption of prisoners manipulating the system. Elizabeth Mawer (2006) in her autobiography of life as a prison officer in a prison for women, argued that some prisoners are 'general attention seekers who would scratch their skin, and then you would have those who would go the whole way. They would slice their skin open with whatever they could find' (Mawer, 2006: 26). That prison officers do not take the self-harm of prisoners seriously is further reinforced in the testimony of Rod Caird when he talks about problems in prisoners receiving appropriate assistance in response to the ringing of their cell bells:

There are many stories about the bells. They often break down, for example, and are said to be left deliberately out of action by officers. Or in the same vein, officers are said to put pieces of cardboard in the bells to silence them. The delay between a prisoner ringing his bell and an officer coming to the cell is a source of great bitterness. (Caird, 1974: 44)

In his prison officer autobiography, Douglas provides a disturbing account of a time he, with another prison officer, went to check the cell of a prisoner named Williamson:

> 'Brace yourself' [the other officer] says and unlocks the door. There's Williamson 'anging from the window bars!' Used 'is torn-up pillowcase', he 'ad Face blue, tongue 'anging out. 'We'd better get 'im down,' I says, 'might still be a chance.' He puts a hand against my chest. 'He's dead as a doornail, son,' he says. 'Remember when I put the tally down and said, leave this 'un?' He looks at me. 'Yeah. Was he already hanging?' 'No. When I looked through the spyhole, he's standing on the chair watching the door. Soon as he sees me look at him, he knows next thing is I'll be opening up—so he kicks off. 'Spects me to dive in and rescue him doesn't he? He got that wrong!' I just reached up and pulled the tally down. He mustn't have known who was on the wing tonight.' (Douglas, 2008: 68)

According to Douglas (2008) then, prison officers sometimes do nothing to prevent prisoners taking their own life. Samworth (2018) has a similarly disturbing tale of prison officer moral indifference:

> Cell doors have an observation panel, vertical slits behind the metal flap, so you can see what's going on. I had a look in and he was already in the corner, he'd only been with us for half an hour, rocking away and cutting himself with sharp objects he found somewhere. Superficial scratches, well, maybe a bit more, there was some claret, but what he was doing it seemed to me, was splashing water on his arms on the cut to make it look like blood was pouring. Fuck me, I thought this is no way for the wing staff to tolerate that, he's going back to healthcare, but whoever found him would have a lot of paperwork. So, I walked back and leaned on the stairs, the guy wasn't dying, I'm not evil, I was just getting one up on my mate. (Samworth, 2018: 81)

Ethical questions

An ethical encounter is one which is grounded in human relationships formed through respect of human dignity. Ethical encounters lead to recognition of shared humanity and a sense of responsibility for those less powerful than us (Dussel, 2013). There are of course clear power dynamics between prisoners and prison officers hence, the responsibility for ethical engagement and recognition of the suffering of those below them in the organisational hierarchy is even greater for officers; because they have more power and more ability to help alleviate pain than prisoners. Though there are examples of prison officers and prisoners showing kindness and mutual respect and support, these are exceptions which prove the rule. Violations of human dignity are deeply engrained and rather than reflecting natural human sympathies around care, compassion and empathy (Kropotkin, 1924) the prison place socially produces cruelty and indifference (Bauman, 1989).

For people who are vulnerable, rather than exploiting, humiliating and perpetuating the indignities in an institution steeped in social death, we should aim to acknowledge suffering, meet human need and facilitate the paradigm of life. Prisons structurally deny this kind of ethical encounter and in so doing, the very basis of the formation of the human self is undermined. When situating the prison within the four key socialist principles of freedom, empathy, dignity and the right to life, questions about the moral and political legitimacy of penal confinement inevitably are brought into sharp relief.

Prisoners have phantom faces because in an environment soaked in human suffering and misery, the easiest thing to do is to become morally indifferent and switch off to even the most extreme forms of harm. In the prison place it is almost impossible for another person to adequately address the needs of others or fully acknowledge their pain. The only conclusion that we can reach from this is that neither prisoners nor prison officers have the ability, opportunity or resource to voluntarily meet the needs of others they encounter on a day-to-day basis. Thus, if people are effectively unable to act with care, empathy and kindness in response to the suffering of others, then prisons must be considered as profoundly immoral institutions.

CHAPTER 5

Prison is Not a Home:
Estrangement and the Prison Zone of Abandonment

> The fact is that prison eats your insides out, and ties your stomach in knots, leaving your heart very heavy. All of this takes place when you are alone...(Boyle, 1977: 107)

One of the defining aspects of imprisonment is the deprivation of liberty. But prisons are never just about the physical removal of a person from society. There is much more to penal confinement than this. It may be helpful for us to conceive the prison place as a 'zone of abandonment'; that is, as a specific spatial, moral and social location from which the broader community withdraws support, empathy and care and where the sovereign state suspends certain legal protections (Adelsberg, 2015). In the prison zone of abandonment, prisoners are not just of lesser value, but often are people devoid of any value at all. Reduced to the objective of 'survivalism' and living a 'bare life', the prisoner becomes merely a nameless individual whose life (or death) is no longer deemed of any significance (Carlen, 1996; Agamben, 1998).

Uprooted from their social milieu and former life-world, the prisoner is Othered and turned into a *stranger* who is likely to experience social death—the 'death' of human relationships, status and moral standing and in its extreme, the non-recognition of shared humanity (Patterson, 1982; Scott, 2018b). Specifically, imprisonment inevitably results in 'natal alienation' and estrangement (Ibid). Estrangement is to shut out and separate someone from their previous close and intimate relationships, such as with family and kin (Scott and Codd, 2010). It is also to be 'out of place', to shift from familiarity to strangeness and to be re-assigned to a new devalued status. The process of estrangement, in short, is premised on the process of becoming a stranger from that which was previously inhabited as home. The abandonment of the 'estranged Other' in the prison place can weaken the sense of self and result in deep seated anxieties, fears and personal insecurity (Salerno, 2003). The deprivation of liberty and the traumatic emotional constellations it engenders, impact upon abilities to exercise negative freedoms (such as freedom of speech, voluntary associations and freedom of movement) and positive freedoms (such as fulfilling human potential and human wellbeing).

The prison place, as a zone of abandonment and estrangement, also invisibilises social problems. Prisons have always been warehouses for the unwanted. The homeless, and especially those who are rough sleepers, comprise a disproportionate number of people in prison. For many homeless people in prison, the process of Othering, estrangement and social death has, at least to some extent, already taken place before confinement. The prison sentence merely exacerbates already existing personal troubles and health problems and does very little to address the existential crises generated by being without a home. Indeed, the prison has never been an environment which can deliver the beneficial place characteristics of a home.[1] Through inherent violations of human dignity and the fear, or actual presence, of violence, the prison place blocks the ability to be emotionally vulnerable or open when encountering others. The prison cannot be a place of sustained habitation and dwelling, nor are prisons environments conducive to showing vulnerability and care or the generation of a sense of 'belonging' and inclusiveness. Instead, the prison place is characterised by discomfort and an absence of security and safety. In other words, *the prison is not a home.*

This chapter starts by discussing the meaning of 'place' and the importance of habitation in a home for human identity formation and personal growth. The chapter then proceeds to focus on the 'homeless', noting not only the similarities between being a rough sleeper on the streets and being imprisoned (for both are abandoned, estranged and separated from a previous life-world whilst at the same time often denied voice), but also that a disproportionate number

---

1. This chapter refers to 'home' as a place of emotional intimacy, support and connectedness. This discussion is not intended to detract attention away from some of the serious problems that can plague the patriarchal family home, such as domestic violence and/or emotional and sexual abuse. The following discussion of the home is then an 'idealised' one, highlighting the positive place characteristics that result in human growth and wellbeing, rather than a discussion of how some women, children and men may negatively experience the 'family home'.

of homeless people receive prison sentences. The chapter also brings attention to the violation of dignity and the presence of *'institutionally-structured violence'* (Scott, 2015a) in the prison place, which rather than being perverse or pathological aberrations, are inevitable and legal features of prison life. It is argued the daily workings of the prison place systematically undermine human wellbeing and the possibilities of securing place characteristics of a home. Drawing once again on prisoner and prison officer autobiographical accounts, the chapter illustrates the feelings of abandonment, alienation and loss of sense of place. The chapter concludes by calling for empathy, solidarity and understanding of the suffering of the estranged Other.

There is no place like home

The human life-world is essentially a shared world, encompassing the people we encounter in our daily lives. As humans are embodied subjects, any conception of our being is also inseparable from the specific spatial and situational contexts we inhabit—what is referred to here as 'place' (Malpas, 1999). All humans need care and love to become secure and well-grounded people and the meeting of the requirements for positive freedom of human wellbeing should be understood in relation to the 'places' where people dwell and how that shapes their emotional constellations and inner experience (Medlicott, 2001). The vitality of our life-world, how we engage with others and the fostering of emotional bonds and attachments are closely associated with having a strong a 'sense of place' (Das, 1997) and the feeling of being at 'home'.

Home is a place of intimacy, familiarity and meaning. It is a place of openness and essential to the foundation, development and stabilisation of human identities (Yi-Fu Tuan, 1977; Jencks, 1994; Carlen, 1996; Scott, 2020) and creating a sense of 'rootedness' (Creswell, 2015). Home is about generating safety and feeling part of a wider community. As a place of dwelling, unsurprisingly, people think of home as a place of special significance in their lives and are often strongly attached to their home (Medlicott, 2001). One reason for this strong connection to home are the deep and nurturing human relationships, happy memories and emotional bonds that arise within (Relph, 2008). A home is safe, familiar and comfortable. Home is also a place of rest, recuperation and respite, something essential for human wellbeing.

The process of becoming human is always a relational and ongoing process. To grow, humans need to adopt a radical openness to others (Shildrick, 2002; Stauffer, 2015). The embodied self is made through relationships with others and human identity is necessarily situated within a co-joining relational context. As inter-connected beings, human identities take shape and grow through open and unguarded encounters with other people (Malpas, 2012). It is only by being open, and hence vulnerable, that human identities are nurtured. We have then an ever-present interdependence with others and cannot persist unhindered without such a shared world. If separated from others and our sense of place, the very fabric of a human identity can come under threat (Medlicott, 2001).

There is then an inherent vulnerability or precariousness to the human condition. It is only through life-affirming ethical encounters with others in the everyday that humans can effectively generate and reinforce feelings of love, safety and security. Encounters with others must be in a place and the home is one of the key locations for this. A home has positive and nurturing place characteristics, as previous encounters in a place impacts on the expectations and hopes regarding encounters in the present (Ahmed, 2000). To engage in an encounter at home is to feel safe and secure and to reconnect with the past, live in the present moment, and anticipate the future. Fostering a sense of home strongly connects to the affirmative ethics of libertarian socialism and the promotion of the paradigm of life, dignity and empathy. Human life involves the ongoing struggle to create and maintain meaningful and empathetic relationships with others grounded in respect, dignity, mutual support, care and compassion. In the same way human life and wellbeing are threatened by isolation and removal from existing relationships. Violations of dignity, moral indifference and the removal of the positive place characteristics of home 'can lead to the unravelling of identity' (Relph, 2008). This chapter focuses on highlighting the failure of the prison to provide such life-affirming place characteristics—that is, its failure to become, over a sustained period of time, a home. To consider this claim let us focus on both *people and places*. Let us start with people.

Warehousing the unwanted

There is overwhelming evidence that prisons, in the main, hold unwanted people for whom nobody feels ethically or politically responsible (Prison Reform Trust, 2019). Prisons reflect and reproduce social divisions in advanced capitalist, patriarchal and neo-colonial societies; and the extent of accumulative social disadvantage among prison populations is staggering. People in prison have had difficulties in families, schools, workplaces or communities. They may have already experienced years of hostility because of their perceived 'race', gender or sexuality, which has fundamentally undermined their health and wellbeing. Many prisoners in England and Wales today were formerly in care homes; have experienced emotional, physical or sexual abuse; were unemployed before custody; or have a physical or mental disability. Prisoners have often been failed by the schooling and welfare system and many people in prison can barely read or write. Prisoners are also disproportionately from black, Asian or minority ethnic groups (Scott and Codd, 2010; Prison Reform Trust, 2019). Basically, prisons function as *warehouses for the unwanted*. They are an expensive means of removing and silencing 'unproductive' people who are considered a nuisance and of limited (financial) value to society (Mathiesen, 1990).

The prison has a long history of controlling and 'invisibilising' the poor (Rusche and Kirchheimer, 2003). A significant number of imprisoned people were without access to basic resources and security that most of us take for granted prior to incarceration. Such people — most notably the homeless — live without a home. The nature, extent and definition of homelessness[2] is hotly contested, but it is clear that people living on the streets — the 'literal rooflessness' (Carlen, 1996) or 'rough-sleepers' (Harding, 2020) — face considerable deprivations and experience great hardship as a result of such extreme poverty.

---

2. There is no agreed definition of homelessness. Struggle over the meaning of homelessness and the number of homeless people is very important for policy decisions. In the UK statutory homelessness increased from 40,000 in 2009/10 to 59,000 in 2016/17, whilst the recorded number of homeless people on the streets increased from 1,767 in 2011 to 4,571 by 2017 (Harding, 2020: 206). Following Watson and Austerberry (1986), who identify a homelessness continuum ranging from living on the streets at one end of the spectrum to secure tenancy at the other, includes those: people without shelter now or in the future; people without security of tenure; people living in emergency accommodation; people living in homeless shelters, squats, unlicensed hostels, cheap lodging houses, boarding houses; and people stopping with friends or relatives in cramped living conditions. With such an expanded definition, in 2018 there were estimated to be least 320,000 homeless people in UK (Butler, 2018).

Rough-sleepers and people living on the streets are largely without work, privacy, decent food, or shelter and are often without good health. Further, rough sleepers and people living on the streets have been estimated to be eleven times more likely to have mental health problems than the general population (Bines, 1994); and many homeless people die young through disease, substance usage, and/or a lack of basic human necessary needs.

Focusing on day-to-day 'survivalism' (Carlen, 1996), homeless people are unwanted, lost and abandoned; and almost without exception, a homeless person is estranged, dehumanised, othered and denied voice. Rough-sleeping people on the street are denied dignity; are vulnerable to violence; are perceived as socially insignificant; and have little or no hope in the future. Homeless people on the streets are 'death-tainted, as living dead or as non-living dead, in some symbolic way' (Lifton, 1992: 141). They are socially dead (Patterson, 1982). Staying physically alive, especially in the long cold nights of winter, takes good fortune and fortitude, which at some point is likely to run out. People living on the streets may have the appearance of considerable autonomy, but they live constantly in the context of both legal and illegal coercion, domination, hostility and exploitation. They are physically free, but at the same time without most negative and positive freedoms. People living on the streets are often 'invisible victims' (Huey, 2012) of physical, emotional, sexual and psychological violence. Their suffering is ignored or treated with moral indifference. Yet homeless people living on the streets not only fail to be considered as 'ideal victims', but are also often seen as 'suitable enemies' and face considerable negative engagement with the law through police surveillance, state regulation and legal punishment (Christie, 1986). Unsurprisingly perhaps then, there is a strong connection between homelessness and imprisonment.

Prison is at least a partial cause of homelessness. Imprisonment is likely to result in prisoners losing their former homes alongside loss of significant interpersonal relationships in their life-world. Data on homeless prisoners is fraught with difficulties, so the full extent of the relationship between imprisonment and homelessness is difficult to assess. For example, prisoners may give their parents' or former partners' address rather than officially record they are homeless when first imprisoned (Carlen, 1996) and much evidence of homelessness post-imprisonment is based on self-report studies. A national prisoner survey by the Prison Reform Trust in 1991 found that 12 per cent of convicted prisoners had no permanent accommodation at the time they were imprisoned (Prison Reform Trust, 1991). More recently, the Chain Report (Greater London Authority, 2018) found that 15 per cent of newly sentenced people in prison reported being homeless before entering into custody. They also found that a third of the people sleeping on the streets in London in 2018 had served some time in prison.

Further, official data indicates that of the 7,745 women sent to prison in 2018, 3,262 were recorded as 'being of no fixed abode' when arriving in custody, which is approximately 42 per cent of the prison intake in that year (Grierson, 2019). It is also estimated that about 60 per cent of women ex-prisoners have nowhere to go on release from prison (Homeless Link, 2018). Broader data on the homelessness/accommodation status of prisoners is also only partial, with currently there being missing data on the accommodation status of 10,000 prisoners, but it is estimated that between 2016–2018 more than *100,000 prisoners* were released to 'unsettled or unknown accommodation' in England and Wales (Walker, 2019). Homeless Link (2018) found in a self-report study that 15 per cent of men and 13 per cent of women in prisons listed 'no fixed abode' as their accommodation status when leaving prison. With only a discharge grant of £46 (and a further £50 that can paid in advance to a landlord if this can be arranged whilst in prison), it is perhaps unsurprising that so many ex-prisoners sleep on the streets, or that more than two thirds of homeless ex-prisoners — 67 per cent in 2016 (Walker, 2019) — reoffend within one year of release. A lack of home is hugely damaging for homeless people and also generates harms, troubles and problems for the wider society. But the relationship between homelessness and imprisonment goes much further than invisibilising socially-dead populations. The prison itself systematically fails to generate the place characteristics of a home, thus mirroring some (but not all) of the symbolic and existential aspects of being homeless on the streets. Let us now consider further some of the characteristics of the prison place in more detail.

Institutionally-structured violence

Prisons are a specifically designated coercive *spatial order* controlling human choices, actions and relationships. External physical barricades regulate the conditions of social existence through sealing the prisoner off from their previous life-world, whilst internal control mechanisms survey and place constraints on the minutiae of the prison day. Security restrictions on prisoner movements — such as access to educational and treatment programmes; religious instruction; work and leisure provision — are carefully structured and regimented around predetermined orderings of time and space (for further on space-time, see *Chapter 6*). The architecture of the prison place determines the location of events and the distribution of bodies and in so doing also highly regulates relationships.

Prisons are places of legal *repression, exploitation and domination* (Scraton et al, 1991). Such repression can be explicit, as for example through the structured humiliations and denials of dignity within the daily role of the prison officer — strip searches; cell searches; control and restraint; locking people into a cell which has little more than a toilet, bed, belongings and so on. The sense of powerlessness that arises through such legal repression is well illustrated in the writings of Victor Carasov (1971) below, when he describes his brutal experiences of being strip searched:

> 'Stand there, shut your mouth up, empty your pockets…strip off…any ailments? Turn round…bend down' [the prison officer] *looks up* your arsehole…'cough'…he looks at your prick…'All right you can go.' (Carasov, 1971: 24)

In everyday situations, *legal repression* — even if it is just a cloak of legitimacy for terror, torture and abuse of power — undoubtedly shapes the conduct and acquiescence of prisoners (Cover, 1986). The acquiescence of prisoners can thus be understood in the context of the potential threat of an 'overwhelming array' (Cover, 1986: 11) of practices of state violence and the *fear* of state violence: 'prisoners walk into prison because they know that they will be dragged or beaten into prison if they do not walk' (Ibid). Such analysis points to the permanent and irremovable legally coercive situational contexts of penal confinement.

Prisons, as places which morally condemn and coercively deprive liberty, are inevitably structured through an 'unequal exchange' between people ranked differently, which creates a form of involuntary structural vulnerability. The general lack of privacy and intimacy; the 'forced relationality' (Guenther, 2013) between prisoners sharing a cell; insufficient living space and personal possessions; the indignity of eating and sleeping in what is in effect a lavatory; living daily and breathing in the unpleasant smells of body odour, urine and excrement; the humiliation of defecating in the presence of others, these are all institutionally-structured situational contexts that are profoundly harmful to human wellbeing. The deprivation of liberty is then exacerbated by further denials of both positive and negative freedoms.

This 'institutionally-structured violence' (Scott, 2015a) arises in the prison place when actions structured into the daily operations of penal institutions constitute a violation of human dignity and/or prevent the fulfilment of basic human needs. Permanent, ubiquitous and operating independently of direct human action or intention, institutionally-structured violence slowly but surely eats into people 'from their insides out' (Boyle, 1977: 107) and is perhaps the most insidious of all forms of violence in the prison place. Central to this discussion is the claim that institutionally-structured violence fundamentally undermines the necessary place characteristics of a home.

Legitimate abandonment

In the previous two sections we have separately considered people and places. Let us now consider both together. For prisoners who have previously experienced a sense of 'home', the abandonment, loneliness, dehumanisation and structured violence of the prison place may now be felt as something akin to being homeless. Like homeless people living on the streets, prisons can destroy human world and leave people struggling for survivalism; existing with only a 'bare life' (Agamben, 1998) rather than truly living. Whereas it does provide shelter and some basic necessities; the prison 'zone of abandonment' can also lead to rootlessness, the breakdown of human intactness and a penal abyss of hopelessness and death (see *Chapter 6* for discussion of death consciousness).

It was highlighted earlier that penal institutions are rooted in legal repression and institutionally-structured violence. In other words, whilst they are lawful and widely considered as legitimate responses to human wrongdoing, they often produce violent, harmful and deadly outcomes for those they contain. The prison place is a warehouse inflicting pain and suffering upon the abandoned, but significantly, prisons are *legal* institutions of '*legitimate abandonment*' (Salerno, 2003). Abandonment, which is when someone is banished from society or forcefully separated/estranged from previous human connectedness, can dislodge the constitution of an inter-corporeal being and attachments to their previous sense of place and time. The prisoner inevitably experiences abandonment, estrangement and natal alienation as they are no longer part of their former world and have no prior claims on the wider community for help or assistance; as prisoners are to be neither seen nor heard. Abandonment can result in detachment, loss and desolation and the prisoner may become a de-socialised and depersonalised enforced stranger. Further, ethical responsibility for the abandoned is abdicated as they are no longer considered valued members of the moral and political community. Indeed, perceived as an 'enemy within' who is hostile to the norms and values of law-abiding culture, the prisoner is the known stranger — the person who, because of certain characteristics, is considered a threat or danger to the moral and political community.

It has been argued in earlier chapters of this book that the daily operational practices of penal regimes can be hugely harmful to prisoners (and probably prison officers too) and may result in significant physical and/or psychological injury that undermines human wellbeing and other positive freedoms (see also *Chapter 6*). The emotional constellations characterising the prison zone of abandonment are those of sadness, melancholia, insecurity and a sense of loss. Perhaps one of the most significant problems generated by the prison zone of abandonment is the grief generated by the loss of a previous home (Medlicott, 2001). Prisoners long for a secure dwelling place where they can just be themselves, but the institutionally-structured violence of the prison place prevents this. As Ruth Wyner (2003) wrote in her autobiography, the prison is a place always filled with 'constant tension' (Wyner, 2003: 148) and somewhere where it is never possible to feel 'properly relaxed' (Ibid). It is undoubtedly hard to find connections and a sense of place within the prison environment and the sense of connectedness with others, which characterise a home. For Wyner (2003) when writing during her experience as a prisoner: 'I feel my exclusion acutely, cut off from the outside world, by the bars of the jail and inside by my complete lack of relatedness to this place.' (Ibid: 67).

One of the greatest hardships is the removal from former loved ones and a sense of home. Prisoners may still try to hold onto their previous life-world and keep in touch with family and friends on the outside, but this is not always possible; and through its physical constraints the prison can destroy hope and, in the worst case scenario, may even may lead to a partial unravelling or complete disintegration of human identity. In the words of former prisoner Trevor Hercules (1989) in his personal experience:

> Prison is a lonely life. You arrive on your own without your real friends and family and the people you do meet in prison you mostly tolerate as opposed to welcome. It's lonely because you and you alone have to come to terms with your freedom being taken away, with being locked up and confined in jail. Other people don't wish to hear your problems, they've got problems of their own. A late letter or a cancelled visit is enough to give a prisoner a nervous breakdown wondering what happened. Are they all right, why didn't they come, why didn't they write? Your mind, already wracked by prison tension, becomes alive with ill fate. Only you can deal with it and you had better be strong. You feel so frustrated when you receive a letter or visit and something's happening out there which you could have prevented if you had been free. You feel so useless at not being able to help your family or friends. (Hercules, 1989: 86–87)

Prisons create a new community of strangers, who share a common set of pains and deprivations. The deprivation of goods and services and heterosexual sex are of course significant (Sykes, 1958), as are living in physically degrading conditions, but these deprivations alone cannot explain why the prison is such a toxic environment. Conditions can be improved; conjugal visits arranged; more goods and services provided, but none of these will even get close to the inherent harms and loss of love, autonomy, nurture and care. A prisoner is often reduced to simply a person who is barely existing in a place which can never be a real home. The thing is the prison just cannot provide the positive and life-affirming emotional constellations required to be a genuine home. For Wyner, the prison place is characterised by an overwhelming sadness:

> …we all had to cope with the waves of sadness that came upon us, often when we least expected it. I imagined that there was a spirit of despair inhabiting the prison and that it moved indiscriminately from inmate to

inmate [read prisoner to prisoner], so you never knew where it was going to descend next. When it was my turn I could feel it knitting my brows, churning my stomach, pulling every part of my body into itself. All I could do was endure, and await its departure. I fought it in the gym and worked furiously in the gardens, but this demon spirit made its own choices about when to move on. (Wyner, 2003: 148)

This account almost implies that prisons are haunted and trapped within the terribly sad and lonely experiences and memories of those who have been imprisoned before. What is certain though is that the prison place is a pale imitation of a natural home (Medlicott, 2001). It cannot reproduce, at least for any significant time, the emotional, spatial and physical place characteristics of a home. Rather than building relationships, the prison place is often the cause of their dissolution. For Edward Relph (2008), speaking more broadly about the loss of home, 'some places have died—the world is indeed full of skeletons of dead places' (Relph, 2008: 32). Prisons may well then be best described as *dead places* that overwhelmingly lead to endings and the breaking of ties and bonds, as well as being haunted by the pains and sufferings of their past generated by institutionally-structured violence and hostility.

The inability of prison to be a home is in part reflected in the sanitised blankness of the physical prison environment itself. The 'bare life' (Agamben, 1998) of a prisoner is exacerbated by living within an environment of 'bare otherness' (Switzer, 2015). According to Adrian Switzer (2015), the physical bareness of the prison place is a constant reminder to prisoners that prisons are artificial environments where daily life is structured in ways that are different to the world outside. This inauthenticity of the prison place is constantly revealed through its architectural blandness. The enforced sterility and emptiness of colour of the prison place makes it feel like a non-home; a place of non-belonging or rootedness. The artificiality and emptiness of prison life are key then to the 'irreversible alienation' and estrangement from home that the prison represents. Consequently, the difficulties that prisoners face in attempting to transform the austere physical and spatial environment of the prison place (whether on the landings or in each individual prison cell) into something that resembles personal tastes, identity and life-world outside of the prison, and hence reminders of home and life-world, are almost certainly *deliberate and inescapable* (Switzer, 2015).

The rules against allowing prisoners to personalise, paint or decorate their cells is a constant reminder that prison is not home (Meyer, 2017). Prisons systematically deny prisoners the personal possessions that are needed to create a strong sense of a place of dwelling. The lack of control that prisoners have to create a genuine sense of home is vividly illustrated when attempts to habituate living spaces are destroyed by prison officers when they remove home posters and pictures from the wall, personal possessions and other furnishing, because such 'pictures on the wall [are] now regarded as an infringement of the rule prohibiting cell adorning' (Kane, 2011: 233). This is exacerbated further by cell searches. Paddy Kane (2011) eloquently conveys the manner in which prisoners:

> …deeply resent the cell spins as they know just as a screw does that they have little to do with security and are mainly intended to humiliate and remind the prisoner who is in charge. The integral part of prison management thinking, whereby control is maintained by not only locking up a bloke one hundred percent of the day, but also fitting in a whole range of dehumanising practices. Reading private letters; listening in on telephone calls; constant rubdown searches, plus impromptu full body searches; regularly ferreting through personal belongings; peering through peepholes, having to explain to a child at visits why dad has to wear a silly bib, are just a few examples of the extensive range employed. In addition to the spins, our Saturday morning will be completed when the screw checks the steel bars on the windows to make sure you have not got through them with your plastic fork. (Ibid: 233)

Norman Howarth Hignett describes the way in which the searching of prison cells can also be a form of humiliation, even though this is not something that is deemed as inappropriate practice because it is justified within the lens of security. Like strip searching, cell searches are legal intrusions of personal space, yet may in fact be used as an 'unofficial punishment' by prison officers:

> The unofficial punishments are one of the worst features of the system, as an individual officer is in a position to victimise any prisoner for whom he

conceives a particular dislike or disapproval. There are a hundred and one ways in which this can be done and it's a matter about which the prisoner has no redress. It may take the form of constant and unnecessary reprimand, the turning off of the cell light to leave the prisoner sitting in semi-darkness. The holding of him to ridicule or humiliation in front of other prisoners or the deprivation or restriction of privileges. I have seen men unjustly deprived of association and similarly deprived of education facilities of books and periodicals. I've seen men deliberately provoked to anger and then delightedly marched away to the strong cell, a dark and dismal dungeon of stone and even to bed. I have seen men beaten up, I've known even worse, I have known razor blades to be placed in the pages of a man's library books and subsequently found upon a search. No prisoner, however clean his conscience, can be entirely at ease during the searching of his cell, he is utterly at the mercy of the search officers. (Hignett, 1956: 117–8)

So, prisoners are vulnerable and their powerlessness is further exacerbated by the actual prison regimes around security. John McVicar (2002) describes one particularly violent set of prison searches in HMP Durham where a 'few of the screws had gone the rounds of the cells smashing record players, ripping up letters and photos, burning private towels and so on' (McVicar, 2002: 92). Hostility, violations of dignity and disruptions of a sense of home are then structured with the very daily workings of the prison place. That cell searches are not an absolute security necessity, is illustrated in the words of Elizabeth Mawer, a former prison officer:

> … Every so often we would have to do cell searches. You had to do so many per month. Many officers couldn't be bothered with this so they would just sit on the prisoner's bed for 20 minutes watching the T.V. You were supposed to leave the cell in the same condition that you found it, but some officers would trash it, simply because they could get away with it … (Mawer, 2006: 34)

Prisoners are also confronted with an almost constant sense of place precarity, because they can be 'moved on' from their cell, landing or even the prison in which they are housed at extremely short notice. This 'ghosting' of prisoners makes it difficult to establish a deep connection and sense of safety within a given cell or even penal institution, assuming of course that their current living space has not been subject to an encounter of physical, sexual or emotional exploitation, abuse or physical violence. The regular prison practice of moving prisoners from cell to cell is a way to profoundly destabilise relationships and such enforced *nomadism* and hostility are structured within the very workings of the prison place itself. The precariousness of place undermine habituation. Basically, there is just never the stability and permanence that is required to establish a sense of home and dwelling. Such upheaval can also deeply undermine any feeling of personal security and the destabilising prison environment can generate insecurities. The prison place can then become uninhabitable, inhospitable and totally unsuitable to make a home (Medlicott, 2001; Switzer, 2015).

The constant undermining of the prison cell as a home is also illuminated in the way in which it can become a site of resistance. Few people wish to trash their homes and personal possessions and the sense of security that such things bring. But in prisons, cells can be the site of a dirty protest, where excrement is smeared on the walls and furnishings (Boyle, 1977; Leech, 1992), or maybe the location of a 'smash up'. The testimony of a further prison officer, Jim Dawkins indicates that the outcome of a cell 'smash up' may even sometimes be the result of a deliberately hostile ploy:

> When a prisoner gets frustrated over not getting a valid explanation to a certain problem, the main way that he can get heard is by smashing up his cell. I have witnessed many, many officers refuse to speak to an inmate [prisoner] and forcibly lock him up to get rid of the problem. They then ignore the cell call bell that inmates use to get a member of staff, and sit and wait until the prisoner gets so frustrated and angry that he starts to smash things up. This then gives those officers who love to wind up inmates the 'valid' excuse to get on their riot gear and go into the cell to remove the inmate by force. (Dawkins, 2006: 201)

The consequences of the prison not being a home are extremely important for penal abolitionists inspired by the normative and meta-ethics of libertarian socialism. If the prison cannot provide a nurturing and loving environment;

if it destroys rather than builds meaning; if it undermines previously existing opportunities for the fostering of positive identities rather than providing the resources to rebuild new positive identities; and if it is grounded in a hostile environment which encourages watchfulness, anxieties, fear and the erection of defences against self-disclosure rather than the openness and ability to be vulnerable that personal development requires, then prisons can never be places of rehabilitation, human wellbeing and the respect of inherent human dignity. Rather they will always be brutal and dehumanising places of useless and unnecessary suffering that snuffles out hope and perpetuates social death. The pathologically negative and dehumanising characteristics of the prison place can result in the destruction of the self, the weakening of important human bonds and ties and the creation of alienation, powerlessness, violence, exploitation and estrangement. The prison place cannot be a place of healing and rehabilitation because it is not directly connected to life-affirming human relationships. It erects numerous blockages to being vulnerable that cannot be undone and therefore prevents the very incorporeality and intersubjectivity that is necessary for human growth and wellbeing.

Solidarity with the unwanted

The problem of people being without a genuine home is considerable in modern societies. They are abandoned and largely without voice. Some of these people are 'made invisible' through penal incarceration. But we also need to think about the place characteristics of a given physical space of a dwelling and the emotional constellations that they generate when reflecting about the absence of a sense of home. This chapter has identified how there are certain continuities between the problem of homelessness and the failure of the prison to provide the necessary place characteristics for it be a habitable dwelling generating security, love, care, respect of dignity and the requirements of positive freedoms. Positive freedoms, such as emotional and physical wellbeing, personal growth and development, require our life-world to be situated in a place of safety—what we call our *home*. Prison cannot be a home for any sustained period of time and therefore should be problematic for socialists not only politically, because it is an institution which soaks up unwanted populations, like people living on the streets, but also on ethical grounds, because it inevitably is a place which generates harm, violence and social death. As such, the prison should be abolished and more life-affirming alternatives promoted, which can deal with private troubles and public issues in a more humane, non-violent and effective way.

So where do we go from here? Socialist ethics dictate that our first ethical responsibility is to hear voice and meet others, including those strangers or people who have broken the law and thus society has made estranged, with peace, friendship and non-violence. The ethical encounter with others should be based upon kindness, respect, generosity and hospitality (that is the right not to be treated as an enemy). This requires that we approach the estranged other with an ethics of care and understanding. Crucially this non-violent approach to our encounters with others (including strangers/the estranged in considerable hardship and great need) should be grounded in non-reciprocity. For Maurice Blanchot (1995) when presented with such an encounter, we should approach the other with solidarity, empathy and friendship; for it is only 'in friendship that I can respond, a friendship unashamed, a friendship unshared, without reciprocity, friendship for that which has passed leaving no trace' (Blanchot, 1995: 27).

This empathy, solidarity, and friendship for unwanted people means promoting and facilitating their voice (see *Chapter 2*). Following the insights of Edouard Glissant (2000), responses to social harms and human wrongdoing should be guided by an ethics of care and sense of solidarity with unwanted sufferers. In so doing, we should demonstrate our empathy by embracing the distinctive voice and standpoint of the person (*victim*) who has been harmed (Dussel, 2013). But this means reconstructing the 'victim' to include all people who have experienced a form of social injustice. When it comes to those without a home—people who are merely surviving, facing social death within a coercive and hostile daily environment—we should encourage the transformation of current social circumstances so that all people can genuinely have a home; a place where they can be vulnerable and open so that they can learn, grow, heal, and build their life-world through mutually constitutive relationships. This should entail providing the appropriate environment so that those who have done wrong can be open and vulnerable, and thus be able to genuinely reflect upon and change the way they relate to others. In other words, it means calling for changes that meet the demands of the 'paradigm of life' (Dussel, 2013).

For penal abolitionists, whilst it is impossible to change all the structural arrangements of the prison place, there are still contradictions and inconsistencies within daily operational policy and practices that can be exploited in the here and now. Humanitarian changes can be introduced that can mitigate some of the worst excesses of institutionally-structured violence. Some of the current intrinsic deprivations of the prison place (Sykes, 1958) can be easily removed in both policy and practice; and many daily infringements of human dignity can be greatly reduced. Further, cultural changes can be made to the prison place, where a democratic culture providing first a voice to prisoners and then a commitment to become virtuous listeners to that voice with respect and due consideration, can enhance recognition (see also *Chapter 2*).[3]

But any promotion of non-violent conflict resolution and transformative justice must also at the same time draw upon a negative consequentialist ethics that question the very existence of state institutions which generate useless and unnecessary suffering and extinguish life. Prisons can have devastating impacts on existing human relationships and create further harms by undermining the normal habitation of daily existence. The prison cannot be a home and thus produce the life-affirming positive changes to human character that its proponents have longtime claimed. Rather than being a conduit for the creation of a new life for wrongdoers or provide a sufficient response in terms of rebuilding and repairing the lives of those who have been harmed, the prison is a morally questionable state institution steeped in violence, suffering and death.

---

3. Further, finding new non-violent ways of dealing with personal conflicts and troubles in prison drawing upon principles of discourse ethics would also almost certainly reduce the extent of physical violence (by both prisoners and prison officers — see *Chapter 3*) and would help de-legitimate existing cultures of violence (see also that chapter).

CHAPTER 6

Falling Softly to Your Grave:
Time Consciousness and the Death-bound Subject

> You can feel the creeping numbness, the memory of life growing weak. Burial. Each hour is like a shovelful of earth falling noiselessly, softly, on this grave. (Serge, 1929/1970: 57)

Affirmative socialist ethics indicate that society should be organised in a manner which promotes human life. Following the insights of Peter Kropotkin (1924) and Enrique Dussel (2013), 'life-affirming' ethics demands that material, emotional and psychological resources are freely available to facilitate the life and wellbeing of all. Negative socialist ethics, however, are also important for shining a spotlight on what is most important in life by creating awareness of its exact opposite—the 'death-bound subject'. A death-bound subject is someone who is without hope and consumed by thoughts of death, which is referred to in this chapter as *death consciousness* (Holland, 2000; JanMohamed, 2005). Death-bound subjects are socially dead and 'falling softly to their grave' in the prison place because they are haunted by past trauma and drained of hope in the present and the future.

Human life is dependent upon the constant pursuit of new meaning[s], purpose and direction and these are largely produced through engagement in rewarding and life-affirming interactions in our life-world. Our life-world is a shared one, where our lived consciousness and understanding of self are embedded within our relationships with others. Life is continually renewed like a flowing river. If that river is blocked and people are no longer able to freely pursue new meanings, their life-blood runs dry and they are likely to experience an existential crisis, evaporating hope, and possibly leading to thoughts contemplating death. Our life-worlds are predicated upon certain negative freedoms, such as voluntary choices, associations and agreements. Indeed, our sense of purpose and very being-in-the-world, is underscored by such personal and collective negative freedoms. This is not to deny the determining structural contexts shaping our choices (and how this has implications of thinking about the idea of 'free will'), nor that the 'choices' available within the prison place are different and more limited to those on the outside, but that the way in which we live in freedom is crucially important for our wellbeing.

Experiences of freedom also influence how we experience time. Time is finite and human life-course is all about the amount of time people have and how they spend it. As people grow older they naturally have increased awareness of the limited amount of time, and whilst this awareness can weigh heavily on the shoulders of some, it is also something which can have positive implications for human motivation and influence wiser uses of time. However, consciousness of time is not a stable and constant phenomenon. Time, and especially time consciousness, are experienced differently depending upon the negative freedoms possessed by an individual, especially with regards to diverse and voluntary choices and associations. Human meanings are generated through the combination of a sense of freedom and the security and safety of living in a place which is a home. Freedom and sense of place provide foundation stones for someone to subsequently engage in diverse and stimulating life experiences, as well as form new positive life-affirming relationships. The removal of freedom, de-habitation of home and severing of intimate relationships are profoundly painful and have a negative impact upon not only how we conceive present time, but also hopes and aspirations for the future. Coupled with an absence of diversity or mental stimulation, a person may become trapped within a never-ending and monotonous present, resulting in mental and physical lethargy, as well as opening a window to constant reflections on past mistakes, harms and trauma.

The greater the diversity of stimulating options and choices, the less conscious we are of the passage of time. Hence, negative freedoms and time are key to understanding how a fulfilled human life is lived. But, drawing upon negative ethics, it is also important to be aware of the opposites to a fulfilled human life: death consciousness and the sense of a wasted or miserable existence. Human identities are in constant danger of unravelling because unmet human needs and vulnerabilities remain always just under the surface. There remains the constant danger of being dehumanised; of losing meaning; of losing purpose and direction; and becoming a lost soul without any hope of a better present or future. Losing all sense of hope is hugely significant, in terms of failing to generate the continuance of life in the future.

This chapter is particularly concerned with the connections between 'mental time', legal coercion and thoughts of death. It has four parts. The first part considers the prison as a place of death and connects this understanding with the insights of the three dimensions of space-time identified by Henri Lefebvre (1991) in his classic text *The Production of Space* and subsequently applied to the prison place by Roger Matthews (1999) in his book *Doing Time*, which informs the remainder of the chapter. Part two reflects upon the interconnections between freedom, relationships, place and the lived experience of prison time; and draws extensively upon prisoner autobiographies to illustrate this. Part three points to some strategies of 'psychological survival' in the prison place, which for some prisoners at some points in their sentence, may help them cope with prison time. Finally, part four draws the different strands of the discussion together to argue that the lived experience of prison time can result in prisoners being hurtled towards death consciousness; that is consumed by thoughts of death.

Time and the death-bound subject

Prisons are state institutions, which sometimes lead to people wanting to abandon the journey of life. The prison place propels them down a pathway to death. Penal institutions are characterised by what Orlando Patterson (1982) refers to as 'social death' (see previous chapters for discussions on violence; the systemic violations of dignity and estrangement). One aspect of social death not fully explored by Patterson (Ibid), but which seems to be pertinent to the social death of prisoners, is the manner in which under certain circumstances, people in prison can also become 'death-bound subjects' (JanMohamed, 2005). The death-bound subject is a human being estranged from loved ones who is held in a violent institutional context, which systematically generates feelings of worthlessness and humiliation. Such feelings of powerlessness and vulnerability (i.e. violations of dignity) can lead to the exhaustion of meaning and hope. The death-bound subject turns away from life (meaning) and towards death (hopelessness and despair). Sharon Patricia Holland suggests that state institutions, which systematically erode hope and engender overwhelming thoughts of ending life, such as the prison place, should be conceived of as 'spaces of death' (Holland, 2005: 4).

Prisons systematically destroy human world. All prisoners are vulnerable to the unravelling of hope and the dissolving of meanings that are required to continue on the journey of life. Caleb Smith argues that the 'reformed prisons', which evolved in the early-1800s, were always intended to create social death, as 'living death was neither an accident, nor an excess, but a fundamental part of the institutions design' (Smith, 2009: 39) from the very beginning. The historical lack of interest regarding the corporeal death of prisoners continues to be of great concern. It is likely that the literal death of a prisoner is already preceded by their social death; the estranged Other with a phantom face who is consumed by loss and endings has ceased to be considered as a fellow human being worthy of our care, compassion and empathy. Death-bound subjects are produced through a combination of coercive place characteristics and a saturation in now-time consciousness. Prisons, which are rooted in violence, estrangement and violations of dignity, socially produce 'death consciousness' in abundance. The prison place has such an undesirable impact on perceptions of time because it removes negative freedoms and intimate relationships and as a result can also undermine the sense of relatedness to the life-world which prisoners inhabit.

The passing of time is not just an objective, external and physical phenomenon, but is also interpreted and experienced subjectively and as a lived event. The great socialist thinker, Henri Lefebvre, identified the 'dual lens' (Lefebvre, 1991: 175) and 'double surface/double appearance' (Ibid: 181) of 'space-time'. For Lefebvre time 'is solidified and fixed within the rationality immanent to space' (Ibid: 21); yet though time is 'concealed in space' (Ibid: 96) and 'space is the envelope of time' (Ibid: 339); time is 'distinguishable but not separate from space' (Ibid: 175). Though space and time imply each other, it is possible to explore the experience of time within a specific space/place. Such consideration is important in the struggle to avoid the 'erasure of time' (Ibid: 96) and reverse the current lack of understanding of time in modern societies.[1] Lefebvre identified three different dimensions of space-time: first there is physical space-time; second there is mental space-time; and third, there is social space-time. These three dimensions are further elaborated on in the context of 'doing prison time' by Roger Matthews (1999), upon which the following discussion also builds. *Physical space-time* is something that can be measured quantitatively because it refers to how long it takes us to do things. The passage of physical time can be objectively quantified in terms of days, hours and minutes and as it reflects the 'natural rhythm of life', it can also be calculated in terms of months, seasons and years (Lefebvre, 1991).[2] It is through physical time that the ticking of the 'biological clock' during the human life-course is measured; and hence consciousness that human existence is finite and time bounded. Yet whilst physical time can be viewed objectively, there is much more to time perception than merely a mechanical passing of physical time from the start to the close of the day. All that lies in-between must be interpreted and experienced and thus has subjective dimensions.

The insights of Roman Ingarden (1964) are also helpful here. Ingarden (1964) indicates that when we are separated from the natural rhythm of life the sense of how life unfolds cohesively can be replaced with one which is increasingly conscious of the fact that the passage of time is being destructive. People can start to notice the deteriorating impacts of time (Cohen and Taylor, 1972) and for some the heavy weight of wasted and empty time can prove to be (almost) too much. This leads us to consider what Lefebvre (1991) calls *mental space-time*. This is basically how we experience time. The social construction of mental time indicates that in certain ways our understandings of the passing of time are subjective rather than objective. In mental time, perceptions of time can speed up or slow down and may vary considerably between people, even in the same place. This of course is directly related to whether a sense of time (time consciousness) is largely present or absent; and if its passing generates meaning or is simply empty and wasted. Mental time, as discussed below, is relational and how it is experienced provides an index of our relatedness to others and the world more broadly.

---

1. For Lefebvre (1991) 'Time may have been promoted to the level of ontology by philosophers, but it has been murdered by society' (Lefebvre, 1991: 96).
2. It is the focus on Rhythm that is widely considered as one of most important intellectual contributions of Lefebvre (1991).

The third dimension of time identified by Lefebvre (1991) is *social space-time*, which is particularly significant for understandings of how the experience of imprisonment can result in the annihilation of hope and the creation of death-bound subjects. Social time refers to the manner in which we construct time along the lines of 'past, present, and future'. Now, of course, time is only ever experienced within in the present; it is always about what is happening in the now, as this is where our feelings and emotional constellations emerge and develop. Understandings, interpretations and meanings in present time are undoubtedly reflective of the circumstances of a person in that given moment, as well as drawing upon accumulative experiences from the past. Whilst the present is something which is constantly moving through physical time from one minute to the next, it *always feels as if it is in the same moment*, because we are always in the present. How we construct and interpret the past is open to change and may be influenced by the quality of relatedness to the life-world. The same is true for hopes and fears for the future. How 'prison time' (the mental experience of time in the present and its implications for social time conceptions of the future) is conceived and its potentially deadly implications, are shaped by inter-connections between freedom, sense of place and relationships.

Freedom, relationships, place and the lived experience of prison time

It is natural, indeed healthy, to have a certain level of the consciousness of time and the finite nature of life. Reflecting on the passage of time can provide a sense of continuity, identity and narrative for the life journey (Ingarden, 1964). However, it is possible for people in prison to become saturated in time consciousness; and this heightened awareness of the passage of (wasted) time can be debilitating and sometimes deadly (Ingarden, 1964; Cohen and Taylor, 1972; Matthews, 1999; Medlicott, 2001; Scott and Codd, 2010). Perceptions of the passing of time are linked to freedom of association and to who people spend their time with. As discussed above (and in previous chapters), prisons, by default, result in estrangement, as prisoners have been forcefully separated from their friends and family. As intersubjective beings, the loss created by this separation is hard enough to cope with, but the resulting emotional gap left by the removal of close bonds and interactions cannot be filled in the soulless abyss of the prison place.

Freedom of association—especially spending quality time with people we are intimate with or have other strong emotional ties—strongly influences time consciousness in the here and now (Bouton, 2014). The weight of the passage of time is so unburdensome that it may be barely noticed at all and yet may be filled with meanings and treasured memories. In contrast, 'forced relationality' (Guenther, 2013) and the denial of freedom of associations can result in time devoid of meaning and value, passing at a sluggish rate. This unwelcome 'empty time' is experienced as 'heavy time'. When the *heavy weight of time* passes painfully slowly there is a heightened sense of time consciousness. This can influence how people intentionally relate to those around them and generate/exacerbate emotional fragilities; leave people vulnerable to revisiting unwelcome thoughts from their past; or undermine their ability to cope with life in the now and/or the future (Medlicott, 2001; Meyer, 2017).

Habituating a home—a place of relaxation and intimacy—and our relatedness to given places are also crucial to how we conceive time and intentionally relate to people around us (see previous chapter). Certainly time, relationships, freedom and place all closely interconnect. As well as restrictions on associations, those confined in the prison place also have severe constraints on movement and choices, which can also have an impact on perception of time. Institutionally-structured violence is as pleasant as walking through fragments of shattered glass. For wellbeing, people need to relate to the world and each other in life-sustaining ways; and this means having genuine choices; which allow people to feel a close sense of relatedness to their life-world. To feel attached to a place—for it to 'feel alive'–requires positive interpersonal associations, which respect dignity and generate a sense of security and safety. The converse—a 'dead place' (Relph 2008)–is a characterised by loss, loneliness, disruption, the dissolution of pervious meanings and hauntings of past trauma. It puts into jeopardy relatedness to the world and hope for the future (Meyer, Ibid).

Jones and Schmid (2000) succinctly note that prisons 'terminate intimate relationships' (Jones and Schmid, 2000: 26) and that enforced separation from, or the ending of, relationships with significant others can alter meanings and sometimes the direction of a life journey. Significantly for us here, it also impacts upon how people conceive time. Time spent in an intimate relationship and the meaning that this creates is in effect *a form of freedom*, at least in the sense that it frees people from the heavy weight of experiencing empty time. Intimate relationships generate an emotional constellation in which people feel like they are alive and can look forward to repeating this feeling in the future. Broken and estranged relationships can have the opposite effect; they can lead to a greater sense of heaviness and weariness of time and negatively transform how the future is conceived. Freedom, time and sense of place are all relational (as is of course human dignity). It is important then to consider the way a prison sentence will inevitably impact upon freedom, place, time and relationships and recognise that any deprivation of freedom and restrictions on choices; loss of sense of place; and removal of previous intimate human interactions—all part and parcel of the legal coercion of the prison place—impact upon time-consciousness. A prison sentence may also result in someone finding themselves at a crossroads. Some may have the resolve and ability to continue on their life journey, whilst others, alternatively, may lose hope and become death-bound subjects.

If perceptions of time are profoundly influenced by our relations with others and freedom is at least in part found in the relishing of those opportunities to spend time with intimates and those to whom we are bonded; then it is not surprising that relationships with abusive, disrespectful and hostile people increase *time now awareness*. If relatedness to place and the life-world is created through life-affirming human relationships and indeed, if the emotional constellations arising from given place characteristics provide the basis for such relations to be formed (see previous chapter), then conversely the place characteristics of state institutions, which deny negative freedoms, such as the deprivations of liberty, can result in a negative and distorting context that dissolves relatedness and sense of place.

Diana Medlicott (2001) explains how people confined in the prison place can become trapped in *now-time* (the present). Let us therefore now consider what prisoners have had to say about this experience of now-time. For Christopher Burney (1962) 'time in prison was endless' (Burney, 1962: 65) whereas Victor Serge, whose prisoner autobiography remains one of the most eloquent and powerful ever written, gives us some indication of the heavy weight of now-time in the prison place when he notes that all he knew was that 'the next hour [in prison] will be exactly like this one' (Serge, 1929/1970: 10). He continues:

> The contrast between this vacant, empty prison time and the intense rhythm of normal life is so violent that it will take a long and painful period of adaption to slow down the pulse of life, to deaden the will, to stifle, blot out, obliterate every unsettling image from my mind. (Ibid)

Here then is an application of what Lefebvre called mental (space)time and how the experience and anticipation of time can speed up and slow down. Jack Abbott (1981) puts it like this: 'time descends in your cell like the lid of a coffin in which you lie and watch as it slowly closes' (Abbott, 1991: 4–5). Time in prison for him was oppressive, almost claustrophobic and weighed him down. In a slightly different context, Viktor Frankl describes his experiences of time within another form of confinement, the concentration camp:

> The events and the people outside, all the normal life, there, had a ghostly aspect for the prisoner. The outside life, that is as much as he could see of it, appeared to him almost as it might to a dead man, who looked at it from another world. (Frankl: 1959: 80)

Here we are getting a sense that by the very nature of being estranged from society, becoming placed away from the very normality of physical time, the prisoner becomes almost like a ghost, standing outside of physical time and the normal rhythm of life (Ingarden, 1964; Cohen and Taylor, 1972). Mental time, the lived experience of time, is relative and impossible to generalise, but both Serge (1929/1970) and Frankl (1959) indicate that the experience of confinement dominates their conception of present time. This indicates that when thinking about 'prison time', it may be sensible to look at this as distinct from both physical time and the subjective and socially-constructed mental time and social time in the wider society.

In effect, the prison place creates its own situationally and contextually bound 'modus operandi' of how mental time is experienced. That the prison 'imposes, in an important and dramatic way, certain time relationships upon the life of the prisoner' (Lewin, Meyers, Kalhorn, et al, 1944: 158) is something that has been long recognised by those studying prisons (see also Cohen and Taylor, 1972). But the point is, prison time not only results in useless and unnecessary suffering, it can also be deadly.

The more time you have, the less it has value, especially if it is empty time devoid of meaning. The subjective and inner-experience of 'prison time' seems often to be one where prisoners consider their time spent in institutional confinement as tainted, destroyed, stolen, taken away, or wasted (Goffman, 1961). The prison stretch of time is bereft of freedom and (largely) loving, caring and supportive human relationships. The passing of objective physical time in prison is largely subsumed beneath the more profoundly subjective mental time, which in turn has an impact on understandings of social time. Thoughts about the past, present and future are hugely distorted in the prison place and the present, or *now time*, becomes all consuming (Matthews, 1999; Medlicott, 2001; Scott and Codd, 2010).

As noted in *Chapter 4*, the daily lived experiences of the prison place are shaped by an institutional context of indifference, cruelty and indignity; and the longer that a person is exposed to such a toxic environment, the more likely it is that it will start to undermine and dissolve their identities. *Chapter 5* added to this understanding by situating violence in prison within the context of institutionally-structured violence. As evidenced in prisoner autobiographies, serving time in prison can result in a kind of paralysis to the sense of self where the building blocks of life are removed one by one and replaced with a sense of purposelessness, powerlessness and despair. In terms of taking the life journey forward and looking to the future, the existence of a sense of hope is absolutely essential. The problem is that endless and empty time pass in such a way that any such hope for the future can become felt by prisoners as being futile. Rupert Croft-Cooke refers to this aspect of prison time as 'suspended animation' (Croft-Cooke, 1955: 91):

> It is because in prison a man ceases to live, in anything but the organic sense. He merely waits, lets time pass over him, remains supine and spiritually comatose until enough months or years have passed by. If he could lose from his life-span the length of his sentence, even if it brought him to the very last margin of his existence, he would do so. He does not regard his time in prison as anything but a period of suspended animation from which he scarcely hopes, one day, to emerge and to breathe and think again. (Ibid)

So, the prison place, according to Croft-Cooke, is lost from life. Time is *erased* as Lefebvre warns us. Indeed, prison time is serving a sentence out of life. It is serving a sentence out of place. It is serving a sentence where time is ultimately wasted and lost. The inordinately heavy weight of time in punitive state institutions like prisons is something which has also been identified by those who have experienced other forms of confinement. Frankl, when describing his experience of concentration camps points to the torture and fatigue of endless time. For him, the passing of time in confinement seems to lose its natural flow (i.e. that physical time is distorted):

> A small unit of time, a day for example, filled with hourly tortures and fatigue, appeared endless. A large time unit, perhaps a week, seemed to pass very quickly. My comrades agreed when I said that a day lasted longer than a week. How paradoxical was our time experience. (Frankl, 1959: 79)

So, here we have this notion that physical time is completely lost within the subjective experience of life within coercive state captivity. Prison time, in other words, can become limitless, but without meaning and paradoxically passed both slowly and quickly. Subjective mental times seems to slow down creating a weariness of the loss and waste of life. Physical time, whilst still passing in fact at the same rate and tempo, is experienced as though it is speeding up.

The lack of choice and privacy and virtual absence of meaningful experiences, associations and/or purposeful activities, ultimately generates exhaustion, stress and anxiety. What is significant here is the removal of freedom of choice and the loss of a sense of place where prisoners can relax, feel safe and secure and reflect upon past loving memories associated with a given place (Medlicott, 2001). Prison time not only alters the way in which people in prison engage with the present; it also, through the stifling boredom of useless time, creates a sense of exhaustion, fear and lethargy.

The prison place intensifies a sense of despair. Jim Phelan in his prison autobiography indicates that when people were housed within a jail machine it systematically created a debilitating form of penal stasis, which prevented full engagement with life:

> We will put you in our jail-machine. You will be squeezed of all initiative and resource, till you become like a mummy or an automaton; or you will be driven into neurosis, perhaps insanity… (Phelan, 1940: 22–23)

Idleness and inactivity lead to chronic tiredness or lethargy and add to the weight of doing time. Such feelings of heaviness may come from the lack of meaningful activities in which to engage and the monotony of their surrounding daily routines. Rod Caird puts it this way:

> In prison, there is no hurry to do anything—what is the point of rushing anywhere when you have years to spare? I noticed that only the new arrivals were impatient; all the other prisoners such as the one who brought our tea—were going about their work in a slow, steady way. Never moving faster than absolutely necessary. (Caird, 1974: 11)

Ultimately, prisons lead to people focusing on the pointlessness of engaging in life and the destroying of dreams. Prison time, then, is melancholic, monotonous, and mundane. Time drags because there is an absence of stimuli and a constant repetition of the same routine. In other words, people in prison are bored. There is a constant waiting for nothing to happen. As prisoners no longer have genuine freedom of choice or association with others, they are no longer in charge of their own time. Harvie Fergusson (2006) describes this as tedious time: time detached from relationships, human intentionality and/or a strong relatedness to their coerced life-world. The prison may fail terribly at its stated aims (Scott, 2018a), but it is an institution which is enormously effective at exhausting and preventing the construction of meaningful human interactions. The 'suspended animation' and literal emotional and physical freezing of penal stasis arise through deprivations of negative freedoms; the prevention of prisoners from undertaking fulfilling and meaningful tasks; and not only the estrangement from home and relationships with significant others, but also the forcing of prisoners to spend large amounts of time with people against their will.

When we hear prisoner voice, especially in terms of how prisoners understand their lived realities within the jail machine, again and again a similar message is conveyed: time in prison is lost; stolen; or it just slowly slips away into nothingness. The deadening routines of the jail machine generate a sense of being 'buried alive' and that the predictable, boring and inescapable nature of prison time becomes almost suffocating. It can also lead to a 'saturation of time consciousness' (Cohen and Taylor, 1972; Medlicott, 2001; Scott and Codd, 2010).

Let us consider some further illustrations of this problem in prisoner autobiographies. Croft-Cooke provides powerful testimony when he writes:

> [Prisoners] know that for three, five, seven years, for eternity in fact they will follow the same deadly routine, eat the same food, do the same dreary tasks, sleep in identical cells. They have nothing to live for, and they are made to remember it hourly. Their will to rise, their self-respect, their pride—all these have been broken, not by any overt act of cruelty, not by any physical punishment or individual show of malice, but by an inexorably grinding system which, while hypocritically proclaiming its good intentions, continues to confine men in grey limbo, without relief, or hope of variety. (Croft-Cooke, 1955: 113)

The suffocating prison regime, through its boring and dull atmosphere, destroys meaning. Trevor Hercules, put it this way:

> The claustrophobic intensity of every day being the same, of having nowhere to go, of seeing the same faces doing the same things, of having the same meals, time after time after time—after a while it takes its toll. (Hercules, 1989: 101)

Florence Maybrick, when recounting her experiences of prison in the early-1900s, had something similar to say:

> The routine reeled itself off with mechanical precision. The rules were enforced and carried out to the letter. The deadly monotony never varied. All days were alike, weeks, months, years, slowly accumulate, and in the meantime, the mental rust is eating into the weary brain, and the outspoken cry is rising up, daily—'How long, oh Lord? how long?' (Maybrick, 1905/2012: 29)

For Abolition

What is interesting about these accounts is this focus on dead time; that the prison routine is monotonous and boring, something which in a profoundly harmful way distorts perceptions of time. Ruth Wyner describes her experiences in the following manner:

> During my first few weeks in prison the days passed excruciatingly slowly, but then time seemed to find a pace of its own; the individual hours were long but the weeks went by fast. I wondered whether this was because prison was such an empty routine existence; there was so little stimulation, so little going on; just drudgery, boredom, and restriction; nothing of note to fill the days. (Wyner, 2003: 150)

The prison writings of the imprisoned libertarian socialist Victor Serge remain one of the most powerful and eloquent testimonies of the hardship and harms of prison time. Below are three examples of the penetrating and poetic nature of his insights:

> Minutes, hours, days slip away with terrifying insubstantiality. Months will pass away like this, and years. Life! The problem of time is everything. Nothing distinguishes one hour from the next. The minutes and hours fall slowly, tortuously. Once past, they vanish into near nothingness. The present minute is infinite. But time does not exist. (Serge, 1929/1970: 30)

> How is the pulse of life extinguished? It is impossible to say: with time. The same feelings, repeated indefinitely, grow dull. You lose count of the hours and the days. What moved or terrified you during the first days no longer moves you. Suffocation? Drowning? A torpor sneaks into your veins, between your temples. All of life takes on the faded-ochre hue [winter colour] of the cell. You can no more escape this torpor than you can escape from these four walls. The rhythm of your inner life slows down…Their rhythm is slow too; they come and go against this unchanging background without shattering the deeper torpor. (Ibid: 55)

> The unreality of time is palpable. Each second falls slowly. What a measureless gap from one hour to the next. When you tell yourself in advance that

six months—or six years—are to pass like this, you feel the terror of facing an abyss. At the bottom, mists in the darkness.

Months have passed like so many days: entire days pass by like minutes. Future time is terrifying. The present is heavy with torpor. Each minute may be marvellously—or horribly—profound. That depends to a certain extent on yourself. There are swift hours and very long seconds. Past time is void. (Ibid:56)

The lived experience of the prison place is coloured by the 'faded-ochre hue' (Ibid: 55) of the winter season; where time is frozen and very little of meaning can grow or survive. These writings of Serge connect and illustrate the arguments of Lefebvre, indicating the crucial importance of grasping fully the nature of 'doing time' in prison and its potentially deadly consequences.

Psychological survival—coping with prison time?

There have been various penological studies exploring prison time and how prisoners cope with the repetitive, monotonous and boring aspects of daily prison life. As Cohen and Taylor (1972) rather poetically put it, psychological survival is difficult because 'every total institution can be seen as a kind of dead sea in which appear little islands of vivid, en-capturing activity' (Cohen and Taylor, 1972: 64). The metaphor that prisons are oceans of despair, interspersed with small islands of hope, graphically illustrates the burden of time. It also pictures to us how swimming in these dead seas of hopelessness can increase the *weight of imprisonment*. Whilst for some the burden of time becomes too heavy to carry, others find their respite by somehow creating little islands of meaning.

Cohen and Taylor (1972), in their book, *Psychological Survival*, are focused on the existential challenges prison time creates for prisoners and how they cope, or otherwise. Cohen and Taylor (1972) note that one way of coping with prison time—and especially how this is experienced differently to the flow of physical time in the outside world—is to *internalise prison time* by cutting off contact with personal relationships on the outside. Rather than continue to deal with the stresses of the limited contact that people have with family members, for long-term prisoners, the easiest thing to do is actually just get your mind off your family. This way of surviving the prison place means internalising the prison situation and its social construction of mental time. Whilst this may numb the pain, it can result in institutionalisation and, on leaving the prison place, result in difficulties coping with freedom and the creation of new intimate relationships. This strategy then deepens estrangement and social death in other ways.

Yvonne Jewkes (2002) discusses two further ways in which people in prison cope with the way in which the prison place distorts the subjective experience of 'mental (space) time': *killing prison time* and *marking prison time*. 'Killing prison time', is where the painful prison time is managed by simply removing consciousness of large chunks of its passage. This includes excessive sleeping and sometimes a combination of drug usage that induces sleep and other, potentially more harmful substance usage, which can release prisoners from the present by changing their consciousness and perception of prison life (Cope, 2003; Scott and Codd, 2010). This of course means that large chunks of a human life are wasted; and can also mean that prisoners' intellectual and personal development can become retarded or that a mismatch evolves between the physical ageing of a person in prison and their skills, knowledge and life experience; not to mention the possibilities of drug overdoses both inside and outside of the prison place.

'Marking prison time' is a further strategy for coping and is a more constructive way of responding to the challenges of prison time than internalising or killing it. According to Thomas Meisenhelder (1985) rather than taking drugs or sleeping, prisoners also attempt to take hold of prison time, and 'mark' the time by doing something positive. This again is something that Cohen and Taylor (1972) identified. They point towards various different strategies of psychological surviving, from body and mind building, through to campaigning, legal petitions and letter writing; and sometimes through more direct acts of resistance in the prison place. Whilst resistance and strategies of survival in prison can be internalised through self-harm and injury or hunger strikes, it can also manifest itself in rebellion, such as through prison labour strikes and disturbances. For Meisenhelder (1985), 'marking time' was characterised by constructive and productive ways of trying to generate some meaning within the prison place. This involved a whole range of various things, like developing skills, becoming involved in various educational or musical projects. Marking time is illustrated in a number of prisoner autobiographies. Hercules provides a very clear example of how he tried to mark and give some kind of meaning to how he spent his prison time:

> The days, weeks, and months rolled on by and I decided to forget about time. After all, one day or one week was the same as the next. Time has no meaning in prison, not in hours, days, weeks, or months, and if you ask a prisoner what month it is not many will be able to tell you. The days become monotonous, one sliding into the next, except for weekends when there is no work. I became bored and restless, moving from one cell to another until chatting also became tedious to the point where seeing the same faces day after day drove me to hide in my cell. I read books. Much to the horror of my near neighbours I purchased an acoustic guitar from a guy for two ounces of tobacco and for a time I was bored no longer, the thrill of learning to play keeping me occupied for hours and carrying me into a world of my own. (Hercules, 1989: 86)

Being able to get some sense of fulfilment or even enjoyment in now-time is really important with regards to coping within the prison place. The difficulty is that prison coping ebbs and flows in ways which mean that sometimes a prisoner is coping, but other times they are not (Medlicott, 2001). The little islands of hope where time can be marked or killed, after a while, are sunk beneath the high tides of the penal ocean of despair. But more than this, Meisenhelder (1985), also charts the collapse of physical time and how both mental and social time are transformed in the prison place. In short, following Lefebvre (1991), what this implies is that the way in which prisoners construe the past and future is fundamentally distorted and can lead to the generation of death consciousness—where in 'spaces of death' (Holland, 2000: 4), thoughts, meanings and interpretations are swamped by a focus on death rather than life.

Hurtling towards death consciousness

Thinking about the first dimension of space-time from Lefebvre (1991)—physical space-time—helps to establish that there is a difference between time spent in the outside world and prison time. Consideration of Lefebvre's second dimension of space-time—mental space-time—gives us some indication of why the prison place is so painful, whilst at the same time appearing so bland and ordinary. The third dimension of space-time identified by Lefebvre (1991), social space-time, provides, however, insights into why the prison place has proved to be so harmful and deadly. Medlicott (2001) powerfully argues that all prisoners are vulnerable to the sense of loss and wasting effects of excessive time consciousness. People in prison fluctuate between coping and not coping with now-time. In particular, Medlicott (Ibid) highlights the existential angst of being trapped in the present—in the here and now. But this is not just about the distortion of the flow of time. It also about considerations of past; future; and feelings of hope.

Meisenhelder points to the disruption of the 'natural flow of time' (Meisenhelder, 1985:92) in prison as one of its central place characteristics. Whilst prisoners may initially believe that the prison is a place of omnipresent physical violence, it is actually characterised by the less visible institutionally-structured violence. Prison life is largely boring and unstimulating. Time, estrangement from intimate relationships, loss of negative freedoms, violations of dignity and deprivations of necessary needs are, for most prisoners, the major threats to their wellbeing. For Meisenhelder, it is the very 'blankness' (Ibid: 53) of 'now time' that is most dangerous, for it is not only painful, but can transform understandings of 'social time' (Lefebvre, 1991). The future can no longer be conceived for it is also nothing more than blank and absent of meaning, and it is no longer possible to look ahead in an optimistic way, if indeed at all. *Now-time*—the present—for some prisoners becomes all-consuming; and develops into something blocking the search for new life-affirming meanings. How people in prison experience the present then leads to ultimately a disintegration or collapse of time more broadly and in particular, future time. To a certain extent, what happens is that prisoners become ultimately trapped in 'now time' or the past. Cohen and Taylor (1972), referred to this as prisoners becoming 'ghosts of time', no longer able to actually exist in the future. They had become a ghost in their own lives.

With thoughts of a positive future annihilated, their only escape is to drift back into the past. The danger here is that the prisoners' past could be filled with trauma. A window opens through which freely flows thoughts of previous harms and hurt encountered by that individual. It leads, not to an energising and meaningful engagement with life, but rather, a slow and elongated drifting away from life. The danger is that a prisoner can find themselves at a crossroads. They may take a step on the journey of life, but also may go in the other direction and become a death-bound subject, turning away from life. This is the danger which is inherent within the saturation of time consciousness in the prison place and how this may turn into death consciousness (a preoccupation with thoughts of death, endings and suicidal ideation).

When we look at the prisoner population, it is a historical fact that large numbers of people in prison have been subjected to various forms of neglect of their needs, be it the educational, material or emotional; have internalised or 'acted out' all sorts of interpersonal and relational difficulties arising from an absence of care and love as both children and/or adults; and whilst themselves have engaged in problematic and troublesome conduct, are likely to have experienced various different forms of physical and psychological harm, injury or trauma in the past. To then place them into an environment where they are subjected to enormous lengths of time alone, with no hope for the future and without anything to do but reflect on their past lives, is a recipe for intense anguish, pain and suffering. In prison time, the past can become almost frozen and start to consume the mind. Indeed, rather than remaining simply empty and blank, these moments of being trapped in the present may be filled with traumatic memories re-emerging from the past into the here and now (Herman, 2015).

In prison time the past interrupts the present, haunting it, as manifested in flashbacks or nightmares. There is no immediate stimulation in the prison place to block out these negative, emotional and perhaps guilt-ridden forms of trauma. Thus 'now time', rather than simply leading to boredom and the waste of life, can also become a conduit for the resurrection of previous harms, hurtling the prisoner towards becoming a death-bound subject. The harms and injuries of the past and the present can be projected into a bleak and meaningless future that may be too difficult to face. A lost future may then become literally no future.

Living daily in a context where there are swift hours and long seconds is profoundly dangerous. Kurt Lewin's and others study from 1944 (Lewin, et al, 1944) was one of the earliest studies to identify that the emotional suffering arising from prison time was the salient feature of prison life. What Lewin and colleagues found was that the way in which the past and the future are constructed are dependent upon the present. They noted that in the prison place the present is undoubtedly one of great suffering and hardship and that prisoners had considerable difficulties in dealing with the prison time perception because their sense of the future might be negated. Lewin et al wrote:

> Prison behaviour appears to be dominated by the need to get out and the perceived paths towards this goal. Factors in the immediate day-to-day situation, despite continued exposure to them, are not of importance. Rather, the crucial ones are factors involving time perspective, particularly the future outlook, and factors involving the position of the person on his path to the goal as measured by his complicated and complex valuational yardsticks. The date of release represents the boundary of the effective future time perspective, the date the sentence was imposed the main boundary of the effective past. (Lewin et al, 1944: 208)

The future is locked within the very prison sentence itself. This may lead to penal paralysis and an inability to see beyond the bland and melancholic daily grind of imprisonment. Medlicott (2001) similarly indicates that there is a freezing and ruining of time in the endless present of the prison place. Prisoners become 'saturated in now time awareness: they cannot move through time but must endure the feeling of its slow passing as a kind of personal torture' (Ibid: 143). With no future, there is no hope of better times to come or a sense of purpose or worth. The absence of freedom, intimate relationships and sense of safety and security as found in a home, mean that unless prisoners kill time in some way or other, time kills. The future can become an object of dread, almost like a living hell. In such circumstances suicidal ideation is likely and the prisoner becomes soaked in death consciousness

Prisons are suffocating institutions that challenge the very basis of a human's sense of self. The desolation and abandonment of wasted and empty prison time leaves all vulnerable to its harms. For Abdul JanMohamed (2005) 'the death-bound subject designates the kind of politically and existentially aporetic subject position that somebody, akin to slavery, is forced to occupy' (Ibid: 26). The death-bound subject is somebody who ultimately is socially dead. The prison place estranges people from intimate relationships; subjects them to violence; and coerces people to live their days in torture, humiliation, and indignity. Through lack of a meaningful existence and through the absence of strong human relationships and strong human bonds, spending time in prison is likely to take some people down the path of existential crisis and the sense that there is no point in continuing. The usual factors which protect us from the presence of death are stripped away within a prison; as the prison becomes an abyss, where life is emptied of value. There remains the ever-present danger that some prisoners will become death-bound subjects, who, without hope of a better future, will contemplate death and sometimes act upon this impulse. What is required is a radically alternative philosophy of hope grounded in the socialist ethic of freedom as a means of finding renewed hope for the future. It is to this liberatory philosophy and its calls for freedom from state coercion that we now turn.

For Abolition

CHAPTER 7

Abolitionism as a Philosophy of Hope:
System 'Inside-Outsiders', Freedom and the Reclaiming of Democracy

> Democracy is a perpetually unfinished system...[It] is not merely a procedural system—a simple form for arriving at consensus—but also a normative one. The fact of [democracy] is always seeking an increased symmetry and participation among citizens—[something which is] never perfect, always perfectible...(Dussel, 2008: 51)

Penal abolitionism promotes the lived realisation of both negative freedoms (like hearing voice and promoting democratic dialogue) and positive freedoms (such as developing the capacities and capabilities necessary for fulfilling human potential and democratic participation). In so doing, penal abolitionism rejects punitive judgements, legal coercion and criminal blame. The penal abolitionism advocated in this book draws inspiration from socialist ethics exploring both 'negativity' (the negation of life) and 'affirmativity' (life-affirming values and principles that build a sense of hope for the future) (Dussel, 2013). *Chapters 3 to 6* have each, in turn, problematised the four dimensions of social death in the prison place: violence; violation of dignity; estrangement; and death consciousness. This chapter, and the two that follow, reflect upon how penal abolitionists can work towards both further visibilising and de-legitimating the iatrogenic harms of the penal rationale (the logic of punishment) and promote life-affirming ethico-political interventions through a pedagogy of freedom in the here and now. Rather than chart specific penal reforms, the remaining chapters are intended as a call to arms for socialist activist-scholars and organic intellectuals in their struggles for freedom and social justice.

Penal abolitionists are conscientious objectors to punishment and call for its replacement in the form of non-punitive interventions of repair and redress as legitimate responses to wrongdoing, troubles, and problematic conduct (Scott, 2018a; see also *Chapter 9*). Penal abolitionists are often cast as 'system *outsiders*' when it comes to debates regarding the role and legitimacy of the penal law because they question the very existence of the penal rationale. Through their critique of the penal apparatus of the capitalist state, penal abolitionists aim to reveal the contradictions and inconsistencies within the application of penal law, often by drawing upon evidence from people who have directly experienced its full force. By providing a platform for the often marginalised or discredited knowledge of prisoners and their families (and sometimes prison officers), penal abolitionists help shine a light on the hideous realities and negative consequences of the prison place, thus opening it up to democratic scrutiny and public debate.

However, penal abolitionism is not just about abolishing legal repression or even facilitating alternative ways of thinking about and responding to human wrongs; penal abolitionism is a *philosophy of hope* looking to promote the good society, genuine human freedom and the paradigm of life (Dussel, 2013). Underscored by libertarian socialist principles of freedom, empathy, dignity and the right to a fulfilling human life, penal abolitionism aspires towards an emancipated and truly liberated humanity grounded in non-hierarchical, anti-oppressive and non-exploitative human relationships. Emancipation is to come through a free and thoroughly democratic society organised around human wellbeing and the meeting of our necessary needs.

The ideas of penal abolitionists should not be restricted to bookshelves in university libraries or student seminars, but rather should be infused into popular culture and be drawn upon to influence the way that people think about crime and punishment. In this sense, penal abolitionists should work from '*inside*' the system, they should perform an active role in society and contribute towards everyday cultural and ideological battles for hearts and minds through a pedagogy of freedom. Such an understanding of the role penal abolitionists should perform in public debates means having a very broad understanding of what abolitionist activism and interventions entail. Abolitionist and socialist activism, as understood by this author, ranges from delivering public speeches, seminars, research, briefing papers, journalistic writings and other media engagement as well as community organising and providing a platform for subjugated and subaltern voices. Further, many prominent penal abolitionists today teach in an institution key to modern day knowledge production and dissemination: the university. The penal abolitionist is then a *system inside-outsider* who should be committed to further enhancing democracy and building public spaces for critical reflection by being both *tactically inside* and *strategically outside* the system at the same time.

Following the insights of Edward Said (1994), the penal abolitionist should deliberately *not* fully belong to a given society. It is only by sitting on the margins of the system that they can appreciate the problems confronting the society in which they live; and understand the world view of underrepresented or disadvantaged groups. This approach can help facilitate uncovering hidden or 'alternative' truths to dominant narratives, assumptions and underlying structures of power. Being a system outsider is also the best way to avoid co-option (Mathiesen, 2006). Yet penal abolitionists must also find the courage to both testify against oppression and engage in struggles for freedom in the here and now. They must exploit opportunities for progressive social change and attempt to implement their vision for social transformation across a range of different sites of engagement. Abolitionist ethical hermeneutics dictate that a penal abolitionist should explore the past and present from the point of view of the subaltern (those without a voice) and speak truth to power in the cause of freedom and social justice (Said, 1994; Scott, 2016c). These ethical hermeneutics inform abolitionism as a pedagogy of freedom.

As Vincenzo Ruggiero (2012) has argued, penal abolitionism is the only criminology he knows of that has always adopted a public stance. Like 'public criminology' (Loader and Sparks, 2011) more broadly, penal abolitionism aims to raise questions about common sense assumptions, generate new evidence and knowledge to debunk punitive myths and ultimately help reframe the debate about crime and punishment. In so doing penal abolitionism proposes a kind of imagination that can locate individual experiences within broader social and economic contexts and thus help transform currently neglected private troubles into public issues (Mills, 1959; Drake and Scott, 2019c; see also *Chapter 9*). Democratic engagement with the general public through a pedagogy of freedom goes then to the very heart of abolitionist praxis, but it is an approach which differs from 'public criminology' in one very important way:

penal abolitionism aims to deconstruct the ontological and epistemological assumptions of the logic of crime and offer alternative ways of thinking about and responding to problematic human conduct beyond the criminal process (Scott, 2018a). Drawing on grass roots emancipatory politics and praxis, penal abolitionism does not conform to the criminological doxa that knowledge is generated from value free, objective and scientific inquiry whose relevancy is shaped by government agendas and priorities. In this sense, penal abolitionism aims to foster a vision of society, political action and human relationships, which is 'against criminology' (Cohen, 1988).

This chapter discusses some of the ways that penal abolitionists as system inside-outsiders can challenge dominant understandings of crime and punishment through a pedagogy of freedom. A 'pedagogy of freedom' (Friere, 2001), emphasises the aspiration of building greater political freedoms for a genuinely healthy and democratic society in the future. This implies the importance of developing widespread intellectual curiosity and asking difficult questions about the justifications of the penal rationale; a commitment to the truth and a critique of power, domination, and exploitation; the development of educational interventions that can reverse the 'learned ignorance' (Davis, 2012: 141) of advanced capitalist societies; the instilling of collective responsibility through informed democratic dialogue and the building of skills and capacity for engagement in emancipatory struggles against (penal) coercion in everyday life; and a willingness to dream of a better future filled with hope and the furtherance of human wellbeing (Friere, 2001).

This chapter has three main parts. It starts with a brief consideration of the current limitations of institutionalised education, knowledge production and dissemination in the neo-liberal university (which is when an institution ostensibly designed for public education is grounded in the principles of the capitalist market place, private gain and accumulation of profits) and the importance of considering radically alternative ways of organising public education in the community. This is followed by an exploration of how penal abolitionists as system inside-outsiders can help facilitate a new critical pedagogy about human conflicts, troubles and problematic conduct as a 'collective organic intellectual' committed to both positive and negative freedoms (Giroux, 1988). Seven abolitionist activist interventions are then discussed that have been adopted by the author to illustrate how penal abolitionists can work towards promoting a pedagogy of freedom and reclaiming democracy through reinvigorating existing or creating alternative forms of knowledge production and public spaces for rational dialogue. Finally, the chapter concludes with a brief discussion of the importance of connecting abolitionist theory with public participation in democratic debates.

Pedagogy beyond the neo-liberal university

The central argument of this chapter is that penal abolitionists should position themselves both inside and outside the university (academy) at the same time. As an ideal, the university *should* work for the public good, helping to facilitate emancipatory knowledge as well as fostering and nurturing an ethico-political commitment to social justice, human rights and democratic accountability (Giroux, 2006). Whilst this aspiration for the university should not be abandoned, it should be located in context. One of the most enduring concerns raised against knowledge production and dissemination in the university is that it is an institution that reproduces and distributes power and cultural capital, thus performing a key part in legitimating values necessary for maintaining economically and socially unequal societies (Illich, 1970; Giroux, 1988, 2013a, 2013b). Through top-down hierarchical management styles and the centralisation of power, in recent times anti-democratic and authoritarian tendencies have increasingly been deployed by university management, resulting in limitations in professional autonomy and the standardisation of curriculums (Walters, 2003). The demand for income and immediate results has also reduced opportunities for in-depth theoretical studies, which require several years of work.

In our time of market-led criminological research, research designs and methodologies can increasingly come to reflect the interests of corporate power (Walters, 2003). As a result, research independence can be fatally undermined by the external constraints of government authorities and research funders. The basic concern is that intellectual labour and knowledge production are being used to serve corporate and technocratic priorities of neo-liberal political economies, rather than the interests of the people (Giroux, 2006; Sudbury and Okazawa-Rey, 2009). Fusing knowledge production with the logic of the capitalist marketplace (i.e. privileging the pursuit of profit and an overarching business culture) leads to a market-driven enterprise that maximizes profits through the commodification of knowledge and turns this educational institution into a space focused on service-delivery (Giroux, 2014), which then redefines students as either clients or customers.

Significantly, the neo-liberal university also fails in its basic democratic mission to be an institution that can inculcate civic values and ethical principles and generate concern and responsibility for tackling social problems and social divisions (Giroux, 2013a, 2013b). It is not very effective at turning students into critical citizens who can recognise the importance of participating in political culture to defend negative freedoms; or defending the human rights of socially marginalised groups; or holding those in positions of power to account (Giroux, 2013a, 2013b). Indeed, for Henry Giroux the neo-liberal university is part of a broader 'disimagination machine' (Giroux, 2014: 27) that is blocking potential for future political consciousness and public engagement. The neo-liberal university undermines critical thinking and impinges upon the mental faculties required to imagine a different kind of world grounded in empathy, respect for dignity and the paradigm of life. It can thus become a conduit for a *politics and philosophy of despair* rather than instilling a *philosophy of hope* committed to a pedagogy of freedom.

Following the insights of Ivan Illich (1970), it should be recognised that institutionalised forms of schooling, including the university, sometimes hinder learning skills for democratic participation rather than facilitate them. For Illich (Ibid) most learning occurs *informally* and people often learn best in direct reciprocal dialogue and engagement with others in everyday settings rather than through formal timetabled educational classes. Talk of engaging in informal apprenticeships in non-traditional educational settings where the goal is skill and knowledge transfer without a focus on formal educational qualifications stands in stark opposition to working in the neo-liberal university. For Illich (1970) such a scenario could be understood as a kind of learning web that connected people with the resources they need. The vision is for learning to be a positive, liberating and life long experience, which matches a persons' interests and motivations with the expertise and skills of those who inspire them. Underscoring an abolitionist pedagogy of freedom then is a commitment to capacity-building and sharing knowledge and expertise outside of the university so as to secure positive freedoms for all.

The vision presented by Illich is clearly appealing, yet we should not necessarily throw the baby out with the bath water. There have been times (such is as in the 1960s and 1970s) when universities have been at the forefront of developing radical and emancipatory thought and a key player in generating student protest, resistance and dissent. This radical history also reminds us that the university is an arena for struggle and intellectual freedom rather than an inherently conservative institution. There should be attempts to transform the neo-liberal university so that it can once again be a vibrant resource in the struggles to address injustices, oppression and exploitation (Scott, 2016b). As system inside-outsiders, penal abolitionists should look to work within the academy to help reclaim universities as public spheres. Following the insights of Illich (1970), penal abolitionists should also step outside of the university and participate in a broader revitalisation of public engagement in emancipatory politics and be prepared to engage in non-traditional educational settings. This suggests that penal abolitionists should transcend the boundaries between formal and informal education and between the university and the community.

Penal abolitionism therefore looks to challenge the generation of scientific knowledges within the neo-liberal university that serve the interests of the powerful and whose research agendas are shaped by governmental policy priorities (Walters, 2003). Instead, penal abolitionists aim to incorporate emancipatory politics into the education process (both formal and informal) where social and economic inequalities can be challenged. Rather than just working within the existing spaces for knowledge generation and exchange, which are set apart from the community (i.e. the university), as is often the case with public criminology, penal abolition presents a new challenge that demands new forms of genuine democratic engagement that are explicitly directed at facilitating emancipatory knowledge and praxis through a pedagogy of freedom which can aid the freedom of subjugated and oppressed groups.

Organic collective intellectuals

As a system inside-outsider committed to facilitating negative and positive human freedoms, the penal abolitionist should aim to abolish categories, barriers, boundaries and walls regarding educational theory and practice. This includes abolishing widely-held distinctions between intellectuals and non-intellectuals. Thinking, acting, interpreting and giving meaning to life are all intimately related and we all undertake mental labour in our ongoing everyday experiences (Mayo, 1999). For the great Italian socialist philosopher Antonio Gramsci (1971), every human relationship is educative and has an influence on the kinds of political debates that develop in civil society. Education, then, is not restricted to formal educational settings, but can take place informally in the community and in ordinary human interactions and conversations. Nor for Gramsci (1971) is there an obvious distinction between the teacher and the learner, as learning can and should be a two-way process. Gramsci (1971) did, however, identify a person who offered moral leadership and facilitated informal education through direct engagement in a social movement as an organic intellectual. Through the organization of people and dissemination of knowledge, the organic intellectual was an insider to a social movement who became an integral part of the local community, rather than someone from the outside simply bringing knowledge to the masses. The overall objective of the organic intellectual is not just political engagement on a specific topic, but the transformation of an entire way of thinking about the world. Building on the insights of Gramsci (1971), Giroux (1988) talks about the importance of learning collectively and the cultivation of a collective social awareness and consciousness-raising operating along horizontal lines (i.e. non-hierarchical relationships). For Giroux the end result of this collective learning process, where groups of people rather than individuals worked together collectively to build capacity among all of its members, is the creation of an 'organic collective intellectual' (Giroux, 1988: 23).

To become an organic collective intellectual means participating in and facilitating the emergence of a collective voice that can contribute towards the deepening of democracy and the facilitating of human freedoms. The penal abolitionist should work collectively, cooperatively and in a spirit of solidarity with oppressed communities in an attempt to help find common ground for alliances and the promotion of a collective vision of a non-punitive and inclusive society (Ibid). The penal abolitionist should be prepared to provide moral leadership in terms of raising ethico-political awareness and consciousness of social injustice and the harms of the penal law, but to do so in a way which is consistent with the broader framework of abolitionist hermeneutics (see

Chapter 2). This means witnessing and engaging in struggles for social justice and facilitating attempts to imagine a different kind of world through creating a coalition of progressive forces. As a system insider-outsider, the abolitionist should use their privileged position (be that their educational background, networks, communication skills, knowledge, or organizational experience) to build capacity through informal ties and learning networks in the community (Illich, 1970). This sharing and building of collective power and capacity can be achieved through helping to build the self-esteem, skills and confidence of individuals, or through historical recollections of past struggles and radical cultural heritage that show that another way of living and dealing with human and social troubles is possible.

This all points towards the importance of cultivating an abolitionist critical pedagogy beyond the (neo-liberal) university setting. Paulo Freire (1970) highlights the importance of connecting politics, culture and education together and raising the critical consciousness of individuals so they can understand their own oppression and subsequently undertake emancipatory transformative action. The liberation philosophy of Freire (1970), like that of Gramsci (1971), is intended to give hope and disrupt current understandings by looking beneath surface meanings to try and uncover the root causes of social problems. It is crucial that penal abolitionist interventions promote experiences and help transform feelings of subjugation into concrete action (Freire, 1970). This means highlighting the dialectical relationship between critical consciousness and social action in a penal abolitionist pedagogy of freedom (Ibid). Listening, learning and reflecting are all essential for the project of radical social transformation. For Said (1994), the aim of public engagement is to redraw the narrative—to cut against the grain, question received and 'common sense' ideas and engage in a critical encounter through dialogical transformation, which means for the penal abolitionist changing the way of seeing the world and ultimately awakening a new cultural consciousness among the masses. This can, but does not need to, take place in the university as different sites of social practice, such as the workplace, can be transformed into sites of informal learning.

For Freire, however, the community is required to be an active participant in the process of their own learning. Those engaged in critical pedagogy should actively participate in reciprocal dialogue, whereby every teacher is also a student, and look to promote critique and political engagement. Education itself was an inherently political act with the ultimate goal being freedom and emancipation from subjugation through the 'awakening of a critical consciousness' (Friere, 1970: 36). Friere, (1970) referred to this process as *conscientisation* (the deepening of the coming of consciousness). Following Gramsci (1971), the educator, whose role is almost interchangeable with that of the learner, should engage in reciprocal learning—learning the unique language and culture of a given community or group of people—so as to be able to convert common sense into good sense (Mayo, 1999). But this is more than just critique of the prison place. It is also about trying to deepen understandings and develop the possibilities for deliberative democracy (that is informed discussion about the key issues of the day) and the realisation of the principles of libertarian socialism. Democracy is a constant and ever unfinished struggle that needs to be reproduced on a daily basis, which requires skills and knowledge among the people. Democracy can only survive if it is constantly reconstituted in the here and now (Giroux, 2013a, 2013b).

For the penal abolitionist, then, hierarchical forms of public engagement—that is vertical relationships between a knower (i.e. a bearer of knowledge) and a learner—can never be enough. The distinction between knower/educator and learner is a false construction, which individualises knowledge production and dissemination. Public engagement for the penal abolitionist should be conceived as part of a collective and organic process, which can raise the consciousness of the populace through the principles of critical pedagogy. Through working cooperatively and collectively with marginalised groups and engaging in the process of dialogical transformation, hidden or alternative truths, assumptions and underlying structures of power, can be revealed. Placing themselves *both inside and outside the formal educational system*, the penal abolitionist should aspire to be an 'organic collective intellectual' speaking truth to power in the cause of freedom and social justice (Said, 1994). In so doing, public engagement can be a way of helping to facilitate the reclaiming of democracy from below and the promotion of the paradigm of life.

Reclaiming democracy

To culturally embed the ideas of penal abolitionism requires the existence of appropriate public spheres through which new non-punitive meanings and understandings can be formed and popularised through a democratic and reciprocal dialogue. A meaningful understanding of democracy can only arise when it is instituted in concrete spaces that allow people to come together to discuss, think and reflect upon social issues and their values, beliefs and responsibility for the existence of such circumstances. These public democratic spaces, what Zygmunt Bauman (1997) refers to as an *agora*, can allow for debate and scrutiny of hegemonic ideas around punishment and facilitate opportunities for the public to encourage decision-makers to justify their actions — in other words call for accountability and answerability. Democratic debate should always engage with a diverse range of dialogical encounters firmly grounded in day-to-day struggles around the meaning and interpretations of harms, troubles and conflicts which shape contemporary society. What is also crucial is the development of a critical vernacular that is understandable to the masses; 'penological illiteracy' must be eliminated by developing accessible language so that oppressions and penal injustices can be named, shamed and eventually tackled (Drake and Scott, 2019b, 2019c). Effective communication and the development of an abolitionist pedagogy of freedom is essential on the path to direct action (see also following chapter).

Any such democratic interventions cannot be technical or merely reformist, but must also aspire to a form of human living that enshrines empathy for human suffering, the respect of human dignity and that everyone has material resources to meet their necessary needs — the paradigm of life (Dussel, 2013). These new public spaces must allow for both oppositional knowledge that can challenge state-corporate and penal power and promote more utopian aspirations. In this sense, public spaces must also be both an 'oppositional space' for highlighting problems and penal controversies and a 'dream space' that can cultivate a radical imagination and inspiration for the transformative potential of human agency and the fulfilment of a philosophy of hope. It is essential in such a real utopian vision of freedom to link critical scholarship to broader forms of oppositional and idealist knowledge. Doing so allows those advocating prison abolition to accomplish three things: 1) facilitate concrete and pragmatic transformations; 2) expose and uncover how domination and oppression are produced and reproduced; and 3) ensure that in the long-term commitment to the penal rationale can be broken (Scott, 2013b).

Below are seven examples of how the abolitionist as a system inside-outsider can help work towards greater human freedoms and reclaim democracy. Whilst the suggestions below are by no means comprehensive (indeed they draw upon examples from personal public interventions) they collectively illustrate that it is possible and desirable for penal abolitionists to make immediate and direct interventions in the public sphere and give some indication of how an abolitionist pedagogy of freedom can be mobilised in the present.

We should hear diverse voices and write what we like

The place to start with reclaiming democracy is the contested space of the neoliberal university. Abolitionists with tenure in a university are in a privileged position; and should use this to help generate momentum for the creation of organic collective intellectuals. Penal abolitionists should write not for their institution or for state sanctioned research exercises, but for the broader goals of human rights, social justice and democratic accountability. They should write about what they consider to be the most ethically and politically important issues of the day and focus should be on movement building and local community organising. There should be an attempt to integrate organising into their everyday life rather than engage in organising for 'impact' or as a career vocation. The political commitment of the penal abolitionist should be to support all those, both as formal students and activists in the wider community, who are engaged in democratic struggles. The first step is to make strong connections with local abolitionist networks and directly participate in the everyday organising of community activists. This includes organising, publicising (such as through leafleting and the creation of pamphlets), participating in public meetings; and direct community engagement through both informal dialogue with activists and members of the public (for further discussion see *Chapter 8*). 'Joining in' and doing the 'behind the scenes' work required for the building of public meetings are essential for building trust and strong relationships with community activists.

Despite the commodification of education, there remain opportunities to *deploy* university resources to support community activism (Sudbury, 2009). Working in collaboration with local activists, the abolitionist as a system inside-outsider can create spaces for critical inquiry and the sharing of wisdom through collective organising by promoting social justice and emancipatory knowledge (Scott, 2018a). To subvert the logic of the neo-liberal university it is important to avoid drawing any boundaries of exclusion and creating new ties and solidarity with activists based on difference rather than sameness. This approach also requires working with a diverse group of people outside of the academy/university. Bringing the community into the university can add a level of commitment against penal injustice that can send a powerful message and provide inspiration for all who are prepared to listen. One example would be the London International Conference on Penal Abolition (ICOPA) (June 15–18, 2018), which was organized by two universities (The Open University and Birkbeck University London),[1] but which reached out to local and national abolitionist campaign groups, activist networks and pressure groups. Here academics, including this author, worked closely in a university setting with more than 40 activists to deliver an activist-centered conference that was attended by more than 300 delegates from all around the world. Characterised by horizontal (non-hierarchical) relationships, the aim of the organisers was to provide an opportunity for abolitionist activists to come together in solidarity and hopefully build new networks to help the UK abolitionist movement move forward.[2]

As system inside-outsiders penal abolitionists should always provide assistance to those working for liberation and freedom in the community. Whilst it is important to recognise the limits of the university and how they currently devalue activism, it can also offer legitimacy to community organising. By engaging the university as part of a pedagogy of the oppressed, new spaces can be opened up for critical pedagogy. This should entail drawing strength and inspiration from social movements to challenge elite institutions and privileged sites of expert knowledge and utilising activism within the curriculum.

Researching and platforming subjugated and marginalised voices

The penal abolitionist should also aim to facilitate a platform for subaltern (marginalised and currently unheard) voices. As discussed above, widening

---

1. The conference was also organized in collaboration with the Centre For Crime and Justice Studies (CCJS).
2. The ICOPA conference organization may, however, have focused too much towards accommodating the interests of London activists, with a consequent devaluing of the role and contribution of abolitionist academics and activist scholars across the rest of the UK.

participation in democratic dialogue is a key aim of the inside-outsider. Enhancing the diversity of voices heard in penal debates should also involve providing a platform for prisoners, ex-prisoners and the families of prisoners, but can also include doing research with prisoners (Scott, 1996). This means challenging the silencing of people in prison (Sudbury, 2009). Given the nature of the prison place, it is almost inevitable that the prisoner will be structurally prevented from participation in conversations with members of the general public and there may be no or only limited access to spaces for dialogue with debating partners within the prison place. Further, given the social backgrounds of prisoners and their broader social exclusion, many of those behind bars have found it difficult to perform the language games of normal society. Prisons are places of civil and social death and are powerful determinants of an individual's location within the knowledge economy. Engaging with prisoners establishes a new social relationship and transcends social death.

When individuals speak, they thus engage in a political process that not only starts a conversation, but which may also *ultimately lead to a* new way of conceiving the world being fostered. Hearing the voice of families, ex-prisoners, and sometimes the voice of researchers and those who have worked in the prison place, can provide powerful testimony of the damage prison creates both for prisoners and the wider community (as evidenced in *Chapters 3–6* of this book). It is essential that society hears and listens to the voice of experience when it comes to prison realities. To address the potential silence, abolitionist activist scholars must use qualitative research methodology to gather testimonies of people in the prison place, such as carrying out collaborative research with people in prison, so that the testimonies of prisoners are at the forefront of current debates. There are abolitionist prisoner voices and it is important that the voice of the 'abolitionist in prison' is given due prominence in collections of abolitionist writings (Coyle and Scott, forthcoming) and also at abolitionist gatherings, such as at ICOPA annual conferences. In the *International Handbook of Penal Abolition* there are 20 contributions from abolitionist prisoners from countries including Germany, the USA, Spain and Argentina (Ibid). These papers were selected from more than 140 letters, which were written to the editors of the volume in 2018 and 2019.[3] At ICOPA in London, abolitionists activists created

---

3. A number of these letters are to be subsequently published in a further volume by Routledge entitled *Contesting Carceral Logic*.

and published a special prisoner voice zine; facilitated ex-prisoners and prisoner families to speak at the event, which also included the reading of testimonies of currently serving prisoners.

It is crucial that this view from below is given a platform in any public spaces dedicated to debating the legitimacy of punishment, whether this be in the media or, most importantly, at public events and community meetings; the most effective way to generate connections and understandings. Readings from prisoner autobiographies, interviews and collaboratively published work with activists are all important for the wider struggle for freedom and social justice.

Expert witness to the courts

Whilst it is then essential that the voice of the estranged Other (the prisoner) and the activist is heard and responded to appropriately, penal abolitionism is not just restricted to listening to and interpreting the view from below. It is also important for penal abolitionists to 'speak truth to power'. This can be done in various ways (see also the following three examples), but one is through supporting prisoner legal petitions by providing expert witness reports and testimonies. Up until the 1970s prisoners were considered to possess only privileges and that once the gate closed behind them those confined were beyond normal legal remedies. This first started to change with the case of *Golder v United Kingdom* in the European Court of Human Rights in 1975 and the opening to claims from prisoners was further established in the domestic courts of England and Wales in the third ruling of the *St Germain* cases in 1979 following disturbances at Hull Prison in 1976. In this ruling Lord Justice Shaw (1979, cited in Scott, 2013a) held that 'the rights of a citizen, however circumscribed by a penal sentence or otherwise must always be the concern of the courts unless their jurisdiction is clearly excluded by some statutory provision' (Ibid: 235).

Penal abolitionists have rightly expressed concerns that *legal rights* agendas do not sufficiently encompass the values underscoring emancipatory moral visions of human rights (Scott, 2016a). This critique of rights has thus focused primarily on the *limited existing content and restrictive judicial interpretations of prisoner legal rights and the long-standing almost automatic judicial deference to penal authorities* (Scott, 2013a). Further, Carol Smart has strongly argued that using law to advance emancipatory goals is 'hazardous' (Smart, 1989: 138), as law constitutes an 'institutionalised and formalised site of power' (Ibid). For

Smart (1989) legal rights are too easily appropriated by the powerful and used to reflect their interests. This being said, there are possibilities for progressive judicial decisions and the law remains an important arena of struggle and contestation. Although only limited and partial, the very admittance of prisoner legal petitions in the courts challenge 'civil death' (death in law) and are one means of questioning state power.

One recent example of expert witness legal activism by penal abolitionists came in *R v Secretary of State for Justice (ex parte Davis)*, Queens Bench Division, April 2020, during the early days of the COVID-19 pandemic. This case called for a judicial review of the decision to deny a prisoner in HMP Stocken who was terminally ill with bladder cancer (and was estimated to have only between three to 18 months to live) compassionate release under the provisions of Paragraph 12.1 of Chapter 12 to Prison Service Order 6000 and Section 248 of the Criminal Justice Act 2003. Two abolitionists (Professor Joe Sim and this author) researched, prepared and wrote an affidavit (Scott and Sim, 2020b) and two reports for the High Court (Scott and Sim, 2020c and 2020d) in March and April 2020 highlighting the limitations of the government's current policies on containing COVID-19 in prison and the broader limitations of both risk algorithms and the historical failure of prisons to deliver appropriate standards of care within the prison place. Drawing upon official discourse, the court reports also pointed to an absence of appropriate cleanliness and poor sanitation, ventilation and hygiene in the overcrowded prisons in England and Wales[4] (see *Afterword* for further discussion of COVID-19 crisis).

Testifying for freedom in official submissions to the state
The above example of providing expert legal evidence as a form of abolitionist activism highlights the significance of testifying against penal oppression, exploiting opportunities for progressive social change and directly engaging in struggles for freedom in the here and now. The voice of the abolitionist can also be felt in other aspects of the 'view from above' and official discourse through submissions of evidence to government and other public inquiries.[5] The authors

---

4. On 8 August 2020, Roy Davis was eventually released from Stocken Prison on compassionate grounds. Although the High Court case itself did not directly result in his release, it did put pressure on the Ministry of Justice/HM Prison Service to reach this decision.
5. *Chapter 3* indicates though the significant limitations of official discourse when it comes to revealing hidden truths and delegitimising brutal penal policies and practices.

of these official reports act as 'authorities of delimitation' (Foucault, 1972: 41), authorising a particular knowledge as the 'true' version of events. The key to understanding their role is through grasping the complex relationship between power, knowledge and the production of 'truths' (Foucault, 1980: 133). This 'regime of truth' (Ibid) operates in an exclusionary manner in that it places narrow confines on what can be deemed worthy of attention. Only certain ways of thinking are considered appropriate and the discursive structure both rules in and rules out certain ways of interpreting events and lived experiences. The statements of official reports and governing authorities are thus instrumental in the production and reproduction of power relations.

Official reports define and set the parameters or scope of a problem and possible means of resolution. As a result, certain ways of conceiving imprisonment are presented as legitimate whilst others are de-legitimated and effectively defined out of the debate or marginalised as 'irrational' social policy options. For Burton and Carlen the function of official inquiries is 'primarily to allay, suspend and close off popular doubt' (Burton and Carlen, 1979: 13) through representing 'failure as temporary, or no failure at all, and to re-establish the image of administrative and legal coherence and rationality' (Ibid: 48). Yet official reports do not normally provide a whitewash. More likely, the danger is that they incorporate and re-articulate criticism in a way that certain problems and social harms are re-contextualised so that their potential to undermine the legitimacy of the penal apparatus of the capitalist state is dramatically curtailed (Scott, 2006c). Official discourse often privileges certain voices and explanations, whilst subjugated voices and knowledges are denied space, which can result in the production of sanctioned knowledges, circumventing acknowledgement of the crises of penal legitimacy. At the same time, it is also essential to expose the contradictions and inconsistencies within official narratives and to question their claims and evidence. Though it remains a high-risk strategy—concerns around co-option must be taken very seriously—it is undoubtedly of the greatest importance in terms of abolitionist activism to confront the state on its own terms and rationale, which includes providing evidence to official inquiries and politicians in the hope of rational discussion.

There are various ways abolitionists can engage, of which examples from this author include providing evidence for the Harris Review of Child Deaths in Custody (Scott, 2014) and the Joint Committee on Human Rights (Drake and Scott, 2017b); providing evidence on 'controversial issues in prisons' and other assistance for the United Nations Special Rapporteur on Health, Dainius Pūras, prior to his public call in June 2018 for the abolition of child custody; submissions to politicians, including the Minister of Prisons, on how to radically reduce the prison population (Scott, 2018c, 2019b); providing evidence for politicians to engage in rational debate (House of Commons, 2016; Scott, 2019b); and either undertaking private consultations with senior parliamentarians about abolitionist agendas (Scott, 2019b) or sharing a platform with politicians in the House of Commons to argue for abolition (in this context the abolition of child life sentences) (Scott, 2017). Whilst the co-opting and incorporation of abolitionist ideas is always possible, principled engagement is undoubtedly essential as part of a strategy to deliver 'real utopian' polices that can reduce human suffering in the here and now.

Contesting state-corporate power

Since the early-1990s, the private and voluntary sectors in England and Wales have had increasing influence on the workings of the criminal process. Yet the private companies running prisons are not and cannot be held directly to account by the general public; and this deficit in accountability is significant and should be addressed. *Democratic accountability* requires a public forum where the managers of corporations can be directly questioned and confronted by members of the public. In general, such opportunities are denied to citizens in relation to private companies. However, it is possible for shareholders—those with a vested interest in a private company—to challenge and question the way that a company conducts its business. This can, generally, be done through the forum of the company's Annual General Meeting (AGM). Whilst shareholder scrutiny is in no way a satisfactory alternative to public scrutiny, it is one means by which a privately-run corporation can be asked to account for their actions. Of course, the problem is that the AGM is a private space with access restricted to shareholders only (including activist shareholders aiming to tell truth to power) as opposed to an open and public space for all citizens. Yet possibilities remain; over the last few years, members of the Reclaim Justice Network have been activist shareholders at the G4S AGM (Drake and Scott, 2017a).

Unsurprisingly, questions have been raised about whether the AGM could ever provide a forum for genuine accountability. Though much evidence points to how actual levels of transparency are low and not openly available to shareholders, there have been some small, but significant victories for accountability through Reclaim Justice Network shareholder activism at the 2017 G4S AGM. For four years, shareholder activists requested data on self-harm of prisoners published in the annual reports; and for the first time, in 2017, G4S published details of all the prisoners who had died in their prisons in England and Wales (G4S, 2017). G4S (2017) has also continued to talk about having a policy of 'zero harm' (G4S, 2017) for all of their services, although when under questioning, they were unable to provide specific policies in which this was being implemented in their custodial services.

Following concerted protests from a range of activist groups at the G4S AGMs from 2014–2016, the company withdrew from its controversial delivery of child detention in Israel. Ironically, whilst this one decision clearly indicates the real potential of the AGM to respond to the calls of shareholders, it now means that the only protest group that is still attending the G4S AGM from 2017 is the Reclaim Justice Network. Though it is not without its limitations, shareholder activism can provide a means of creating a limited version of a 21st century agora that can be part of the wider struggle to challenge the dehumanising and sometimes deadly pursuit of profit. With the announcement in October 2020 that G4S has been given the contract to run one of the new mega prisons in England and Wales, the continuation of this kind of abolitionist inspired shareholder activism remains of considerable importance.

Selective engagement with the existing media and creating new forms of media

A further form of state-corporate power shaping our understandings of democracy is the media. Despite its limitations, penal abolitionists should have a direct and concerted engagement with the media so as to question the current forms of penological illiteracy and open the debate to a more nuanced and informed debate about penal realities (Drake and Scott, 2019b, 2019c). The exposures of inhumane prisons in the media in the UK in recent years is significant politically because the message that the public are receiving about the prison estate is one of chaos, harm and inefficiency. The public then are slowly being educated about what prison is today through such representations of a prison system in crisis. To create the appropriate public environment for downsizing the criminal process requires an informed and rational debate about the strengths and weaknesses of punishment in the mainstream media.

Penal abolitionists should selectively engage with both the local and national media; and independent media — such as radio, TV, newspapers, podcasts, documentaries and internet blogs. This can also mean building and using their own media. *EG Press* is a good example here. Established by three academics (J M Moore, Emma Bell and this author) as the publisher of the European Group for the Study of Deviance and Social Control in July 2015, this radical and independent publisher utilises existing technologies on a voluntary basis to publish radical books by critical scholars and activists as well as the journal *Justice, Power and Resistance*. The other intervention that is of great significance is the short film/documentary. These may range from a few minutes to perhaps 60–90 minutes in length, depending on the time required. With mobile phone technologies and the ease of uploading to YouTube, the short films at least are now within the production capabilities of activists. One example of this is the *Why We Should Abolish Imprisonment for Children and Young People* film made by the author with The Open University in March 2019. The film, which was relatively quick and economical to make, was utilised in social media and also on websites of anti-prison and penal reform groups in 2019 to highlight the violence of incarceration and the pressing need to end the penal confinement of children and young people (Open University, 2019). Another recent example is the author's collaboration with the BBC (2020) on the short animation *A World Without Prisons* in early-August 2020, which was platformed on the BBC Ideas website and raised in mainstream forum some of the key ideas of penal abolition.[6] Some medium of getting the message out is essential, but we must not become mere technicians of the state and the powerful and must be aware of pitfalls. Whilst the media is important, it must always be secondary to the main tasks of the organic collective intellectual; which is building relationships and understandings within the community.

The media, then, can be utilised most effectively to publicise activism in the community and to project the event to a wider audience.[7] Engagement with

---

6. This film became the fifth top story on the BBC homepage /BBC News website on 17 August 2020. Further evidence of how the media is starting to mainstream abolitionist ideas in the UK.
7. In the context of COVID-19, there has been a large increase in activists engaging on webinars. This important innovation has seen their talks reach international audiences through the summer and autumn of 2020.

media can also help to place abolitionist arguments on the agenda and can open up abolitionist ideas to a wider audience, but interviews with the mainstream media (especially TV and radio) alone can never be enough.

Building communities and the production of insurgent knowledge

Finally, penal abolitionists need to engage with activists inside and outside prison to create counter-carceral knowledge (Sudbury 2009). It is important that democracy grows from the grass roots upwards and that any organizing against the prison is thoroughly democratic in philosophy and practice. Abolitionists should build towards creating their own autonomous power bases that can foster visions of emancipation, freedom and liberation beyond the academy/university. This should be self-reflective as there can be no social change without also transforming ourselves. Education of the masses should be the core goal of penal abolitionism and for that to be achieved education about the distorted logic of crime and punishment should become part of everyday life (Scott, 2018a, 2019a); it should not be exclusively institutionalised within specialised places of learning. Therefore, penal abolitionists envision a very different kind of educational and political participation in the community that should exist alongside the university as the foundation stones of a pedagogy of freedom. This starts, as discussed earlier, by helping community-based actors build political and intellectual capital. It means sharing know-how, skills and resources with ordinary people so that we see the creation of organic collective intellectuals. But this educational approach is not just about knowledge production, rather about building solidarity movements that can lead to liberation. Constructing a pedagogy of freedom means engaging in organizing and activism that do not have formal ties to the capitalist state, but rather are part of a given community. This is something which is at the heart of the following chapter (see *Chapter 8*; Scott, 2019a) on the importance of abolitionists connecting with the struggles for freedom of 'ordinary rebels'.

This vision of an abolitionist pedagogy of freedom requires the building of learning communities where people can teach each other and where people can make resources available for radical interventions. This leads us back to the ideas of Ivan Illich (1970) and his notion of the learning web. Rather than focusing on formal qualifications and a formal teacher-learner model, the learning web is predicated on self-motivated learning and on giving individuals opportunities to link with people, places, and ideas that can help them grow at their own pace. This is a kind of apprenticeship in the community, where people learn about prisons and punishment through workshops and talking face-to-face with people who have been incarcerated.[8] This approach would also encompass what Illich (1970) called skill exchanges and capacity-building where abolitionists can identify their skills, the conditions under which they are willing to serve as models for others who want to learn these skills and through peer matching communications networking and how this can be achieved. In short, it means collectively learning together and engaging in reciprocal dialogue as organic collective intellectuals.

Freedom, hope, and praxis

Prisons devour the public resources necessary to restore communities devastated by racialised gendered violence, economic restructuring and discriminatory criminalisation. The goal of the penal abolitionist is to challenge the deadly harms of incarceration and to help build the mechanisms that can be put in place to create freedom, liberation and, most of all, human vitality and wellbeing. It means imagining a world without prisons and promoting radical but plausible alternatives to the criminal process (BBC, 2020). Abolitionists, though, cannot do this alone as there need to be agents of change—ordinary rebels—who can work together to transform communities. This work becomes increasingly necessary as the struggle from below is essential not just for democracy, but also for recapturing resources for communities in terms of promoting the paradigms of life. It is not just about dismantling the prison; it is about building communities and building hope, social justice and a commitment to common humanity. The philosophy of hope requires collective knowledge, trust, solidarity and listening. It cannot be driven from afar or via centralised forms of control, but must grow and be locally based, drawing upon intellectual solidarities that work against broader forms of inequitable social relations. If any form of abolitionist democracy is to work, it is of crucial importance to build the cultural capital of activists.

---

8. It is also important for this to be a dialogue with members of the local community and that they have the opportunity to express their lived experiences and understandings.

Penal abolitionists should therefore be prepared to take intellectual and political risks. The promotion of (non-penal) real utopian alternatives to prison that have demonstrated their effectiveness in addressing human conflicts, troubles and illegal behaviours should be a top priority (Scott, 2013b). Prisons do not create safer communities, but there are many different avenues that can be pursued to help build safer communities. This means investing in community projects and in the lives of people so that they have a better future. Given the widespread knowledge of the humanitarian crisis confronting prisons, it is likely that if some of the myths surrounding the idea that 'prison works' were cleared away there would be public support for fiscally prudent non-punitive interventions. Any effort to reduce incarceration must begin with an investment in community welfare service, but it must also recognise the many deep wounds and traumas created from prison life, as well as the previous trauma that many of the people who are sent to prison have experienced.

Penal abolitionism is not only a philosophy of hope engaged in a wider struggle for social justice, freedom and the recognition of human dignity for all, but is also a form of pedagogy and praxis and as such abolitionists must reflect and act in the world in order to transform it in a progressive direction. It is also necessary that penal abolitionists work with people where they are at; whilst it may well have a utopian element, abolitionism is profoundly realistic in terms of what it can (indeed must) achieve in this historical conjuncture. One of the tasks of the abolitionist is to identify what is possible and how. Through understanding present conditions, it may become possible to highlight pathways for the democracy that is still yet to come (Said, 1994).

Reclaiming democratic spaces so that genuine dialogue and reflection can take place is a key starting point. We can only collectively move away from our current reliance on punishment and prisons once these issues have been debated and exposed for their true nature. This requires the formulation of a counter-hegemonic collective imagination and the building of alliances and relationships so that new agents of change can promote transformative political programmes. The oppressed individual must perform the central role in their liberation. The penal abolitionist as inside-outsider and conduit for the formation of organic collective intellectuals can help to raise consciousness and offer some ideas that could be developed further through democratic dialogue and participation (Freire, 1970, 2001).

Penal abolitionists must continue to engage in the battle for hearts and minds in the university/academy and beyond its walls and aim to further develop its pedagogy of freedom. They should provide scholarly and nuanced accounts of the problems we face today; and do the groundwork to help communities work together to find ways to address them as best we can. Critical analysis drawing upon the ethico-political insights of libertarian socialism remains intellectually powerful, for understanding its implications can change people's lives and influence government policies. Critical criminological writings in the past have predicted, with somewhat disturbing accuracy at times, many of the problems we face today (Hall, Critcher, Jefferson et al, 1978). Critical criminological and penal abolitionist scholarship will continue to be acknowledged and have impact in the real world and we should face the future not with trepidation, but with confidence that our arguments are strong and that collectively we can start to challenge problematic policies and practices of the corporate university. It is also essential that, as a society, we put human need and inclusion before reciprocal dialogue. The first priority is to make sure that people have the right access to the democratic process (Dussel, 2008). This is part of our collective responsibility in the struggle for freedom, democracy and the creation of socially just society. Just talking about democracy, dialogue and voice can never be enough; the material conditions must be met first for all so that people can engage in reciprocal dialogue. A firm political commitment to social justice and meeting human need is the only way to ensure that voice is heard and that democracy is genuinely reclaimed for all (Dussel, 2013).

To achieve these ambitions and aspirations, penal abolitionists must work collectively and collaboratively with the community and help to generate an organic abolitionist social movement, which can operate as a genuine agent for transformative social change. As discussed in *Chapter 2*, abolitionists must not only be legislators (offering ideas and helping to shape organic abolitionist social movements) but also interpreters (providing a way of translating the ideas of abolitionist activists into different public idioms) as well as using their position as system insider-outsiders to provide a platform for prisoners, ex-prisoners and anti-prison community activists. This requires political commitment, hard work and above all, the recognition that abolitionism is a future-orientated *philosophy of hope*.

CHAPTER 8

Ordinary Rebels, Everyone:
Abolitionist Scholarship and the Struggle for Freedom

> Everything ends sometime. Prison will end someday. But men remain, men move on. The old structure is cracking. Perhaps only one good blow is needed before everything changes. It's worth living for, and maybe even dying for. When there is enough bread for everybody, no-one will steal any more. When women no longer sell themselves, when reason prevails, there will be fewer vices and fewer murders. Prison will be destroyed. People will come and stare at the stones that are left, and they won't be able to imagine what we are living through. They won't be able to conceive of our misery… (Serge, 1929/1970: 241)

There can be little doubt that we currently have an excessive and unhealthy commitment to punishment. Over the last couple of decades, collectively our society has come to think that punishment is somehow invested with magical powers that can not only solve our deep-rooted social problems and ease our anxieties, but also provide a secure platform for a better future. In fact, it can do none of these things. It has long been recognised by prisoners and prison administrators alike that prison is a cesspool hindering positive reformation of character. Even the most well-respected penal reformers of the past, such as the famous Prison Commissioner Sir Alexander Paterson, have argued that prisons are costly environments (both in human and financial terms) that are only likely to make people reoffend in the future (Paterson, 1951). Talking up punishment's magical powers is just a clever illusion, masking the fact that our excessive commitment to punishment actually exacerbates existing social problems, anxieties and insecurities (Scott, 2018a). One of the most pressing pieces

For Abolition

of evidence of this *punishment fetish* in the modern day—and more broadly the development of an increasingly punitive state—are the current government plans to build six new 'mega prisons' in England and Wales.

The locations of the new mega prisons were announced between November 2016 and March 2017. They were Wellingborough, Northampton; Glen Parva, Leicester; Full Sutton, Yorkshire; Rochester, Kent; Port Talbot,[1] South Wales; and Hindley, Greater Manchester (Travis, 2017a). Four of the mega prisons were also originally planned to be built on sites of existing prisons (HMP Wellingborough, HMP Glen Parva, HMP Full Sutton and HMP Hindley). The intention of this chapter is to focus on the encounters with ordinary people as one aspect of an abolitionist pedagogy of freedom in the campaign from March 2017 to November 2017 revolving around the rebuilding of HMP Hindley, in Bickershaw.[2] Although full details of the proposed redevelopment at HMP Hindley have not been made public (and indeed plans appear to have stalled entirely at the time of writing in September 2020), the new mega prison, if building does go ahead in 2022, would have capacity to hold at least 1,300 prisoners.[3]

For penal abolitionists the prison—whatever the size—will always be an inhumane and immoral institution. Consequently, prisons should be closed down and life-affirming alternatives promoted in their place (Scott, 2018a). Abolitionism is about raising political consciousness and the realisation of humanity for all. Thus, a key goal is to render visible broader issues around social and economic inequities and the commitment to social transformation. An abolitionist pedagogy of freedom should aim to awaken our cultural consciousness and to change the direction of the punitive wind by changing the way people see both the punitive state and the role of the prison within our society. The struggle then is ultimately one of liberation, freedom and social justice as their view of the prison is not as the protector, but *the enemy of ordinary people*.

The punitive state and its punishment fetish present a clear danger to democracy because not only does it disenfranchise large number of people but also leads to the racheting up of a punitive culture at all levels of society. The aim for abolitionists is not just to dismantle the prison, but also to generate a

---

1. It was announced by the government in January 2019 that because of a strong local campaign, plans to build the new mega prison at the Port Talbot site had been abandoned.
2. Bickershaw is a small village in the borough of Wigan, Greater Manchester.
3. For a further discussion of this campaign, including a detailed account of the arguments used by local activists to challenge the mega prison, see Scott (2018a).

philosophy of hope, building communities and fostering a widespread commitment to acknowledging common humanity for all through a pedagogy of freedom. Abolitionism aims to strengthen democracy by building stronger bonds and networks of voluntary association in the community, developing community-based models of resistance and organizing political activities that can work towards improving the safety and wellbeing of neighbourhoods. There are clear advantages for abolitionists, especially those inspired by socialist ethics, to engage in political activism — *being part of the community and networking with like-minded people can renew energy as well as a mutually affirming position that challenges legal coercion.* So, whilst aiming to produce politically useful analysis, abolitionism at the same time recognises the importance of key political agendas being defined by community members themselves. Underscoring this is the strong belief that democratic grassroots socialist activism can be an effective way to challenge the punitive state. Of great importance for abolitionists is to stretch out their hand to activists (who are not abolitionists) and to other members of the community who are neither abolitionists nor activists. Abolitionists recognise that what we require collectively, and indeed should aspire to be individually, is to be *ordinary rebels* fighting for a truly democratic and socially just society.

The discussion below starts with a brief outline of the rules of engagement for penal abolitionists when attempting to build alliances among activists, academics and members of the public. These rules of engagement are specifically directed at the 'activist scholar' (Sudbury, 2009) to ensure that activists, scholars and members of the general public all work equally together for radically progressive transformations as 'ordinary rebels'. This focus on the ethics and politics of abolitionist activist scholars is shaped by the experiences, skills and motivations of the author, who is both an academic working in higher education and also someone who has engaged directly in struggles against the punitive state. The first part of the discussion is therefore reflexive and based on the standpoint of an 'activist scholar'. It acknowledges that whilst academics can bring certain skills and knowledge and can perform an important role in building the capacity of other members of the community, at the same time they are only a very small part of the struggle against the punitive state, whose overall success is dependent upon mutual cooperation and support and everyone working together collectively. Hence, ordinary rebels, everyone. The chapter then moves on to discuss the importance of stepping outside of 'safer spaces' to engage in a critical encounter with people in local communities near to the proposed mega prison site in Bickershaw during the height of the local campaign from March to November 2017. This discussion, then, provides an illustration of several forms of activist intervention highlighted in the previous chapter (see also Scott, 2019c). It concludes with a consideration of how we can all work together, as *ordinary rebels everyone*, towards building an abolitionist future grounded in emancipatory politics and praxis.

Seven rules of engagement for activist scholars

As discussed in the previous chapter, for the great Italian socialist philosopher Antonio Gramsci (1971), everyone in society can be considered as an intellectual, but not everyone in society has the function of intellectuals (i.e. are employed as an academic scholar). By simply using our mental capacities we think and *intellectualise*. A person who engages in writing, organizing and devising socialist political strategies is using their intellectual capabilities. For some activists the term 'intellectual' (and especially the shorthand term 'academic') has become a pejorative one, used today with disdain. Yet the very people who are most likely to be critical of intellectuals are, if we follow the definition of Gramsci (1971), intellectuals themselves. We then have the paradox of the *anti-intellectual intellectual* (Collini, 2002). There is a tendency to construct the 'intellectual' as extra-ordinary—they are either put on a pedestal, romanticised and glamorised, or dismissed, treated with contempt and demonised. What gets lost is that intellectuals are neither. They are just *ordinary people*. The most striking aspect of most people employed as 'intellectuals' (i.e. academics) is their everyday mundaneness. They undertake ordinary tasks and largely live ordinary lives. Some academics are apolitical or attempt to distance themselves from politics, but there are also academics who are rebels—'ordinary rebels'. The ordinary people (like this author) rebelling against the punitive state who work in the academy are referred to in this chapter as 'activist scholars'. They work and campaign alongside other ordinary rebels from the community and non-academic professions, but the term in this chapter is used to refer to academics engaged in rebellious activism.

A major challenge today is to unite as one movement and collectively send the abolitionist message to the people (the general public).[4] The activist scholar should not play the elitist academic game, but rather collaboratively work with others for a more just world. The people with whom the activist scholar speaks should include public audiences rather than just other paid intellectuals; and this engagement should then shape their intellectual outputs and contributions. The role of the activist scholar is therefore the production of knowledge and direct engagement in struggles in the service of progressive social movements fighting for freedom and social justice. This focus on the production of useful knowledge for activists is the focus of the second part of this chapter. Whilst it would be correct to argue that any one of us as ordinary rebels can produce knowledge, activist-scholars have had privileged training and education through the university system.

Drawing upon the insights of Peter Kropotkin (1924) and Enrique Dussel (2013), my focus then is on the ethical responsibility to utilise these skills and knowledge in ways that can best support ongoing struggles against the legal coercion of the punitive state. Other ordinary rebels (especially community activists) may not have had such support. We may well all be equal in certain ways, but at the same time different life experiences (harmful or beneficent) mean we also all remain different. The point of this chapter is to identify how the different skills of the activist scholar can best serve other ordinary rebels in the wider community. Hence, the inequitable power relations invested in paid intellectuals means that there must be 'rules of engagement' for this. Detailed below are seven principles underscoring the political actions of the abolitionist activist scholar.

Challenging privilege

The thorny question of privilege and education should be confronted head on. Privilege is embodied and lived in the everyday (Sudbury, 2009). Privilege reflects life course and access to resources and the privileged university context may be alienating or disconnecting from ordinary people. We may have to just accept that the flattening of privilege is impossible, but it should be part of the daily struggle to live in a genuine democracy. Activist scholars

---

4. The challenge of the 'motivational deficit' to socialist activism is discussed in the following chapter.

should recognise that their tenure, salaries (sometimes with research grants) and technical support from their university give them significant advantages, but it is not impossible for academic activist scholars to support radical social movements and to use their privilege in ethically principled ways. What it does involve though is moving towards ideas that have no connection to university priorities but do have direct relevance to activist concerns that can foster locally based intellectual solidarities. Education is profoundly elitist and can be based on promoting exclusionary and technicist knowledge. There should be no exploitation of community members by those in a privileged position to serve either individual career priorities or the demands of the university research assessments (such as the Research Excellence Framework). Activists (and activist scholars) are right to be sceptical and raise serious questions about the motives of academics in becoming involved in social movements. Whilst it can be difficult to 'fit' rebellious and radical activism within the criteria many universities use to measure impact (hence reducing the attractiveness of such activism to unscrupulous academics) there is always a danger that more is gained by the academic from the community than vice versa. Hence, the importance of reflexivity on the part of the activist scholar—we all must always guard against exploitation and opportunism—and the adoption of an approach of service to others and utilising any privilege possessed (whether that be access, knowledge, skills, networks) to the benefit of all involved in the struggles against the penal apparatus of the capitalist state.

Recognition and the relational dimension

The activist scholar should lead by example. They should give their time generously and be guided by the principles of kindness, care, compassion, love, friendship and the spirit of solidarity. It is essential that horizontal and democratically accountable relationships are fostered; and an anti-hierarchical ethos and the sharing of resources, knowledge and information should be key priorities. There should be loyalty and transparency in all that is done. Recognition of the value of others is key—being involved in local campaigns means being involved in life-affirming and life changing activities and this should underscore all relationships. Community solidarity, shared values and common beliefs in socialist politics and values should form the basis for reconstituting a collective radical agenda as a way of helping *communities to challenge state violence and coercion*. The important value of dialogue and conversation in developing a new consciousness of daily life are an essential part of being of service to the local community. Activist scholars should have a commitment to become a responsible and 'virtuous hearer' (Fricker, 2007: 5), that is someone who is prepared to listen carefully, empathetically, sensitively and without prejudice to not only what is said, but also listening out for what is not said and thus identifying structural denials of voice (see *Chapter 2* for further discussion).

Accountability to the community

Activist scholars must be prepared to unlearn their sense of privilege and instead recognise their accountability to local communities, grass roots activism and struggles for social justice. This entails working towards collective knowledge and the building of trust. It is essential that the abolitionist is prepared to listen and learn from the community, which is exceptionally important in terms of decision-making processes. This means *not being in control* and allowing others to have their voice, enabling them to shape and direct the movement. Local struggles are locally-based movements that require local knowledge and locally-embedded activist scholars. Alongside this, the role of the abolitionist may be, at times, to provide a platform for the voice of others, for example those whose voice is not normally heard, such as prisoners and ex-prisoners. The activist scholar should draw upon their expertise *and ensure* that their work is accessible to the general public.

Levelling up and capacity-building

The activist scholar should aim to improve ordinary people's capacity to function democratically to develop a critical kind of mindfulness and awareness of the socialist vision of justice. Abolitionists should aim to fulfil the potential of people around them and thus provide the intellectual milieu for socially transformative social movements. This means building potential and raising consciousness as a way of creating rebels from ordinary people in the community. Rather than silencing — there must never be levelling down — activist scholars should aim to level up by sharing knowledge, strategies and key ideas in capacity-building workshops. In order to promote a transformative political programme, we need to build a radical historical and cultural narrative uniting abolitionist movement solidarity and providing inspiration for the agents of change for tomorrow — the ordinary rebel.

Consciousness-raising among the populace
Activist scholars must be prepared to challenge dominant myths and official accounts of the prison place, as well as going directly against the received wisdom and common sense understandings to promote penological literacy. The activist scholar must then cut against the grain, questioning received ideas and treating the critical encounter with ordinary people in the local community through 'dialogical transformation' (critical and challenging conversations) by promoting anti-punishment moral education and contributing to the spreading of democratic norms (Freire, 1970). The abolitionist activist scholar should not be a soloist playing their own tune but perform a central role in creating a new abolitionist orchestra. Liberation is of paramount importance in the concept of raising abolitionist consciousness where the activist scholar should attempt to infuse the local community with confidence, renewed belief, pride and dignity.

Building new alliances and power bloc based on difference
To build a new world together we must work towards a solidarity through difference. Activist scholars should promote the importance of building solidarity and recognition of commonality across differences of interests of all in a new coalition of progressive forces. This means building relationships and addressing multiple crises — so when thinking about the penal apparatus of the capitalist state it means creating solidarities with communities who are experiencing the violence of austerity, racialised capitalism and other forms of oppression. We need to co-operate in sustainable ways that can give expression to a collective vision. This means greater collaboration and cooperation, breaking down the silos between academics and activists, framed by activist consciousness and concerns[5] and abolishing the punishment fetish mentality.

Community spaces and the agora
There is currently an absence of an appropriate public arena in which to hold detailed and deliberative dialogues on prisons and punishment. The mainstream

---

5. This includes those highlighted above that infer that academics will be exploitative and focused on personal or professional gain rather than rebelling against social injustice and legal coercion.

media currently hold the monopoly on this, but what we urgently need is an 'agora' (public space for rational debate) where ordinary people can raise discussion of the problems that concern them the most (Bauman, 1997). The activist scholars somehow must find a way to create a public democratic space where people can both question and dream; a space where they can develop and use their imagination to find a new way of doing politics and to awaken and educate new desires for a better world. What is urgently required is a public space that is open to all and guided by the rules of rational discourse. This agora would be a space where informed debate could help convince sceptics that another type of world is possible—a world without prisons, with an authentic democracy promoting the interest of all (see also discussion in the previous chapter).

The encounter: penal abolitionism beyond safe[r] spaces

Emancipatory politics and abolitionist praxis, like all forms of knowledge generation and practical ethico-political engagement, are dependent upon an ethical encounter with someone else. The encounter, by which is meant a face-to-face relationship, is inevitable. We will always have encounters with other people and sometimes those encounters will be with people that we find difficult to understand, or find their embodied privilege problematic for us. They may have done something hurtful to others (or even ourselves) or may simply hold views that we find incomprehensible or morally reprehensible. Yet if we want to create a new and better world, grounded in social justice, we need to generate support from ordinary people who may not think like we do, share our values and principles or have the same interpretation of the world. An inclusionary vision of a socially just, free and truly democratic society must be grounded in reaching out to those who on many issues are on the 'other side' and somehow generating solidarities of difference predicated upon successful engagement with others. Indeed, it is the only way in which activist scholars can help facilitate a radical social movement constituting ordinary rebels.

We need then to ensure that a given community is heard, even when words are not spoken, or they are spoken, but in anger or misunderstanding. We should try and look at the world through the eyes of the ordinary person, adopting or translating their language, meanings and understandings and trying to read unexpected forms of communication. But for Dussel (2013), following ideas rehearsed in *Chapter 2*, we should do even more than this—notably, showing solidarity to sufferers by taking responsibility for facilitating (communal) storytelling that can *rebuild lives and world collectively* alongside the political commitment to attempt to *transform existing asymmetrical power relations* (Haiven and Khasnabish, 2014). As a bottom line, inclusionary visions of social reality acknowledge difference and diversity whilst at the same time recognising what we share: that is, a common humanity. The only way we can challenge the punitive state and build a more progressive and humane future is by reaching out to local communities as they are currently constituted today. But it is also important to recognise that the encounter with other people is a central feature of all of our experiences and not something special. We have encounters with ordinary people every day; sometimes they will be in the context of emancipatory politics and praxis.

Effective activism requires the activist scholars to reach out to the wider community. No struggle against the mega prisons will be taken seriously by local and national politicians unless it is deeply embedded in local communities. The activist scholar must then be prepared to perform a balancing act between listening and learning from the local community and challenging problematic categories and interpretive frameworks. As highlighted above, the activist scholar must recognise and take into account their own privileged position and be prepared to negotiate how they present their political analysis in light of the diverse (and potentially hostile) environment where the community-based activism takes place. There must also be recognition of the oppressive structure of the everyday lived experiences of the community and how that community itself is socially constructed; potentially in problematic ways. Moving beyond 'safe[r] spaces' is inevitable. Safe space policies not only fail to effectively address privilege and power, but in practice means that 'it becomes impossible to develop a revolutionary political programme' (Wang, 2018: 285). Safe spaces cannot remove structural violence—they can only make it less visible and create a little distance from its presence. To bring about the world we desire requires direct encounters, perhaps involving some kind of confrontation in public and undoubtedly less safe spaces.

The following discussion details the engagement with local people in Wigan Borough, Greater Manchester by activist scholars and some of the challenges this presents. The account below is written from the perspective of this author and is based on extensive field notes undertaken during the campaign from March 2017 to November 2017.[6] It follows the emergence of the pressure group *Pies Not Prisons*;[7] the direct encounters with local people in Wigan and Bickershaw; and engagement with local politicians and media. This 'warts and all' account is in chronological order and is followed by a consideration of how well it connected to the seven rules of engagement for abolitionist activist scholars. It is hoped this account will provide useful insights for future emancipatory politics and abolitionist praxis.

Pies Not Prisons

Almost as soon as the plans for the mega prisons were announced in March 2017 (Travis, 2017a) a strategy was put in place by several local activists for a local meeting to be organized. The government plan was to demolish HMP Hindley, the existing prison in the area, and to rebuild a much larger prison (with a possible capacity of 1,300 prisoners) on this land. Knowledge of the local prison area — Wigan Borough — was greatly aided by previous connections to local socialist activists who had been involved in establishing the Diggers Festival[8] in Wigan. Of these connections, the most crucial proved to be with Tony Broxson,[9] a hugely influential local activist who was well-regarded by people in the local community and especially the local left-wing socialist community. Tony Broxson immediately arranged a venue and potential speakers for a Wigan meeting to start the debate on resisting the mega prison. Speakers included activist scholars (including this author); a former prisoner; and a leading member of the Momentum wing of the Labour Party, who acted as chair. At this first meeting on 3 April 2017 people came from around the local area, including activists from Manchester No Prison[10] and activist abolitionists who were based in Liverpool, together with several people from the local community. The

---

6. See discussion in Scott (2018a) for further context of the campaign to rebuild HMP Hindley, Bickershaw, Greater Manchester.
7. Pies Not Prisons is an anti-prison expansion activist group formed in Wigan in May 2017.
8. This is an annual festival which commemorates the life of early socialist thinker Gerard Winstanley, who was born in Wigan; and the social movement the 'Diggers', which was active in England the late 1640s.
9. Permission has been sought and granted to use the real name of this local socialist activist.
10. Manchester No Prison was an anarchist anti-prison group formed in Manchester in 2016 and has close connections to CAPE (Community Action Against Prison Expansion), a national prison abolitionist group formed in 2014.

meeting was attended by 60 people, some of whom were local councillors; and then followed up almost immediately with further discussions at a local NHS crisis meeting event in Wigan town centre a few days later. Here once again concerns about the mega prison were expressed and information was given to members of the socialist and left-wing constituency of Wigan borough.

This was followed by further meetings with members of the Momentum[11] group in Wigan in May 2017, which once again included both long-term socialist activists and left-leaning councillors. The end result of these interventions was the creation of a Wigan Borough based pressure group. This new group was given the rather quirky title of Pies Not Prisons, which reflected the tradition of pie making in Wigan Borough. Underscoring this of course was also a rather simple message: that rather than locking people up, we should feed them. In a town with a number of food banks and high rate of social inequality this message clearly resonated (Scott, 2018a).

The encounter — Bickershaw social club

Although the meetings in Wigan town centre had proved to be hugely successful, both in terms of getting the key message across (Scott, 2018a) and by also generating some 'momentum' towards providing a sustained critique of the proposed mega prison, it was felt essential that Pies Not Prisons should engage directly with the community that was most affected — that is the local community in the area surrounding the existing prison (HMP Hindley) in Bickershaw. A meeting was organised for 29 June 2017 and the local community was widely leafleted with details of the speakers and issues that were to be addressed. Strategically it was felt that it would be helpful to draw upon the relationship between welfare and punishment in order to highlight the social costs of building a new mega prison. Therefore a number of speakers were brought together to explore first of all some of the welfare issues that were confronting Wigan and the area around it of Wigan Borough (which included the village of Bickershaw) as well as issues regarding the closure of HMP Hindley and the subsequent rebuilding of the site as a new 1,300 place mega prison. Speakers were invited to talk about the NHS; the funding crisis in schools; and a platform was also provided for an account of personal experiences of ex-prisoners

---

11. *Momentum* is a radical social group which is closely associated with the UK Labour Party.

and the mother of a currently incarcerated prisoner. One further speaker (this author) was then planning to speak about the social and economic harms of rebuilding the prison and to give the local community as much detail as we possibly could at that point in time, given that the new prison had only been announced a number of weeks beforehand.

The first Bickershaw village meeting perhaps provided a classic illustration of misunderstandings and the difficulties that activists face in terms of trying to read the local community. It also highlighted the democratic deficit regarding the organization of local meetings and a public space for meetings to rationally and collectively discuss social problems and possible solutions (what has been described above as the agora). It also provides an example of an encounter in what ultimately proved to be a less than ordinarily safe space, albeit, one that could hardly be described as dangerous or unsafe. The meeting involved ordinary people coming from both the local community and also a large number of activists who had been inspired to challenge the mega prison from the previous Wigan meetings. The first speaker was the mother of a currently serving woman prisoner. She was allowed to speak, albeit with some grumblings from the gathered local residents. When, however, it came to the following three speakers — who had planned to engage with issues around social welfare, education and health — they were challenged by members of the local community who effectively tried to shout them down.

The local community wanted its voice to be heard and there was clear frustration in the room. The three speakers on welfare spoke more briefly than planned and directed attention more to the local issues of Bickershaw and the prison than was originally intended. To appease the situation one of the speakers (this author) then spoke directly to the most dissident voices in the room, leaving the platform and standing within almost touching distance of a number of the rowdiest members of the local community. There had been a misunderstanding. The local community had thought that the meeting had been organised by Wigan Council and that local councillors would be speaking and giving them direct and specific detailed information on the rebuilding of the prison; and although some local councillors were present, they remained largely silent among the angry voices. The local community were quite vocal in their dissent — shouting 'YES or NO is there going to be a new prison *YES or NO?*' This was something that none of the members of Pies Not Prisons could answer.

What was remarkable from the meeting were two things. First it was evident that the local community was starved of voice; we heard time-and-time-again that there had been very limited numbers of council meetings in the local area and that many people living near HMP Hindley felt as if they had been neglected and denied a voice. Members of the local community also felt that there was a general lack of concern for their interests and, indeed, that the proposed mega prison was going to be rolled through, irrespective of their concerns. There was a palpable sense of passivity and a sense of fatalism when it came to the idea of the new prison. This frustration boiled over on the June 29 meeting; therefore, what Pies Not Prisons encountered was a lot of angry people who did not really know the rules of rational dialogue in terms of a democratic discussion. Nor were they necessarily interested in issues that lay outside of their local remit; their exclusive concerns lay around HMP Hindley and the proposed new mega prison and how that would impact on the local infrastructure and community. This has been widely described in the academic literature as the 'Not in My Back Yard' (NIMBY) agenda. Second, the meeting did not end as a disaster, although it looked as though it may on a couple of occasions; it actually proved to be a great success in terms of building connections with the local Bickershaw village community over the coming months. In the first instance once the local community had vented their anger and it was clear that we were ready to engage in reciprocal listening; they started to respond in a more open manner. It was also evident that Pies Not Prisons was listening and that local activists were responding to what the local people were saying. At the end of the meeting there was much shaking of hands; thanks to the speakers for making the effort to come along; and within only a couple of days there was an immediate call for a follow-up meeting to be once again held at the social club.

The above shows the importance of a dialogical ethics and what situations can arise if dialogue stalls. It is also clear that understanding and engaging in dialogue started to produce results once there was clarity and a sense that Pies Not Prisons was there to work with and alongside the local community; and as a result, a further set of local meetings in Bickershaw village were established before the first meeting closed. At the follow-up meeting, held in the first week of July 2017, 20 members of the local community attended. This encounter started in a very different way. Rather than have guest speakers, organic and collective community meetings were organized. Through this relational dialogue it was possible to establish a sense of what the local community actually wanted and how they thought the meetings could help them try to stop the mega prison being built. More than this, the local community requested practical advice that could immediately and directly be shared with them to help build the capacity to resist. Local ordinary people wanted to know exactly what they could do in terms of challenging this through their local political channels. They wanted their local councillors to be involved; they wanted their local MP to be involved; they wanted the Mayor of Manchester to be involved; they wanted other local councillors who were well known for being dissident in council meetings to be involved; and they wanted more ordinary people who were residents in the adjoining villages to come and join them in their struggle.

Pies Not Prisons facilitated a variety of meetings (details of which were discussed in the engagement with the local political community of Wigan and Bickershaw). But one of the key things that came from the follow-up meetings was a connection with another community only a short distance away in South Hindley village. A campaign group challenging the building on land adjacent to South Hindley village started to make crucially important connections with the Bickershaw community and Pies Not Prisons. A new housing estate was to be situated not far from where HMP Hindley currently stands and engagement in dialogue with local activists in South Hindley village, who were much more organized than the Bickershaw residents, added new strength and vitality to the local campaign against the mega prison. The South Hindley village protest group had come together for quite a number of months before the mega prison was announced, and whilst their focus was not the prison, but rather the building of new houses in a woodland area, their support allowed Pies Not Prisons to extend even further its network of local people. Pies Not Prisons established a small email newsletter putting local people protesting against the mega prison into direct contact with other ordinary rebels; and helped organize further meetings. Significantly, Pies Not Prisons brought together local speakers and made direct connections between the land surrounding HMP Hindley and the issues around asbestos. Through local knowledge, direct action activists and local residents learnt about the harmful legacy of an old Turner and Newell asbestos factory that had been situated just north of the prison and just south of the village of Hindley itself. Thus, a further meeting was quickly organized, which this time involved councillors and a number of local people from both Hindley and Bickershaw.

Although the numbers at this 25 July 2017 meeting were much smaller than the previous big meeting in Bickershaw village, it once again provided an opportunity to hear the views of the local community and what they wanted Pies Not Prisons to help them with. These local meetings quite clearly were not a straightforward political community grounded in values of social justice and human rights. Quite the opposite in fact. The moral and political frameworks held by members of the community were punitive — they did not have a problem with prison, but they did have a problem with it being near to where they lived — the NIMBY (not in my back yard) approach. Pies Not Prison raised an awareness of the harms of asbestos contamination, invited a local asbestos expert to the meeting and also delivered information regarding the practicalities of submitting a planning application objection, all of which it was hoped would be of some direct use to the local community or had been requested by them. In attendance were also representatives of the Prison Officers Association (POA) from HMP Hindley, as activists from Pies Not Prison had leafleted the prison and spoken with prison officers as they were leaving the jail in the days before the big meeting. At this meeting, however, new information was revealed from the POA that a stay of execution had been granted to HMP Hindley. Therefore, rather than close in November 2017, as had been initially announced, the prison was now to stay open until at least November 2019. This news was not officially confirmed until October 2017, when the date of closure was delayed until at least 2022 (Travis, 2017b). Ironically then this disjointed campaign only a few months old had achieved results. But it was a hollow victory at best and, in truth, possibly had very little to do with any of the issues regarding the campaign (Scott, 2018a). More likely a key factor was the broader stalling of the mega prison proposals nationally that occurred in late 2017 and the rising prison population at that time (Travis, 2017b).

Although this third Bickershaw open meeting proved to be the last, what was interesting was that by this point there was a growing sense of community cohesion and that the campaign with the South Hindley group — and especially the concerns raised around asbestos — may actually have proved to have had some momentum. Pies Not Prisons had not seen the radicalisation of consciousness-raising of the community—and certainly no future ordinary rebels had been created—but some solid foundation work had been done that was cut short by the announcement of the stay of execution on HMP Hindley in October 2017.

Engaging in local politics

The encounters with the local community of course were not just about being involved with village residents or organizing big meetings. Encounters during this form of activism also went into the local political community, which itself proved to have various positives and negatives in terms of how the local political process worked. As had been illustrated in the first big Bickershaw meeting, members of Pies Not Prisons found a general sense of apathy and lack of engagement in terms of some serious political support regarding many of the issues that confronted Wigan and also Bickershaw. This was perhaps best illustrated in a meeting with the local MP for the area, the Rt Hon Yvonne Fovargue, MP. Ironically this meeting was set up with the author and local activist Tony Broxson following the first meeting in Bickershaw by the MP. The local MP had a reputation for being on the conservative wing of the Labour Party. However, we assumed that she had some interest in at least finding out what some of the main objections to the mega prison were. It was hoped that she might be interested in coming to a meeting with her constituents or engaging in the broader campaign with Pies Not Prisons. Yet the meeting proved enormously disappointing, at least in terms of the MP's enthusiasm for the campaign.

Almost immediately as the meeting started the local MP said she was not prepared to talk about any policy issues regarding prison building programmes; she was only prepared to talk about practical elements that could lead to an objection to the planning application. That is the 'material conditions of an objection to a prison plan'. The meeting lasted an hour and as time went on it became evident that not only had she spoken with local councillors, but also the local Manchester Labour Party Mayor, Andy Burnham, who had taken an interest in the campaign. The meeting proved to be an obstacle in terms of the MP's position regarding a public objection to the prison (although she did make a statement to a local newspaper about the prison and how she felt this was something that should be open to public debate), but Pies Not Prisons held a follow-up meeting with the office of the local Labour Party MEP (with the hope that perhaps there could be some kind of discussion in the European Parliament) and also had direct liaison with the Manchester Mayor's office, both of which provided encouragement in terms of showing interest in the kind of arguments that would have been raised more broadly against the mega prisons. There were also discussions with Labour Party councillors who, whilst reluctant to engage with many of the key moral and political issues of the campaign, raised question marks about whether the planning application would even go forward; and gave some insight quite early on that they regarded the pathway to the building of the mega prison on the site of HMP Hindley as by no means clear. Discussions and debates were also held outside of the local council offices at times when the local planning committee was meeting (July 18, 2017). The demonstration consisted of approximately 25 people and although conducted in a polite and informal manner, it clearly sent the message that the local community were not going to allow this to happen without some kind of protest (see also discussion below).

Engagement was also made with local unions and with the Momentum group of the Labour Party in Wigan. Talks were given at both Unison's main group meetings (the local Unison group and the Unison Retired Meeting group) and the Trades Council of Wigan, to highlight issues around the problems of building a mega prison. Whilst these talks were largely undertaken by this author, there was also direct connection with local activists—and indeed it was always local activists from Pies Not Prisons who established these meetings in the first instance and local activists, notably Tony Broxson, were always present and contributed to the meetings themselves. There was then a genuine attempt to not only inform the public, but also to try and build capacity in an endeavour to help the local activists themselves build a knowledge base and encourage them to participate in direct dialogue regarding the objections to the mega prison.

There were two further aspects of the political engagement at local level. First of all there was a stall at the local Diggers Festival in September 2017 (and also Pies Not Prisons were represented at the festival in September 2018) which, much to the delight of the local direct action activists, involved the eating of a large number of free pies. Further there was also a fringe event organized at the local Labour Party Conference (North West Region, which was held in November 2017 in Blackpool, Lancashire). This fringe event attracted unfortunately no local MPs, but it did generate debate from a considerable number of people who are members of the Labour Party in the region.

Connecting with the local media

One final area also deserves some brief commentary. Engagement with the local media particularly involved connecting with the local newspaper the *Wigan Post* (which once a week publishes as the *Wigan Observer)*. Over the period of around six months there were 12 separate stories on Hindley Prison that in one way or another were connected to the activities and knowledge sharing of Pies Not Prisons. One of these stories even made it to the front page of the newspaper (as a headline). These stories, albeit quite brief and sometimes offering also a pro prison narrative as an alleged balance to the anti-prison activism of Pies Not Prisons, were often informed by members of Pies Not Prisons and were able to give a critical narrative of the prison as an institution; and also get the message across about both the lack of need for the local prison to be any bigger—indeed it was argued that the prison should be shut down—as well as highlighting the problem of asbestos in the prison and the local community (Scott, 2018a). Pies Not Prisons therefore made direct connections between the corporate harms of asbestos-related deposits and the harms of the prison place. This actually proved to be one of the most significant aspects of raising consciousness because people would start to look beyond the social death of the prisoner and recognise that the issues that were being highlighted in terms of the rebuilding of HMP Hindley as a 1,300 capacity mega prison affected the wider community.

In making connections, local journalists proved to be a useful way of getting the message across and crucially provided a source of credibility in terms of direct engagement with the local community. The Pies Not Prisons, demonstration outside Wigan Town Hall Council Planning Committee meeting on 18 July, attracted local newspaper coverage, including interviews and photographs with activists. However, a critical question was raised by local residents: 'who actually reads the *Wigan Post*?' Some of the other local newspapers also picked up stories, but primarily it was the *Wigan Post* (sometimes when published as the *Wigan Observer*) that provided a platform for the voice of Pies Not Prisons. There was also some minor engagement with local radio in Greater Manchester and Liverpool, including BBC Radio Merseyside about the mega prison, but these interventions were relatively brief and did not really provide what is required for a genuine abolitionist agora.

An ethical encounter?

The 'activist scholar' should provide moral leadership; play a key part in public engagement; provide a platform for the voice of excluded and subjugated voices (which it did on occasion in the above illustration of the campaign Pies Not Prisons with the platforming of ex-prisoner voices); and must ensure that local voices are not silenced, whilst ensuring they too are not silenced; and should channel their privilege into providing resources to engage the interest of ordinary members of the community. It is important however to reflect more generally on how, as an abolitionist activist scholar, the direct interventions of Pies Not Prisons related to the seven rules of engagement detailed at the start of this chapter. Certainly, several processes behind the rules of engagement can be seen to have been followed. There was a strong building of horizontal and non-hierarchical relationships and there were genuine attempts to turn privilege into a levelling up and capacity-building for local socialist activists and people living near the prison. Accountability and answerability to the local community was also evident in terms of the way in which the agenda for engagement was decided and the commitment to supporting local residents who held views diametrically opposed to many of the members of Pies Not Prisons.

For all its strengths though, the activism around the Wigan mega prison made only a small contribution to changing outcomes. It did generate consciousness-raising among the populace, and Pies Not Prisons did at least make good connections with like-minded people and highlight how prisons are a socialist issue. Whilst dialogue between activists and ordinary people in the community was established, it did little to build new political alliances based on the recognition of difference; or create a genuine new space for rational argumentation; though local people were becoming more active and prepared to engage in direct action before the announcement of the five year extension of the existing prison in the village.

The story of the encounter with local residents of Bickershaw then highlights a number of key issues about the importance of working with the community from where it is at. What is required is a negotiating strategy that can both challenge and accommodate the opinions of local people. It is essential to try and build some kind of political momentum by not only working through grassroots connections and local people's views and opinions, but also trying to mobilise local activists who are not necessarily focused on the prison. If there was one big success story of Pies Not Prisons it was that it was able to mobilise members of the Labour Party and in particular members of Momentum and associated unions in a way that meant that challenging prison rebuilding was seen as a major local concern that should be objected to.

Alongside all of this is the enduring commitment to emancipatory politics and abolitionist praxis. Through engaging in praxis, the activist scholars in Pies Not Prisons aimed to build a new power base and generate or tap into existing political consciousness in the community. This meant listening and often carefully challenging the ordinary voices of local people. If we are to live in a different kind of world, we need to create a mass movement that can involve or inspire millions of people. This means developing an 'abolitionist imagination' that can infuse a counter-hegemonic narrative turning penological illiteracy into 'good sense' (Gramsci, 1971). Developing the abolitionist imagination (to which we turn in the next chapter) is not just about the intellectual or those involved in grassroots movements, but reaching out to the general public.

For Abolition

CHAPTER 9

The Abolitionist Imagination:
Ethics of Empathy, Dignity and Life

> This is an ethics of life. Human life in its rational dimensions knows that life, as being in a community of living beings, is ensured through the participation of all. (Dussel, 2013: 108)

It is important not to whisper when speaking of penal abolition. Instead, those who question the legitimacy of the prison place should express commitments as loud and clear as possible *for abolition*. The previous chapters of this book have emphasised the connections between penal abolitionism and socialist ethics, focusing throughout on the socialist principles of freedom; empathy; dignity; and life. This final chapter continues to draw heavily upon the latter three of these to help visualise an 'unfinished' abolitionist roadmap leading towards moral inclusion and social justice in a freer society.

Penal abolitionists argue that not only does the criminal process fail to adequately address social harms, but it also creates new harms. Penal abolitionists aim to expose the domination, abuse of power and exploitation of the penal rationale as well its negative consequences for deepening social and economic inequalities. As discussed in *Chapter 5,* prisons and punishments have for centuries been used disproportionately against people from deprived and impoverished social backgrounds (Scott and Codd, 2010). The criminal process is a way of regulating, controlling and disciplining the poor. It is not just about the people who have done wrong; there are many social harms in society, but only certain harms become criminal harms. Further, only certain criminal harms are enforced by the police and other crime control agencies (Tombs and Whyte, 2015). The criminal process operates in a remarkably partial way and fails to deal with the most serious harms. Many harms, certainly those perpetrated by people in private spaces or by people with power and influence, are very unlikely to be criminalised and sanctioned by the criminal process. It is then, not so much *what* someone has done, but *who* they are. Social backgrounds count.

The abolitionist imagination steps outside the 'logic of crime' and allocation of 'criminal blame' (Scott, 2018a). The current application of criminal blame only morally denounces certain people who have perpetrated certain criminal harms. Indeed, the criminal process has historically failed to reprimand or morally denounce the most serious harms, including those resulting in avoidable and premature deaths. Given that the prison place is characterised by violence, estrangement, humiliation and the creation of death consciousness (in other words, social death), its harm creating daily practices arguably should also be morally denounced. In exploring the above limitations of the criminal process, penal abolitionism utilises the framework of *negative socialist ethics* to shine a light on social injustice and unacknowledged social harms (Dussel, 2013) and provides the bedrock of analysis of social death (see *Chapters 3 to 6*).

Penal abolitionists recognise that activism *against imprisonment* cannot be understood in isolation of other struggles against social injustice. The great Italian socialist philosopher, Antonio Gramsci (1971), argued that as power is dispersed across many different institutions and social networks in advanced capitalist societies, counter-hegemonic forces are required to engage in a wide variety of socialist-inspired struggles. One of the most neglected of these struggles by socialist (collective) organic intellectuals is prisons and punishment. When one engages in an ethical struggle about the 'law and order society' (Kropotkin, 1909; Hall, 1988), there is a damning common sense assumption that those dealt with by the criminal process are morally problematic. Prisoners are socially dead people who are often unable to participate through the hegemonic idiom in democratic debates. Perhaps difficulties arise for many socialists also because penal abolitionists call for the ending of practices which are legal and lawful. This can make public debates more difficult because abolitionist arguments are highlighting state practices, which are taken for granted as being justified. There is often a strong assumption that the moral high ground is on the side of those calling for more and more punishment. However, when people consider the harms created by the criminal process and the limited scope of the people and harms criminalised, it becomes evident that the moral arguments of those advocating the current punishment fetish can in fact be challenged on their own terms. For rather than addressing serious harms and moral problems, in fact, the criminal process is *generating new harms and moral dilemmas.*

Socialist activist scholars may also wish to avoid difficult public debates focused on iatrogenic penal harms because it seems difficult to imagine alternatives, either in terms of principles, policy or practice, to prisons, punishment and the criminal process. This is partly because commitment to the criminal process (and especially attachments to prisons and punishment) seem deeply ingrained in public opinion. Yet the hugely complex 'prison puzzle' remains unsolved (indeed, it is unsolvable). Undoubtedly it is now time to look at the whole project of penal confinement again with renewed energy and urgency. If penal abolitionism is to be a plausible debating partner in democratic dialogue and thus aid wider socialist struggle, there must be a significant shift in public conscience. It is incumbent on abolitionists to perform an active role in any such public education. The moral and political commitments of penal abolitionism require radical root and branch social change; therefore, abolitionists must have a 'public face' where they aim to both engage and persuade not just policymakers or those who work and operate within the criminal process, but also the general public. Such a focus on activist-scholarship was central to the previous two chapters. This chapter builds on these discussions by giving further consideration to 'affirmative' socialist ethics and how they can inspire an abolitionist imagination (Dussel, 2013). For as well as critique, penal abolitionists also advocate non-coercive and life-affirming ways of responding to people who have transgressed laws or societal conventions; as well as promoting social policies addressing human need.

This chapter explores the relationship between socialist ethics and an abolitionist imagination in four parts. The first part of the chapter considers the need for a renewal of socialist ethics and moral education promoting a pedagogy of emancipation and freedom as a way of helping facilitate motivation for radical activism. The second part then focuses on the socialist ethic of empathy and why it is important for abolitionists to reframe public debates towards compassion for the suffering of victims of social injustice, including those currently embroiled in the criminal process. The third part of the chapter shifts attention to the respect of dignity; including a discussion of the importance of taking the indignities of violence against women (VAW) seriously and proposing 'repair' as the guiding principle for intervention. The fourth and final part of the chapter focuses on the socialist ethics of the paradigm of life. It draws upon both negative and affirmative socialist ethics and argues abolitionists should reframe the current focus on 'murder' to include avoidable and premature deaths generated by inequalities and state-corporate harm as well as promote the development of a non-coercive mediator state that can deliver 'equity' and 'answerability'.

The motivational deficit and the pedagogy of freedom

The dismantling of the penal apparatus of the capitalist state requires a counter-hegemonic struggle and a battle for hearts and minds (Gramsci, 1971). This, at least in part, must involve direct challenges against dominant constructions of 'crime' and punishment and questioning the legitimacy of the moral condemnation of people currently defined as 'criminal' (see *Chapter 7*). This requires abolitionists to directly question the coercive power of the state, in terms not only of both its current response to troublesome and wrongful and harmful behaviour, but also its role in perpetrating harms and what more it could be doing to ameliorate a plethora of social harms. To do this requires not only a critique of the prison place and the criminal process through 'negative ethics', but also the visualisation of ethical interventions offering life-affirming 'real utopian' policies and practice; which sidestep the penal rationale and criminal blame (Scott, 2013b).

Radical transformations of society and approaches to justice require both ethical and political engagements. According to the contemporary libertarian socialist philosopher Simon Critchley (2012), at the bottom of the current failings in political engagements with social injustice in advanced capitalist societies is a *moral deficit*. This 'moral deficit' manifests itself as a 'motivational deficit', which leads not only to apathy and disengagement with democratic politics, but also mounting social injustice. Ethical considerations have been squeezed out and the vacuum has been filled by the valorisation of the accumulation of capital. At the same time, the problematic deployment of legal coercion, which is presented as offering security in profoundly insecure times, has trumped calls for autonomy, freedom and non-coercive forms of responding to individual and social troubles. Ethical critique of the 'law and order' society and coercive state power has been effectively silenced in mainstream political debates.

It is though essential for all socialist struggles that assumptions underscoring the law and order society are once again opened up to fierce ethical questioning. This, of course, includes asking why the law and order agenda largely excludes harms of the powerful and is directed almost exclusively against unproductive labourers. Advocating socialist ethical principles and a pedagogy of freedom is essential in our historical conjuncture. The motivational deficit feeds mild moral exclusion, as it categorises certain people as unworthy of our care and kindness. Socialist ethics highlight the importance of not just being aware and conscious of the suffering of others but being directly compelled and motivated to intervene. To help mobilise mass political engagements, socialists must develop a convincing ethical framework that has popular appeal to motivate mass actions and address the current moral malaise. This is an ethics first philosophy, which directly leads to political activism; the generation of an emancipatory politics and praxis; and a pedagogy of freedom (see also the previous two chapters).

The 'negative' ethical critique of the prison place and promotion of life-affirming alternatives cannot be neatly separated out from other socialist concerns about violations of life, freedom and innate dignity; the exploitative logic of capitalist accumulation; and the consequences of both for social and economic inequalities. They must be addressed together through democratically accountable policies grounded in social justice and human rights (Scott, 2013b). The motivational deficit identified by Critchley (2012) seems particularly pertinent when it comes to the question of legal coercion and the curtailment of human freedoms. The moral malaise confronting socialist and abolitionist activists seems to be a lack of understanding for the hardships of other people, especially strangers and the estranged. Advanced capitalist societies are not just characterised by state authoritarianism and turbo-capitalism, but also by a populace which no longer seems to care about or empathise with people who are unable to successfully compete in capitalist economies; and thus, become cannon fodder for state authoritarianism.

Socialist ethics emphasise individual and collective responsibilities to people who are the most vulnerable and have the least power in society (Dussel, 2013). *Abolitionist ethical hermeneutics* start with the aim of fostering greater empathy for others by hearing voice, including people who have done wrong (see *Chapter 2*). Empathy is about looking at the world from the perspective of others. It requires, first and foremost, hearing voice; and then a commitment to listen and acknowledge what the other person has said. For abolitionist ethical hermeneutics it is especially important to hear disqualified and disavowed voice of people who are strangers (or are forced to become strangers) and Othered. But socialist ethics, such as those advocated by Enrique Dussel (2013), ask more of us than to merely just listen to the voice of victims; the socialist ethics of Dussel (2013) require us to empathise and to see the world from the *perspective of the victim*. As explored in *Chapter 2*, this is the only way to ensure that subjugated voices of victims are part of the democratic dialogue.

Socialist ethics are also underscored by a commitment to respect innate human dignity, which means engaging with people in ways that do not make them feel vulnerable or insignificant. For penal abolitionists, everyone should be treated with dignity, even if they have infringed the dignity of others. Rather than criminal blame, socialist ethics also imply the importance of taking responsibility to repair what had gone wrong and to demand answerability, that is, asking those who have generated harms to justify their actions (including justifications of legal coercion and iatrogenic penal harms). As detailed in several of the previous chapters, one of the most significant concerns for penal abolitionists is the denial of dignity in the prison place; but, as discussed below, they are also greatly concerned about other hidden violations of dignity. Calls for the respect of innate human dignity lead us to consideration of affirmative ethics and the paradigm of life. As conceived by Dussel (2013), the paradigm of life requires society, including state institutions, to be organized in such a way that material, educational, emotional and psychological resources facilitating life and wellbeing are delivered for all. This means putting the needs and welfare of ordinary people above accumulation of profit. The paradigm of life commitment to meet human need is ultimately about creating social conditions that protect life; and this requires social policies and commitments to transformative justice grounded in equity rather than equality (Kropotkin, 1913). What this all points towards is the importance of the dissemination in the public domain of a revitalised socialist ethics and a pedagogy of freedom to motivate wider political engagement and activism that recognises the importance of both positive and negative freedoms. This is aided by the mobilisation of an abolitionist imagination.

Empathy

Adopting an abolitionist imagination means to think differently about social problems and how we handle them. It requires us to use our imaginations to step outside the hegemonic norms, conventions and common sense of advanced capitalist societies. An abolitionist imagination invites us to not only reimagine what is possible, but also to reframe some of the most pressing social problems in the here and now. This dualistic approach allows us to consider not only what is going wrong, but also what is required for remedy. In other words, it offers us the mental space to problematise existing hegemonic ideas, policies and practices that result in social injustice and victimhood. But it also provides a *dream space* for imagining what a world without prisons, inequalities and social injustice could look like. This means thinking outside the box and making creative connections that can enhance understandings and motivate action. Using our imaginations is a way of bringing into presence something that was not previously in full sight (Drake and Scott, 2019c).

Developing an abolitionist imagination starts with empathy for others. An imagination grounded in empathy requires us to listen to subjugated voices; adopt new agendas that have clear ethical dimensions; question some of the basic claims and evidence about how both society and the criminal process works; and be open to taking an alternative non-penal pathway when aspiring for justice. Abolitionists should imagine not only how to dismantle the penal apparatus of the capitalist state, but also how to build a more socially just non-coercive state (Cole, 1920).

To empathise is to have a strong commitment to moral inclusion, shared humanity and seeing the world from the point of view of another. The influential libertarian socialist Peter Kropotkin succinctly connects empathy and imagination:

> The more powerful your imagination, the better you can picture to yourself what any being feels when it is being made to suffer, and the more intense and delicate will your moral sense be. The more you are drawn to put yourself in the place of the other person, the more you will feel the pain inflicted upon them. The insults offered at him [sic], the injustice of which [s]he is a

victim, the more you will be urged to act so that you may prevent the pain, insults or injustice. (Kropotkin, 1924: 95)

The more that we develop our imaginations, the more able we are to follow a path towards social justice. In this very short passage, Kropotkin (1924) provides very clear insights into how we can free ourselves from the 'motivational deficit' (Critchley, 2012). Kropotkin suggests we should start to imagine a different way of being—an ethics of life grounded in empathy. If people can find a way of imagining the suffering of others, such as empathising with the pain and hardships of the estranged Other, this may result in a re-sensitising of our collective moral senses and sensibilities. Key to abolitionism is the problematising of unnecessary suffering (Christie, 1981). For abolitionists, the deliberate infliction of pain (including unintended institutionally-structured violence) in the prison place cannot be justified. Unfortunately, the suffering of others is something people largely try hard not to think about (Cohen, 2001). Many block out the suffering of others because it is not always clear how to appropriately respond and it weighs so heavy on the heart (Ibid). At the same time recognition of the suffering of others is important in terms of developing our own moral sensibilities. Both Kropotkin (1924) and Dussel (2013) point to the centrality of victims in socialist ethics, especially if we define the victim as somebody who has experienced social injustice. The greater our ability to empathise with victims of social injustice, the more we can understand the daily indignities, violence and emotional and psychological pain delivered in the prison place (Christie, 1981).

For Kropotkin (1924), the more we picture ourselves in the position of the sufferer and understand their pain, the more we will feel motivated to act. In advanced capitalist societies, with its consumerist distractions and moral focus on merit, desert and success at all costs, it seems harder than ever to put ourselves in the shoes of people who have been victimised by social injustices. If the current motivational deficit is to be overcome, socialists must develop educational strategies and resources that can stimulate empathetic understandings for people who are on the margins of society. Kropotkin (Ibid) is not alone in prioritising empathy. Contemporary socialists, including Zygmunt Bauman (1995) and Dussel (2008) have also advocated empathy, kindness and compassion as important for challenging the moral malaise at the heart of advanced capitalist societies. They remind us that it is important to show solidarity with sufferers, including strangers, the estranged and the socially dead, because we share a common humanity.

The socialist ethics of Kropotkin (1924), Gramsci (1971), Bauman (1995), Dussel (2008) and Critchley (2012) do not restrict ethical choices to individual kindness, but rather indicate *the responsibility to intervene on a collective and political level*. The ethics of care and compassion are most effective when they inform the rationale and the structure of state policies and institutions (Cole, 1920). A commitment to socialist ethics also results in the critique of the imbalances and asymmetrical power relations that pertain within society in our historical conjuncture (Hall 1988). An abolitionist imagination, albeit grounded in empathy, must also reframe harm beyond the current restricted focus on criminal harms and (re)imagine new ways of responding to human failings without recourse to criminal blame by facilitating peace, wellbeing and social cohesion in the future.

The libertarian socialist Charles Wright Mills reminds us that to use our imagination is to draw upon a quality of mind and offer an 'understanding of intimate realities of ourselves in connection with larger social realities' (Mills, 1959: 15). Crucially, what Mills points to is that our imaginations must also help to provide an understanding of how unnecessary suffering is generated. Socialist-inspired abolitionist imaginations should bring into sharp relief the harms and violence of state-corporate power and the exploitative logic of capitalist accumulation, as well as the injuries, insults and indignities generated through social and economic inequalities; whether they be derived through poverty, ableism, racism or sexism. The crucial thing here though is that the understanding of social harms should be underscored by empathy for victims rather than the criminal blame of perpetrators.

It seems to be particularly pertinent for penal abolitionists, as part of the wider socialist struggle, to challenge legalistic understandings of criminal harms and question the legitimacy of criminal blame. It is important for socialists not to be seduced by the logic of crime. Criminal harm and criminal blame remain problematic, whether applied to the harms perpetrated by people in impoverished social backgrounds or the (currently non-criminal) harms perpetrated by states and the powerful; the limitations of the application of the criminal process remain the same. The moral language of criminal blame has been neither successful in holding people to account; sending a clear message that a given behaviour is problematic; nor necessarily a good way of trying to deal with problems in the future. It is a backward-looking approach that does not entreat reformation to ensure people are answerable for wrongdoing (Scott, 2018a). When we start thinking imaginatively and using our 'quality of mind' (Mills, 1959: 15) this helps us to understand the various different forms of problems, harms and troubles that exist today. Whilst reframing harms may well significantly expand the number and range of harms open to formal redress and repair, it is essential to look beyond notions of criminal blame as an effective answer and instead be guided by the socialist ethics of empathy for victims.

Dignity

Innate human dignity should be valued and respected for its own sake. When using our imaginations, one way forward is to consider reframing the most problematic aspects of human conduct through the socialist ethics of dignity. First, the privileging of respect of dignity indicates that whatever society does in response to social harms, it should not systematically violate dignity. Previous chapters in this book have pointed to the daily indignities, vulnerabilities, humiliations and sense of powerlessness that characterise the prison place when dealing with human conflicts. State responses should avoid any interventions that degrade, dehumanise or create new harms, victimisation and injustice through institutionalised violence. What is required is that the voice of the victim is listened to and attempts are made to repair and redress what has gone wrong, rather than create yet more victims whose pain and suffering is hidden and neglected and whose needs are systematically ignored.

Abolitionists should start by deconstructing existing definitions of 'crime' (Barton, Corteen, Scott and Whyte, 2006; Drake and Scott, 2019c) pointing towards the limitations, inconsistencies and contradictions within both the application of the criminal law and also the delivery of punishment. Ultimately, this means drawing attention to the disturbing reality that the people who are sent to prison are not necessarily the people who have perpetrated the greatest harms in society. This deconstruction should be done not to strengthen the justification for imprisonment and widen the penal net, but rather to draw attention to the fact that the criminal process deals in only a partial and relatively insignificant way with violations of human dignity. Let us now take this discussion further by reflecting upon violence against women as an example of a violation of dignity and then discuss some abolitionist real utopian responses grounded in the ethics of empathy (Scott, 2013b).

Penal abolitionists must effectively challenge the myth that the criminal process addresses the most serious forms of (interpersonal) violence in advanced capitalist societies. Violations of dignity arise in relational contexts, including between people in intimate relationships. Many victims of serious violence are potentially emotionally attached to the person who is harming them.[1] One of the first questions abolitionists often encounter in public debates is 'what do you do with the rapists, murderers and/or those who engage in serious violence?'.[2] Perhaps the most obvious response is that most societies do not take sexual violence seriously and that it is wrongheaded to believe that a prison sentence will genuinely address some of the most difficult and problematic harms we face. The criminal process fundamentally fails victims of all violence. One of the reasons is that the criminal law cannot deal very well with forms of interpersonal and intimate conflict. For abolitionists, what is urgently required are interventions which empathise with victims and hold answerable those who perpetrate the most harmful actions in modern society.

Violence against women (VAW) is an everyday and widespread harmful activity, yet it is vastly under-reported and is often understood as an 'invisible crime' because officially recorded police data provides a gross under-estimate of its actual prevalence. VAW violates dignity through verbal put downs, social isolation, public embarrassment, taking away money, spying, kicking, punching, yelling, tearing clothes, destroying possessions, threatening to kill, threatening friends and relatives, pushing, knifing, shooting, burning and so on. VAW can be world or even life destroying—generating trauma, fear, anxiety, insecurity, mistrust, depression, self-harm, sleeping disorders, low self-esteem,

---

1. This discussion does not explore all forms of sexual violence, such as rape, but it is clear from the attrition rate of rape that this is also a violation of dignity that is clearly not addressed by the criminal process. It is estimated that 20 per cent of all women in England and Wales have experienced rape and that 85,000 women each year are raped. It is believed that in recent years only 15 per cent of women who have been raped report the incident to the police and that less than six per cent of reported rape cases end with a criminal conviction (Rape Crisis Centre, 2020).
2. Consideration is given to the deadly harm of 'murder' and other avoidable and premature deaths in the next section on the paradigm of life.

eating disorders, mental ill-health, withdrawal, failure to protect self, suicidal ideation, meaninglessness and breaking previous assumptions about safety. It is now more than 20 years since the *British Crime Survey* estimated that there were likely to be more than one million incidents of domestic violence each year and that one in four women were likely to experience violence from men (cited in Scott, 2018d), with as little as four in every 1,000 incidents of partner abuse reported to the police (Stanko, 1985).

In the year ending March 2017 there were 93,590 prosecutions for domestic abuse-related offences; 70,853 of these resulted in some form of conviction, but this hardly indicates that the vast majority of incidents of VAW are being addressed (Scott, 2018d). For Michelle Maden Dempsey (2009), whilst the criminal process is not going to address all the needs of the victim[3] she argues that successful prosecutions could publicly denounce the patriarchal (male dominance) values underscoring VAW. Dempsey (2009) assumes that successful prosecutions, and thus pursuing the logic of crime, will reduce future incidents of VAW and improve the safety of women in society. This expressive element (expressing social disapproval and condemnation of VAW) is often cited as an important factor for those advocating the use of the criminal law. However, there is much evidence that indicates otherwise (Mills, 2003; Bumiller, 2008). Let us consider briefly how the application of the criminal process to cases of VAW have been questioned by penal abolitionists (Scott, 2018d).

For a start, the idea that the criminal process sends an effective message to society is unproven. People do not necessarily interpret and read the message of the criminal courts correctly (Mathiesen, 1990). Indeed, it is morally unjustifiable to attempt to defend punishment based on moral denunciation alone given it is grounded in blame and moral exclusion (Scott, 2018a). Modern societies must start to critically question the very *ethical basis of the penal sanction* and, as argued below, develop new ways of handling social harms; as the criminal process is not very effective as a means of resolving conflicts between intimates. In fact, the collateral consequences (that is the personal harms) that arise from a criminal conviction (such as loss of job, status, social networks)

---

3. For the sake of consistency, the term 'victim' is adopted in this part of the chapter. It is however important to recognise that feminist scholars of VAW use the language of 'survivors' rather than 'victims'. The terms survivor is deployed as a means of challenging assumptions around passivity and to highlight how an individual has survived a hugely traumatic and potentially life-threatening incident.

means that many victims of VAW are deterred from using the criminal process. People often realise the excessive harshness of the penal law when it deals with the familiar rather than the stranger. The inadequacy of the criminal law as a means of effectively responding or dealing with social conflicts is made abundantly clear when it is used to punish people known well by the victim (Mills, 2003; Bumiller, 2008). Punitive sanctions are unlikely in themselves to foster the kind of acknowledgement of the harm done or generate a commitment to living a life of non-violence that would be desirable outcomes of any direct intervention. Widespread positive imagery building the self-esteem and powerbase of women is much more likely to challenge patriarchal ideas and values than a sentence by the criminal courts.

It should also be noted that only certain categories of perpetrators of VAW are likely to end up being processed by the criminal law. These people are often from low social economic status and have poor inter-personal skills and lack the skills to develop healthy attachments. When the criminal law is applied it is often simply scapegoating the small number of people who it does process and, worse than that, the underlying structural problems remain entirely unrecognised and unresolved. The judgements of the courts may then merely perpetuate inaccurate stereotypes (in terms of both 'race' and class) about perpetrators of VAW that never lead to effective solutions (Scott and Codd, 2010). The patriarchal values underscoring VAW are a distortion of existing social norms that need to be challenged on the basis of their extremist nature. Perpetrators of VAW should not only be understood within the context of existing (and problematic) masculinist hierarchies of power and the way they devalue the lives and knowledge of women more broadly (Jagger, 1983), but also other men, young people and human equalities. The othering of men who have perpetrated VAW is ultimately counter-productive and may even facilitate offending in the future through denials of injury and victimhood (Cohen, 2001; Lacombe, 2008). People reject negative and dehumanising labels — they do not recognise themselves in such a representation and this can lead to perpetrators rejecting the opinion of the courts and accuser, ultimately constructing themselves as a 'victim' in their own mind. If the perpetrator is handed down a prison sentence, then this is likely to only exacerbate the above problems and further entrench patriarchal values and particular constructions of masculinities in a place of institutionally-structured violence. The hyper-masculine environment of the prison only helps to confirm the extreme views of the VAW perpetrator and encourages continued commitment to the social structures that contributed to it in the first place.

Further, the criminal processes cannot meet the needs of the victim; as it does not create the society that we all, surely, want. Women are still left feeling outrage, injustice and pain as the criminal process only provides a fleeting voice for the victim (their day in court) rather than allowing that voice to be appropriately listened to and acknowledged in the long run. Most significantly it does not help to repair or redress the harms and damage that were generated through VAW. Victims of VAW often want to have acknowledgement of the harm done; to know why the perpetrator harmed them; to know they are now safe; and hope that there will not be other people harmed by the perpetrator (Renvoize, 1993). If we are going to address VAW and sexual violence more broadly, then we first need to provide support for victims and recognise their suffering. Kirstin Bumiller (2008) strongly argues that we need to have a more holistic approach to helping women live full and fulfilling lives—this includes making the appropriate social, economic and political supports available to victims of VAW. But most of all we should follow the socialist ethics of empathy and prioritise safety and a victim orientated approach (see also Mills, 2003). There should be immediate increases in funding for 'escape routes' for women and children who are experiencing or witnessing VAW, such as women's shelters, rape crisis centres and refuges and that these genuine places of safety should be run (at least in part) by women who themselves have experienced physical, emotional and/or sexual violence. Socialists, feminists, VAW campaigners and penal abolitionists can work together with other anti-violence campaigners (such as anti-war movements, anti-racists and those advocating peace and transformative justice) to call for the promotion of an *anti-violence alliance*. Here all forms of violence are acknowledged as a problem and that the only approaches that are going to work are those which are grounded in the principles of empathy, moral inclusion and social justice. For Bumiller:

> …[t]he most desirable solutions are neither perpetrator nor 'relationship' focussed but directed to addressing the most persistent problems causing and created by [sexual] violence: the social and economic disadvantage experienced by women and their dependents. The primary goal of a campaign

to prevent [sexual] violence must be to promote the emotional wellbeing and economic sustainability of women who suffer repeatedly from [sexual] violence throughout their lifespan. This certainly involves providing individual women with the emotional, material, and communal support to empower themselves. (Bumiller, 2008: 163)

The criminal process does not protect women who have experienced VAW. It does not create safety or provide the means for helping women leave a violent relationship. Nor does it lead to the respect of dignity for all. The suffering of victims who have been subjected to a harm should be the central focus of the state. It should be trying to fix and put right and prevent future harms that threaten dignity, generate useless suffering and threaten human life.

It is only through a victim-centred approach, adopting forward looking interventions aiming to create safety, peace and support for the person who has been harmed that they can be helped to repair and rebuild ruined lives (Scott, 2013b). This means having an empathetic mind-set, which is one of moral inclusion rather than moral denunciation; an ethics that prioritises restoring the dignity of victims and recognising the dignity of those who have done wrong; and one that looks to repair what is broken and encourage the non-repetition of such harmful behaviour in the future. Many men who have frequent violent episodes require extensive therapy, aid and assistance both in terms of addressing the impulse to violence and other problems of living that they may be encountering (both social and psychological). There should be wider recognition that people who have perpetrated VAW can gain the skills to lead healthier non-violent lives. Interventions, such as those drawing upon cognitive behavioural psychological therapy can help in the taking back of emotional control, challenge denials and acknowledge that VAW is an abuse of power. Yet such voluntarily-chosen interventions, like Strength to Change in Hull are relatively recent and small in number; it was only in 2004 that programmes offering 'intense emotional support' began in England and Wales and there are still only around 40 such groups today.

Ultimately, we need to enhance and develop more men-centred VAW therapeutic interventions and programmes in the community as part of the response (Smallman, 2013). *Repair* in the context of VAW can take the form of therapeutic interventions, or it might be just about restoring confidence, rebuilding new relationships, or providing assistance and support through befriending an individual. It must also mean creating places of care, protection and safety for people whose lives have been destroyed by violence (Stauffer, 2015). Our lifeworld is built around relationships with others. When it is damaged by violence from intimates it cannot be rebuilt by a person acting alone, especially not one with a destroyed self. There is a clear congruence between socialist and feminist ethics, not only around dignity but also empathy and the promotion of transformative justice responses grounded in safety, healing and accountability. Feminist interventions in response to VAW focus first on protecting women who have been harmed and recognise that the transition from surviving to thriving is a long and hard journey requiring time, energy and the support of communities of care (Price et al, 2008). The ethical responsibility falls upon those in the wider society to help with facilitating a dignified life.

Alongside this, socialist feminist philosophies have also informed non-punitive interventions for aggressors that aim to facilitate acknowledgement of sexist hierarchies and the de-valuing of women. Pointing to the importance of personal accountability, the aim of feminist inspired interventions is ultimately to bring about a radical transformation of the aggressor's assumptions about their masculinity. The feminist inspired 'Duluth model' of therapy aims to encourage empathy and the recognition of women as people of equal worth and dignity. The Duluth model is envisaged as a starting point for the deconstruction of masculinist assumptions and as a way to provide the skills and capacity for aggressors to rethink and reconstruct their masculine identity. Despite its merits, this transformative agenda has been open to criticism for not engaging with the full complexity of men's lives or giving full consideration to other non-gender specific factors with regards to why they may have perpetrated violence (Morran, 2013). When determining what is the best intervention for an individual aggressor, it is important to take into consideration social, structural and cultural contexts as well as the significant difficulties that men face in reconstructing their masculinity without ongoing and long-term networks, relationships and communities of intensive support. Enduring specialist assistance for aggressors, perhaps over a number of years, is essential to help reinforce anti-VAW therapy (Morran, 2019).

Feminist inspired interventions remain essential for the development of a libertarian socialist penal abolitionist project. It has long been known that two women are killed by a partner or an ex-partner each week in the UK and many have previously experienced VAW. Any plausible victim centred approach to healing, safety and accountability must ensure these and other avoidable and premature deaths are taken seriously. Let us now give further consideration to the problem of avoidable deaths and the promotion of the paradigm of life.

The paradigm of life

For Dussel (2013) society should be structured around the protection of human life and the fulfilment of human needs. He powerfully claims that human life must come first in any consideration of ethics or politics and that without the material conditions of existence being met, there can be no genuine democracy or moral basis for the state. His arguments draw strong parallels with those of Kropotkin (1913) who maintained some time ago that:

> ...everyone has before everything the right to live, and that society is bound to share amongst all without exception, the means of existence it has at its disposal. We must acknowledge this and proclaim it aloud and act upon it. (Kropotkin, 1913: 28)

Everyone has the inalienable right to live. Mark Olson (2010) embellishes on this idea and notes that the state should not only privilege the 'sacredness of human life' (Olsen, 2010: 43), but should also be committed to ensuring that human flourishing (positive human freedom) is facilitated in the material and structural conditions of a given society. In other words, all humans possess positive freedoms as well as negative freedoms and, as such, all should have the freedom to fully develop their capacities and capabilities. In several chapters in this book, the stand against imprisonment arises because the daily workings of the prison place not only undermine safety, violate dignity and suppress empathy, but also significantly threatens to extinguish human life.

The socialist 'ethics of life' (Dussel, 2013: 108) can further inspire an abolitionist imagination in at least two different ways. First, drawing on negative socialist ethics, it can inform the reframing of intentional homicide (murder) into a much wider focus on avoidable and premature deaths (Dorling, 2005;

Drake and Scott, 2019a; 2019d, 2019e, 2019f, Open University, 2018). Secondly, it can also assist in reimagining non-coercive state response grounded in empathy and respect of dignity, such as abolitionist real utopian policies of equity and answerability. Therefore, let us start this discussion with the reframing of 'murder' in the context of other avoidable and premature deaths.

Whilst politicians and the media focus largely upon deaths that are the result of intentional homicide (murder), this covers only the tip of the iceberg with regards to the numbers of avoidable and premature deaths in England and Wales. Dany Dorling (2005) rightly argues that given the very strong connections between social and economic inequalities with regards to both homicide and reduced life expectancy, it does not necessarily make sense to look at them separately. Indeed, given that by far a greater number of premature deaths are associated with impoverished living conditions and inadequate state welfare provision, drawing upon on the logic of crime to address avoidable and premature deaths seems unhelpful (Scott, 2018a; Drake and Scott, 2019a), as all are non-criminal harms.

In the last decade there have been approximately 700 intentional homicides (murders) in England and Wales each year (Drake and Scott, 2019a). Each death is of course one too many, generating lifelong sadness for bereaved families as well as anxieties and other negative emotional constellations among a much wider community of people. From an abolitionist perspective, it is not enough to just express sympathy/empathy for families and loved ones of victims of intentional homicide. It is important to develop a quality of mind that can widen our understanding to have the same level of concern and awareness about avoidable and premature deaths that occur in other circumstances. Many people die much sooner than they should and only a tiny fraction of this number of deaths arises as a result of the intentional actions of an individual murderer.

For penal abolitionists it is helpful to consider avoidable and premature deaths through the lens of 'structural violence' and social murder. Structural violence occurs at a societal level and arises through 'any avoidable action that constitutes a violation of human rights in the widest meaning, which prevents the fulfilment of basic human need' (Salmi, 1993: 17). Structural violence can, of course, be understood as being a direct form of violence, but most significantly injuries and harms can also indirectly result from the organization of society:

> Indirect violence is a category intended to cover harmful, sometimes even deadly situations or actions which, through one human intervention, do not necessarily involve direct relations between the victim and the institution or people responsible for their plight. (Ibid: 19)

The structural violence of the prison place has been laid open to scrutiny in several chapters of this book and referred to as 'institutionally-structured violence'. Because the deprivation of need is structured within the very fabric of the penal regime, this concept provides the context to understanding the creation of the death-bound subject and the large number of self-inflicted deaths in prisons (Scott, 2015a).

A similar concept, though this time focusing exclusively on the generation of avoidable and premature deaths, is social murder. Referring to a death as social murder is intended to problematise inadequate government policies, regulations and laws that fail to protect human life or prevent certain deaths (Open University, 2018; Drake and Scott, 2019a). Social murder has a long history in the socialist tradition in England and Wales and was first implied by Chartists in 1842 as a critique of the deaths following the introduction of the 1834 Poor Law. Social murder focuses on absences in laws/regulations and the subsequent neglect of human needs and wellbeing. Like in the concept of structural violence, people can die as the result of acts of omission as well as acts of commission. There is no requirement for death to be 'intentional'. Nor does it have to be the result of just one or a small number of people; it can be deployed to refer to avoidable and premature deaths that are the result of the negligence or inactions of the state. Social murder can then refer directly to political decisions that result in unsafe and harmful contexts/deadly conditions, such as through deregulation, or policies like austerity and welfare cuts; and deepening social and economic inequalities. The concept of social murder can shine a light on the deaths of people that arise when the policies of the state do not provide enough care and support to sustain human life (Drake and Scott, 2019a). For example, Watkins, Wulaningsih, Zhou and Marshall et al (2017), who published their data in the *British Medical Journal* in November 2017, argued that due to austerity policies between 2010 and 2017, every day

100 people were dying prematurely. Thus, with both intentional homicides and premature deaths via austerity policies, people are dying too soon.[4]

Penal abolitionists should also point to the data put forward by organizations such as the Hazards Campaign, who investigate deaths of people who died prematurely because of inadequate working conditions. The Hazards Campaign (2018) recently argued that approximately 140 people die prematurely because of work related conditions every day. It does not take a mathematical genius to work out that if you look at those figures independently, there are many more structural and systemic forms of death than in comparison to people who are dying through intentional homicides. Penal abolitionists should then be contributing to the wider socialist struggle to acknowledge state-corporate harms and violence deeply embedded within the social structures of advanced capitalist societies (Tombs and Whyte, 2017). Democratic debate needs to be reframed and rearticulated to shine a spotlight on current inequitable power relations and social and economic inequalities. When the vast majority of avoidable and premature deaths are understood as arising as the result of larger problems at a societal level, it seems more plausible to call for non-penal social policies that can reduce harm, violence, suffering and death. This then leads us back to Dussel (2013) and consideration of the material conditions that support human life in society itself; and the importance of meeting 'necessary needs' (Heller, 1974/2018) above the accumulation of capital, as well as bringing into sharp relief the catastrophic harms of capital for people and the planet.

When reframing avoidable and premature deaths around the broader right to life, it is important, from a socialist perspective, to recognise that the 'problem of riches', as well as the 'problem of poverty', performs a key role in terms of shortening the lives of individuals. Excessive material wealth and power creates its own problems, not least the abdication of responsibilities for the welfare of others less fortunate in society. The paradigm of life provides clear ethical guidance for organizing the economy and the role of the state. For socialists, like Kropotkin (1913), Gramsci (1971) and Dussel (2013) the means of production and economic organization should be connected to democratic ownership

---

4. Whilst it is too early at the time of writing to fully explore this issue in any depth here, the number of premature deaths following the outbreak of the COVID-19 global pandemic could prove to be one of the biggest controversies of the decade. There have been concerns widely expressed in several countries around the world, including the USA and UK, that national government policies have resulted in thousands of avoidable deaths.

and the active and democratic participation in decision-making. It means hearing voices and having freedom of choices. This again takes us down the path towards (positive) freedoms which result in the fulfilment of human potential.

Both the exploitative logic of capitalist accumulation and the repression and domination of the penal apparatus of the capitalist state, ultimately, do the exact opposite — they deliberately deny need and systematically generate deadly harms. Penal abolitionists and socialist activist-scholars are largely engaged in the same struggle — to meet human need and valorise the right to life for all. Unequal societies are much more punitive societies because they are competitive, hierarchical and rooted in status. When people are worried about their job, status and position, they inevitably feel a greater sense of insecurity. Penal abolitionists want to see a true levelling of the social and economic distribution of wealth and power. This, of course, means adopting an equitable approach, which reflects the long held socialist doctrine of 'from each according to ability, to each according to their need'. Justice in the abolitionist imagination should be tied to notions of equity, which recognises the diversity of the human family and calls for society to meet the specific needs of individuals, rather than treating everybody in the same way.

Abolitionists and (a number of libertarian) socialists have historically also shared common ground with regards to questioning the legitimacy of the coercive state. Given the capitalist state is steeped in both violence and death, it should come as no surprise that socialist conceptions of the state not only privilege life, but are also often conceived as non-coercive. George Douglas Howard Cole (1920) was one of the most notable socialist thinkers to highlight the importance of developing a non-coercive state grounded in genuinely democratic principles. Whilst the state would be largely decentralised where power would be dispersed and rooted in local participatory democracy, the centralised aspects of the state would be responsible for the coordination of equitable distribution of material and other resources necessary to meet human need. They would also provide arbitration for various local democratic organizations (Cole, 1920). The state would be a provider of welfare and perform the role of mediator for democratic dialogue, including facilitating the mediation of conflicts, wrongdoing, harms and troubles. In other words, the role of the state is no longer defined by the legitimate use of force and violence, but rather that the state is one which is fundamentally grounded in non-coercion and peace.

Such a vision turns the current role of the state on its head and is clearly attractive to an abolitionist imagination, as it challenges the very existence of the repressive penal law. A non-coercive mediator state could facilitate social organization that prioritises life, acknowledges human dignity and looks to handle troubled and troublesome people through mediation, repair and redress. In terms of dealing with social harm, the state is not just reformed, it is transformed. The moral legitimacy of any sanction of punishment would be open to the greatest of scrutiny and considered as an absolute last resort (Scott, 2018a). Prisons would no longer continue to exist as they are currently constituted because they are institutions that are grounded in punishment and therefore, we should see the end of that form of punitive detention.

It is interesting to note that an embryonic non-coercive form of intervention was also presented at the beginning of the 20th-century by leading penal reformer Sir Alexander Paterson. Paterson (1951: 241) recognised that prisons were potentially a sentence of 'living death', places that could easily become 'unhealthy little cesspools'. By the time he came to the end of his career, he went as far as to suggest that a civilised society should even abandon the way prisons are currently constituted and develop non-penal alternative forms of detention in different sites around training for work, psychiatric care and education (Ibid: 27).

The non-coercive mediator state should find its legitimacy in meeting human need and the facilitation of conflict handling. There should institutionalised forms of state directed redress, grounded in the socialist ethics of empathy and focused first on meeting the needs of the victim. Then, by finding ways that respect innate dignity, consider ways of addressing the needs of the person who is responsible for the injury, hurt or harm, perhaps through voluntary and non-coercive therapeutic interventions (Scott and Gosling, 2016). The non-coercive mediator state will aim to prevent future injustice and where possible help to put right what has gone wrong and help people to rebuild their lives.

The centralised and decentralised components of the non-coercive mediator state, as envisioned by G D H Cole (1920), would be required to be answerable for their actions and decision-making. Answerability is a particularly useful concept for abolitionists in the here and now, because it provides a way of thinking which goes beyond purely that of accountability. Answerability places responsibility on individuals, communities, work-placed organizations and states to explain and justify their actions. Answerability immediately throws back the question of the justification of punishment and prisons to the state. Answerability means challenging power relations because if the exercise of power cannot be justified, held to account and explained, then all in society have a problem.

If appropriate ethico-political justifications for prisons and punishment cannot be found, then their widespread use should be abandoned (Scott, 2018a). It means that the state must meticulously answer for every single instance of the deliberate infliction of pain. Justification is fundamental in terms of why problematic behaviours arose in the first instance and also how they should be responded too. All parties to a conflict have to be heard to allow them to be answerable and attempt to justify what has happened. This not only ties in with this notion of democratic accountability in a decentralised state, but also a victim-focused approach to repair and redress. One of the main outcomes victims want from mediation is for the person who has wronged them to acknowledge what has happened and be prepared to address the problem. Demanding answerability may not only provide justification, but also recognition and responsibility. Answerability, by placing the spotlight on those who have the answers (organs of government state institutions and those at the top of bureaucracies and companies) may be a way of helping to make visible current hidden harms. Finally, answerability may also help to strengthen the link between power and responsibility, because having the knowledge that one must definitely be fully answerable for one's (in)actions may inspire more moral performance; and provide motivation to those who hold power to ensure that appropriate care is taken in the first instance to ensure the delivery of equitable and socially just outcomes for all.

For Abolition

Afterword

> We fight the same battles over and over again. They are never won for the eternity, but in the process of struggling together, in community, we learn how to glimpse new possibilities that otherwise would never have become apparent to us, and in the process we expand and enlarge our very notion of freedom. (Davis, 2012: 198)

A lost opportunity...

A once in a generation opportunity for a radical reduction in the prison population in England and Wales seems to have been missed just as this book is going to press. In early 2020, the UK Government was provided with detailed epidemiological evidence of the ways in which prisons could become hotbeds of contagion during the COVID-19 global pandemic. Government experts advised that somewhere between 15,000–20,000 prisoners of the then 83,000 prisoner population in England and Wales should be released to avoid a potential humanitarian catastrophe of up to 3,000 prisoner deaths. At a time when politically there would have been little concerted challenge to the mass release of prisoners, something perhaps not possible for the last 50 years, the Conservative Government proved unable to escape from its punitive law and order mindset (Scott and Sim, 2020e).

Epidemiologists had noted that COVID-19 could spread rapidly in places that were unhygienic with cramped living conditions. Prisons, by default, also presented basic difficulties in meeting the requirements of 'social distancing' (physically keeping two metres apart) as they are closed and densely-populated institutions. Prisons have numerous shared locations, such as cells, recreational spaces, outdoor areas and so on, that prisoners will inhabit after others (prison officers and other prisoners) have only recently vacated. Given the numbers of people involved, it is virtually impossible for such areas to be thoroughly cleaned. In fact, prisons are cesspools of dirt, filth and rubbish. During the pandemic there were considerable concerns about poor hygiene standards and cleaning regimes across the penal estate in England and Wales. The National Audit Office (2020), when looking more broadly at improving the prison estate, reported earlier that year that numerous prisons were infested with vermin and that prison cells were often damp, wet and cold. Other official bodies, such as Her Majesty's Chief Inspector of Prisons, also raised similar concerns (see Scott and Sim, 2020e), whilst the Independent Monitoring Board (2019), highlighted how cramped living conditions in prisons were. The cells in HMP Pentonville and HMP Nottingham, for example, contravened basic international standards for cell size. Living in a cell which is not much bigger than a small bathroom has of course other structural problems with regards to hygiene. Indeed, in 2020, not only were there still some prisons—notably HMP Coldingley in Surrey and HMP Long Lartin—housing prisoners in cells without any integral sanitation (i.e. toilets) (IMB, 2019), but in April of that year, right at the peak of the COVID-19 crisis in the UK, *The Guardian* (Allison and Pegg, 2020) reported that prisoners at HMP Coldingley were left to defecate and urinate in plastic bags after an automated computer system to give prisoners access to toilets malfunctioned. For other prisoners, spending virtually all day, including meal times, in a cell with a toilet, could hardly be considered as dignified.

Whilst initially there was a commitment from the government to release several thousand prisoners in response to the COVID-19 pandemic, this policy was soon abandoned. Even when this initial commitment held, however, tight restrictions on the risk of future offending meant the number released would always have been significantly smaller than the 4,000 prisoners originally announced. But crucially, this commitment was abandoned only a couple of months into the COVID-19 crisis, when the prisoner population had reduced by only around 3,000 people.[1] The Government revised its claims, arguing that an overall reduction in the prisoner population of around 5,000 would now be sufficient to manage the spread of the disease. The 'law and order' card of the Conservative party trumped broader humanitarian commitments and epidemiological advice. Rather than releasing prisoners, Government policy

---

1. On 17 September 2020 the prisoner population stood at 79,185. However, the significant backlog of cases in the criminal courts and the Government's commitment in their recent white paper *Smarter Justice* to introduce longer prison sentences, indicate that this population is likely to rise again in the near future.

focused instead on authoritarian prison lockdowns, where tens of thousands of prisoners were held for over 23 ½ hours each day in their cell for months at and end. Whilst some prisoners did have access to a phone, TV and sometimes even computer games, many others were given only crayons to help pass the time. Alongside the rigid controls within the prison, there was also the ending of visits for prisoners from March to July; and the building of 500 additional places within the penal estate to enable some prisoners to be isolated in individual cells.

The consequences of the prison lockdown may not become fully obvious till years to come; as being locked in a prison cell for literally months at a time could prove to have devasting implications in terms of mental health. The sense of time consciousness during the lockdown from March to July where prisoners were deprived of meaningful activities and human contact would surely have been extreme. How the consequences of lockdown (which began to be eased from 6 July) will impact on the long-term wellbeing of prisoners may perhaps become at least partly visible in official records of self-harm and deaths in prisons. There are, at the time of writing, concerns that in the immediate context of the prison lockdown, and in the months following, we could witness a significant spike in both prisoner self-inflicted deaths and prisoner self-harm. There are still further concerns that the failure of the government to release thousands of prisoners could yet still prove deadly if there are second or third waves of infections later in 2020 or 2021.

But a world to win...

The COVID-19 pandemic brings into sharp relief the urgent need for a radical transformation in how we treat people who have done wrong in society and the jettisoning of law and order rhetoric. But this is not just significant in relation to the current coronavirus crisis, but also after the crisis. For more than two centuries, prisoners have been regarded as less eligible subjects; and time-and-time-again been considered as socially dead ghosts that are beyond our realm of understanding. There remains a profound moral deficit at the heart of the criminal law, grounded as it is in blame and the deliberate infliction of pain. What we are facing is a moral deficit of empathy for the suffering of others and a subsequent failure to realise in practice an ethics of care. Prison regimes have *always* been unhealthy and unsafe for prisoners which, in turn, has had a devastating impact on their physical and psychological health. When it comes to deaths in custody, this has led to prisoners being blamed for their own deaths either because of individual pathology or they have died 'naturally' (Sim, 1990; Scott and Codd, 2010). There is a clear dividing line between judgements made on human rights and the right to life and those of the current government, which are grounded in security, order, control, discipline and risk. The law and order agenda of the UK Government is firmly focussed on risk of reoffending and ensuring that prisons remain environments characterised by security and discipline. It is an approach devoid of hope and imagination and one which is doomed to fail, at least on ethical grounds.

Yet in all of this darkness, ordinary rebels are fighting back against the legal repression of the capitalist state; and this struggle for freedom is something that is happening all around the world. Ordinary people are increasingly recognising that the 'law and order' rhetoric is shot through with contradictions. But it is not just a critique of 'law and order ideology' (Hall, 1988) that is required; we need to collectively work towards building a more socially just and peaceful future. This requires both hope and imagination; two things which characterise penal abolitionism. Of particular focus at the time of writing is a radical critique of the state police and the political mainstreaming of new and imaginative ways of rethinking how policing can be transformed in the future. Premature and avoidable deaths in police custody have plagued nations such as England and Wales and the USA for decades. In both countries, since at least the 1960s, there have been a larger number of deaths of people from black and minority ethnic backgrounds and impoverished social backgrounds more broadly (Drake and Scott, 2019d). Whilst sadly only one of many, the tragic killing of George Floyd[2] on 25^t May 2020 during a coercive physical restraint by a police officer in Minneapolis, USA resulted in widespread calls to defund the state police and acknowledge the wider harms of state coercion (MPD, 2020) in many countries around the world.

---

2. The final words of George Floyd—'I can't breathe' and the kneeling position of the police officer who had knelt on his neck for over nine minutes until he died have become a slogan and symbol of the anti-racist struggle against legal repression all around the world.

The rationale for the dismantling of the state police and their replacement with non-coercive welfare services is well-established in abolitionist literature (Vitale, 2017). The police are not trained to deal with people who have mental health problems or to effectively negotiate conflicts; and therefore, rather than looking to de-escalate harm and resolve conflicts, state police interventions largely operate within the mindset of crime control. As the state police are not only failing to address the needs of the community, they are generating harm for members of the community (especially those from disadvantaged and minority ethnic groups). As an outcome, today ordinary rebels all around the world are utilising their abolitionist imaginations and thinking about non-coercive alternative means of policing which, if appropriately funded, could serve the community much better than the existing state police. For example, by early June 2020, members of the Minneapolis City Council made a clear and unanimous commitment to dismantle the Minneapolis State Police Department, grounded in legal coercion, and look towards building a new model of public safety policing that actually works (Levin, 2020). Significantly, the shift in emphasis away from 'law and order' towards 'peace officers' focused on 'protection, care and safety' is underscored by a commitment to reallocate funding from the state police to welfare-oriented services around mental health support and therapy; education; employment; and housing.

In the abolitionist imagination, it is essential that connections are made across a wide range of sites of exploitation, repression and domination. When calling for the dismantling of the penal apparatus of the capitalist state, such as the state police and prisons, it is essential that abolitionists consider together the historical legacies and contemporary manifestations of state racism; the insidious masculinist bias within the law and broader society; and the profound exploitation of capitalist labour relations. Further, abolitionism must come from below. Engagement with the political, social and economic elite will not deliver social justice and radical social and economic transformation *unless* it is strongly tied/connected to the 'view from below' and infused with socialist emancipatory politics and praxis. When the ruling elite champion a given moral cause, it may well be for the 'moral capital' that can be transferred to them rather than an honest and principled intervention (Scott, 2020b). Ordinary rebels, everywhere, should utilise an 'abolitionist imagination' that situates the personal within the structural and ideological; and as a consequence, this can inform a pedagogy of freedom and help understand how the intersections of social divisions cut across state institutions and agencies of legal repression.

We are then at a crossroads. In one direction there is more of the same—a failed law and order ideology and an increasingly authoritarian state. In the other direction there are new and imaginative ideas filled with hope, calling for a non-coercive state that aims to actually deal with human troubles and problematic conduct. These radically alternative abolitionist ways forward ground our collective moral and political judgements within the socialist principles of empathy, dignity and the right to life and put both positive and negative freedoms at the heart of social policy. The struggle to abolish the penal apparatus of coercive states in countries all around the rest of world remain as important today as ever. For there to be genuinely civilised and democratic societies in the future, it is a struggle that socialists must continue to fight—and win.

Bibliography

Abbott, J.H. (1991), *In The Belly of the Beast: Letters from Prison,* New York: Vintage.

Adelsberg, G. (2015), 'US racism and Derrida's theological political sovereignty'. In: Adelsberg, G., Guenther, L. and Zemon, S. (2015), *Death and Other Penalties: Philosophy in a Time of Mass Incarceration,* New York: Fordham University Press.

Agamben, G. (1998), *Homo Sacer: Sovereign Power and Bare Life,* New York: Stanford University Press.

Ahmed, S. (2000), *Strange Encounters,* London: Routledge.

Alcoff, L.M. (1995), 'The problem of speaking for others'. In: Roof, J. and Wiegman, R. (eds.) (1995), *Who Can Speak?* Chicago: University of Illinois Press.

Allison, E. and Pegg, D. (2020) 'Discharged UK prisoners with Covid-19 symptoms given travel warrants', *The Guardian,* April 7, 2020: https://www.theguardian.com/world/2020/apr/07/discharged-uk-prisoners-with-covid-19-symptoms-given-travel-warrants (accessed: 30th April 2020).

Allison, E. (2017), 'Prison officers acted unlawfully in restraining prisoner who later died', *The Guardian,* March 31, 2017 : https://www.google.co.uk/amp/s/amp.theguardian.com/society/2017/mar/31/prisoner-acted-unlawfully-restraint-inmate-died-inquest (accessed: 1st May 2020).

Anonymous, [One who has endured it] (1877), *Five Years Penal Servitude by One Who Has Endured It,* London: Richard Bentley and Son.

Anonymous, [One who has tried them] (1881), *Her Majesty's Prisons: Their Effects and Defects—Volume II,* London: Sampson Low, Marston, Searle and Rivington.

Apel, K-O. (2001), *The Response of Discourse Ethics,* Leuven: Peeters.

Barber, M. (1998), *Ethical Hermeneutics,* New York: Fordham University Press.

Bardsley, A. (2018), 'Prison officers cleared of assaulting inmate who tried to throw bucket of poo at them', *Manchester Evening News,* February 15, 2018: https://www.manchestereveningnews.co.uk/news/greater-manchester-news/prison-officers-cleared-assaulting-inmate-14295387 (accessed 1 May 2020).

Barnet, E., Abrams, L., Dudovitz, R., Coker, T.R., Bath E., Tesema, L., Nelson, B.B., Biely, C. and Chung P.D. (2018), 'Child incarceration and long-term adult health outcomes: A longitudinal study', *International Journal of Prisoner Health*, 14(1), January 2018.

Barrett, D. (2015), 'Concerns over "holiday camp" jails', *The Telegraph*, February 11, 2015.

Barton, A., Corteen, K., Scott, D. and Whyte, D. (eds) (2006), *Expanding the Criminological Imagination*, London: Routledge.

Bauman, Z. and Donskis, L. (2013), *Moral Blindness,* Polity Press.

Bauman, Z. (1989), *Modernity and the Holocaust,* Cambridge: Polity Press.

Bauman, Z. (1990), *Modernity and Ambivalence,* Cambridge: Polity Press.

Bauman, Z. (1995), *Postmodern Ethics,* Cambridge: Polity Press.

Bauman, Z. (1997), *In Search of Politics,* Cambridge: Polity Press.

BBC (2002), *The Experiment*, London: BBC: http://www.bbcprisonstudy.org/ (accessed 15 October 2016).

BBC (2020), *A World Without Prisons: A Viewpoint by David Scott,* London: BBC Ideas: https://www.bbc.co.uk/ideas/playlists/made-in-partnership-with-the-open-university

Becker, H. (1963), *Outsiders,* New York: Free Press.

Benhabib, S. (2004), *The Rights of Others,* Cambridge: Cambridge University Press.

Benhabib, S. (2011), *Dignity in Adversity,* Cambridge: Polity Press.

Bines, W. (1994), 'The health of single homeless people', York Centre for Housing Policy, York: University of York.

Blanchot, M. (1982), *The Space of Literature,* Lincoln: University of Nebraska Press.

Bouton, C. (2014), *Time and Freedom,* Illinois: Northwestern University Press.

Boyle, J. (1977), *A Sense of Freedom*, London: Pan Books.

Brocklehurst, F. (1898), *I Was in Prison,* London: Fisher Unwin.

Bumiller, K. (2008), *In An Abusive State,* Durham: Duke University Press.

Burney, C. (1962), *Solitary Confinement,* London: MacMillan.

Burton, F. and Carlen, P. (1979), *Official Discourse: On Discourse Analysis, Government Publications, Ideology and the State,* London: Routledge Keegan Paul.

Butler, P. (2018), 'At least 320,000 homeless people in Britain, says Shelter', *The Guardian,* November 22, 2018: https://www.theguardian.com/society/2018/nov/22/at-least-320000-homeless-people-in-britain-says-shelter (accessed 1 May 2020).

Cacho, L.M. (2012), *Social Death,* New York: New York University Press.

Caird, R. (1974), *A Good and Useful Life: Imprisonment in Britain Today,* London: Hart-Davis, MacGibbon.

Carasov, V. (1971), *Two Gentlemen to See You, Sir: The Autobiography of a Villain*, London: Victor Gollancz Limited.

Carlen, P. (1996), *Jigsaw*, Buckingham: Open University Press.

Cearnaigh, S.U. (ed.) (1874/1967), *O'Donovan Rossa, My Years in English Jails: The Brutal Facts,* Dublin: Anvil Books.

Christie, N. (1981), *The Limits of Pain,* Oxford: Martin Robertson.

Christie, N. (1986), 'Ideal Vctim'. In: Fattah, M. (ed) (1986), *From Crime Policy to Victim Policy*, London: Springer.

Coggan, G. and Walker, M. (1983), *Frightened for My Life,* London: Fontana.

Cohen, S. and Taylor, L. (1972), *Psychological Survival,* Harmondsworth: Penguin.

Cohen, S. (1988), *Against Criminology,* Cambridge: Polity Press.

Cohen, S. (2001), *States of Denial: Knowing About Suffering and Atrocities,* Cambridge: Polity Press.

Cole, G.D.H. (1920), *Guild Socialism Re-stated,* London: Parsons.

Collini, S. (2002), 'Every fruit juice drinker, nudist, sand sandal wearer: intellectuals as other people'. In: Small, H. (ed) (2002), *The Public Intellectual,* Oxford: Blackwell Publishing.

Collins, H. (1998), *Autobiography of a Murderer,* London: Pan Books.

Cope, N. (2003), 'It's No 'Time or High Time': Young offenders' experiences of time and drug use in prison', *The Howard Journal,* 42(2), pp 158–175.

Corsen, G. and Galtung, J. (2016), 'Is Peace Possible? A Dialogue with Johan Galtung', *TMS Peace Journalism,* Dec 5, 2016: https://www.transcend.org/tms/2016/12/is-peace-possible-a-dialogue-with-johan-galtung-on-ukraine-trump-putin-gandhi-and/ (accessed 1 May 2020).

Couldry, N. (2010), *Why Voice Matters.* London: Sage.

Cover, R. (1986), 'Violence and the Word', *Yale Law Journal,* 95, pp. 1601–1638.

Coyle, M. and Scott, D. (eds.) (forthcoming), *The International Handbook of Penal Abolition,* London: Routledge.

Crawley, E. (2004), 'Prison Officers and Prison Work', *Prison Service Journal,* 157, pp. 2–10.

Creswell, T. (2015), *Place,* Chichester: Wiley and Sons.

Crewe, B. (2009), *The Prisoner Society.* Oxford: Clarendon Press.

Critchley, S. (2012), *Faith of the Faithless,* London: Verso.

Croft-Cooke, R. (1955), *The Verdict of You All,* London: Secker and Warburg.

Cronin, H. (1967), *The Screw Turns,* London: John Long.

Das, V. (1997), 'Language and body: transactions in the construction of pain'. In: Kleinman, A., Das, V. and Lock, M. (eds) (1997), *Social Suffering*, London: University of California Press.

Davies, I. (1990), *Writers in Prison*, Oxford: Basil Blackwell.

Davis, A.Y. (2012), *The Meaning of Freedom and Other Difficult Dialogues*, San Francisco: City Lights.

Davitt, M. (1885), *Leaves From a Prison Diary, or, Lectures to a 'Solitary' Audience. Volume 1 of 2*, London: Chapman and Hall.

Dawkins, J. (2006), *The Loose Screw*, Essex: Apex.

Dempsey, M.M. (2009), *Prosecuting Domestic Violence*, Oxford: Oxford University Press.

Dendrickson, G. and Thomas, F. (1954), *The Truth About Dartmoor*, London: Victor Gollancz

Denzin, N.K. (1989), *Interpretive Biography*, London: Sage Publications.

Dixon, K. (1986), *Freedom and Equality: The Moral Basis of Democratic Socialism*, London: Routledge.

Dorling, D. (2005), 'Prime Suspect: Murder in Britain'. In: Hillyard, P., Pantazis, C., Tombs, S. and Gordon, D. (eds) (2005), *Beyond Criminology*, London: Pluto Press.

Douglas, R. (2008), *At Her Majesty's Pleasure*, London: Hodder & Stoughton.

Drake, D.H. (2011), 'The "Dangerous Other" in Maximum-security Prisons', *Criminology and Criminal Justice*, 11(4), pp 367–382.

Drake, D.H. (2012), *Prisons, Punishment and the Pursuit of Security*, London: Palgrave.

Drake, D.H. and Scott, D. (2017a), 'Holding the Corporation to Account?', *Justice, Power and Resistance*, 1(2).

Drake, D.H. and Scott, D. (2017b), 'Mental Health and Deaths in Prison', Official submission to Joint Committee on Human Rights, February 2017: https://www.academia.edu/31070467/Evidence_to_Joint_Committee_on_Human_Rights_mental_health_and_deaths_in_prison (accessed 20 February 2020).

Drake, D.H. and Scott, D. (2019a), 'The Murder Puzzle: Intentional Homicide, Avoidable Deaths and Social Murder'. In: Drake, D.H., Nightingale, A. and Scott, D. (eds) (2019), *Introduction to Criminology (Book 1)*, Milton Keynes: The Open University.

Drake, D.H. and Scott, D. (2019b), 'Contesting Prisons'. In: Downes, J., Kent, G., Mooney, G., Nightingale, A. and Scott, D. (eds) (2019), *Introduction to Criminology (Book 2)*, London: The Open University.

Drake, D.H. and Scott, D. (2019c), 'The Criminological Imagination'. In: Downes, J., Kent, G., Mooney, G., Nightingale, A. and Scott, D. (eds.) (2019), *Introduction to Criminology (Book 2)*, London: The Open University.

Drake, D.H. and Scott, D. (2019d) 'Victims and Perpetrators'. In: Drake, D.H., Nightingale, A. and Scott, D. (eds.) (2019), *Introduction to Criminology (Book 1)*, Milton Keynes: The Open University.

Drake, D.H. and Scott, D. (2019e), 'Dangerous States'. In: Drake, D.H., Nightingale, A. and Scott, D. (eds.) (2019), *Introduction to Criminology (Book 1)*, Milton Keynes: The Open University.

Drake, D.H. and Scott, D. (2019f), 'The Death Penalty: State Sanctioned Murder?' In: Drake, D.H., Nightingale, A. and Scott, D. (eds.) (2019), *Introduction to Criminology (Book 1)*, Milton Keynes: The Open University.

Dussel, E. (1985), *Philosophy of Liberation*, Oregon: Wipf and Stock.

Dussel, E. (1998) *The Underside of Modernity*, New York: Humanity Books.

Dussel, E. (2008), *Twenty Thesis on Politics*, Durham: Duke University Press.

Dussel, E. (2013), *Ethics of Liberation: In the Age of Globalization and Exclusion*, Durham: Duke University Press.

Edney, R. (1997), 'Prison Officers and Violence', *Alternative Law Journal*, pp289–292.

Esposito, B. and Wood, L. (1982), *Prison Slavery*, Washington DC: Committee to Abolish Prison Slavery.

European Committee for the Prevention of Torture and Inhuman or Degrading Treatment or Punishment [CPT] (2020), *Report to the Government of the United Kingdom on the visit to the United Kingdom carried out by the European Committee for the Prevention of Torture and Inhuman or Degrading Treatment or Punishment (CPT) From 13 to 23 May 2019*, Strasbourg: Council of Europe.

Falandsyz, L. (1991), 'Abolitionism: Between Necessity and Utopia'. In: Lasocik, Z., Platek, M. and Rzeplinska, I. (eds) (1992), *Abolitionism in History*, Warsaw: University of Warsaw.

Ferguson, H. (2006), *Phenomenological Sociology: Experience and Insight in Modern Society*, London: Sage.

Fitzgerald, M. and Sim, J. (1979), *British Prisons*, Oxford: Blackwell.

Foucault, M. (1972), *The Archaeology of Knowledge*, London: Routledge.

Foucault, M. (1980), 'Truth and Power'. In: Gordon, C. (ed) (1980), *Power/Knowledge: Selected Interviews and Other Writings 1972–1977 by Michel Foucault*, London: Longman.

Fox, K.J. (1999), 'Reproducing Criminal Types: Cognitive Treatment for Violent Offenders in Prison', *The Sociological Quarterly*, 40(3), pp 435–453.
Frankl, V.E. (1959), *Man's Search for Meaning*, London: Rider.
Freire, P. (1970), *Pedagogy of the Oppressed*, Harmondsworth: Penguin.
Freire, P. (2001), *Pedagogy of Freedom: Ethics, Democracy and Civic Courage*, New York: Roman and Littlefield Publishers.
Fricker, M. (2007), *Epistemic Injustice: Power and the Ethics of Knowing*, Oxford: Oxford University Press.
G4S (2017), *Social Responsibility Report*, London: G4S/Park Communications.
Gaita, R. (2002), *A Common Humanity*. London: Routledge.
Galtung, J. (1994), *Human Rights in Another Key*, Cambridge: Polity Press.
Galtung, J. (2013), 'Cultural Violence'. In: Galtung, J. and Fisher, D. (2013), *Johan Galtung: Pioneer of Peace*, London: Springer.
Gilmore, L. (2001), *The Limits of Autobiography, Trauma and Testimony*, London: Cornell University Press.
Giroux, H. (1988), *Teachers as Intellectuals: Towards a Critical Pedagogy of Learning*, London: Bergen and Garvey.
Giroux, H. (2006), *The Giroux Reader*, Colorado: Paradigms Publishers.
Giroux, H. (2013a), 'The Necessity of Critical Pedagogy in Dark Times', *Truthout*, Wednesday, February 6, 2013.
Giroux, H. (2013b), 'Public Intellectuals Against the Neoliberal University', *Truthout*, Tuesday, October 29, 2013.
Giroux, H. (2014), *The Violence of Organized Forgetting: Thinking beyond America's Disimagination Machine*, San Francisco: City Lights Books.
Glissant, E. (2000), *Poetics of Relation*, Michigan: University of Michigan Press.
Goffman, E. (1961), *Asylums: Essays on the Social Situation of Mental Patients and Other Inmates*, Harmondsworth: Penguin.
Gouldner, A. (1973), *For Sociology*, New York: Basic Books.
Gramsci, A. (1971), *Selections from the Prison Notebooks*, London: Lawrence and Wishart.
Greater London Authority (2018), 'Rough Sleeping in London', *CHAIN Report, 2018*, London: Chain: data.london.gov.uk/dataset/chain-reports (accessed 19 November 2019).
Greenwood, A. (2017), 'How a Brutal Mutiny at Dartmoor Prison Was Sparked by Porridge', *Devon Live*, September 14, 2017: https://www.devonlive.com/news/devon-news/how-brutal-mutiny-dartmoor-prison-480052 (accessed 1 May 2020).

Grierson, J. (2019), 'Number of homeless women sent to prison doubles since 2015', *The Guardian*, Jul 3, 2019: https://www.theguardian.com/society/2019/jul/03/number-female-prisoners-recorded-homeless-doubles-since-2015 (accessed 1 May 2020).

Guenther, L. (2013), *Solitary Confinement: Social Death and its Afterlives,* London: University of Minnesota Press.

Habermas, J. (1994), *Justification and Application,* London: MTT Press.

Haiven, M. and Khasnabish, A. (2014), *The Radical Imagination,* London: Zed Books.

Hall, S. (1988), *The Hard Road to Renewal,* London: Verso.

Hall, S., Critcher, C., Jefferson, T., Clark, J., and Roberts, B. (1978), *Policing the Crisis,* London: Macmillan.

Haney, C., Banks, C. and Zimbardo, P. (1973), 'Interpersonal Dynamics in a Simulated Prison', *International Journal of Criminology and Penology* 69(1).

Harding, J. (2020), *Post-War Homelessness Policy in the UK,* London: Palgrave.

Harm and Evidence Research Collaborative (2018), *International Conference on Penal Abolition (ICOPA),* The Open University, Centre for Crime and Justice Studies and Birkbeck University London, 15–18 June 2018.

Hazards Campaign (2018), 'Deaths at Work': http://www.hazardscampaign.org.uk/ (accessed 15 December 2018).

HC Deb (19 December 1945), 'Inmate's Death', Vol. 417, cc. 1492–3W: https://api.parliament.uk/historic-hansard/written-answers/1945/dec/19/inmates-death (accessed 1 May 2020).

HC Deb (20 December 1945), 'Borstal Inmates Death', Vol. 417, cc1596–605: https://api.parliament.uk/historic-hansard/commons/1945/dec/20/borstal-inmates-death (accessed 1 May 2020).

HC Deb (31 May 1956), 'Liverpool Prison', *Vol. 553 cc427–30*: https://api.parliament.uk/historic-hansard/commons/1956/may/31/liverpool-prison (accessed 1 May 2020).

Heller, A. (1974/2018), *The Theory of Need in Marx,* London: Verso.

Hercules, T. (1989), *Labelled a Black Villain*, London: Fourth Estate. Revised edn. Sherfield-on-Loddon: Waterside Press, 2020.

Herman, J. (2015), *Trauma and Recovery,* New York: Basic Books.

Hignett, N.H. (1956), *Portrait in Grey,* London: Frederick Muller.

Holland, S.P. (2000), *Raising the Dead: Readings of Death and (Black) Subjectivity*, Durham: Duke University Press.

Holt, W. (1934), *I Was a Prisoner*, Bristol: Burleigh Press.

Homeless Link (2018), *Working with Prison Leavers*, London: Homeless Link: https://www.homeless.org.uk/sites/default/files/site-attachments/Working%20with%20prison%20leavers%20March%202018.pdf (accessed 1 May 2020).

Hooks, B. (1991), *Ain't I a Woman: Black Women and Feminism*, London: Pluto Press.

House of Commons (1895), Prisons Committee. *Report from the Departmental Committee On Prisons.* (The minutes of evidence, appendices, and index are published separately}, London: Her Majesty's Stationery Office (The Gladstone Report, 1895).

House of Commons (2016), *House of Commons Briefing Paper 7467, Safety in Prisons in England and Wales*, November 30, 2016: https://researchbriefings.parliament.uk/ResearchBriefing/Summary/CBP-7467 (accessed 20 February 2020).

Hudson, B.A. (1993), *Penal Policy and Social Justice*, London: McMillan.

Hudson, B.A. (2003), *Justice in the Risk Society*, London: Sage.

Huey, L. (2012), *Invisible Victims*, Toronto: University of Toronto Press.

Illich, I. (1970), *Deschooling Society*, London: Marion Boyars.

Independent Monitoring Board (2019), *National Annual Report 2017–2018*, London: IMB: https://s3-eu-west-2.amazonaws.com/imb-prod-storage-1ocod6bqkyovo/uploads/2019/06/IMB-NATIONAL-ANNUAL-REPORT-PUBL-5-JUNE-2019.pdf (accessed 29 April 2020).

Ingarden, R. (1964), *Time and Modes of Being*, London: Charles C. Thomas.

INQUEST (2020), 'Deaths in Prison': https://www.inquest.org.uk/deaths-in-prison (accessed 20 May, 2020).

Jagger, A. (1983), *Feminist Politics and Human Nature*, London: Rowman and Littlefield.

JanMohamed, A.R. (2005), *The Death-Bound-Subject: Richard Wright's Archaeology of Death*, Durham: Duke University Press.

Jencks, C. (1994), *The Homeless*, Cambridge: Harvard University Press.

Jewkes, Y. (2002), *Captive Audience: Media, Masculinity and Power in Prisons*, Portland, USA: Willan Publishing.

Johnston, R. (1989), *Inside Out*, Harmondsworth: Penguin Group.

Jones, R.S. and Schmid, T.J. (2000), *Doing Time: Prison Experience an Identity Among First-Time Inmates*, Bingley: JAI Press.

Joseph, H.S. (1853), *Memoirs of Convicted Prisoners*, London: Wertheim and Paternoster Row.

Kane, P. (2011), *Belmarsh Bang-Up: A Newbies Guide to Prison*, London: Createspace.

Kauffmann, P., Kuch, H., Neuhauser, C. and Webster, E. (2011), 'Human Dignity Violated: A Negative Approach'. In: Kauffmann, P., Kuch, H., Neuhauser, C. and

Webster, E. (eds) (2011), *Humiliation, Degradation, Dehumanisation,* London: Springer.

Keith, B. (2006), *The Zahid Mubarek Inquiry,* London: TSO.

Kimberley, E., Talbot, J.G., O'Conor, C.O., Whitbread, S. and Guy, W. (1879), *Royal Commission on Penal Servitude (1878–99)* (Reported 14 July 1879), London: HMSO.

Kirby, T. (2002), *The Model Prisoner,* London: Time Warner Books.

Kropotkin, P. (1887), *In Russian and French Prisons,* London: Ward and Downey.

Kropotkin, P. (1909), *The Great French Revolution,* London: Black Rose Books.

Kropotkin, P. (1913), *The Conquest of Bread and Other Writings,* Cambridge: Cambridge University Press.

Kropotkin, P. (1924), *Ethics,* New York: The Dial Press.

Lacombe, D. (2008), 'Consumed with Sex: The Treatment of Sex Offenders in Risk Society', *British Journal of Criminology,* 48(1), pp 55–74.

Leech, M. (1992), *A Product of the System: My Life In and Out of Prison,* London: Victor Gollancz.

Lefebvre, H. (1991), *The Production of Space,* Oxford: Blackwell.

Leiblich, A., Tuval-Mashiach, R. and Zibler, T. (1998), *Narrative Research,* London: Sage.

Levin, S. (2020), 'Minneapolis lawmakers vow to disband police department in historic move', *The Guardian,* June 8, 2020: https://www.theguardian.com/us-news/2020/jun/07/minneapolis-city-council-defund-police-george-floyd (accessed 30 June 2020).

Lewin, K., Meyers, C.E., Kalhorn, J., Farber, M.L. and French, J.R.P. (1944), *Authority and Frustration Studies in Topological and Vector Psychology III, University of Iowa Studies: Studies in Child Welfare, Volume XX,* Iowa: University of Iowa Press.

Liebling, A. (2004), *Prisons and their Moral Performance,* Oxford: Oxford University Press.

Liebling, A. and Price, D. (1998), 'Staff-Prisoner Relationships', *Prison Service Journal,* 120, pp. 3–6.

Liebling, A. and Price, D. (2005), *The Prison Officer,* Devon: Willan.

Lifton, R. (1992), 'Victims and Survivors'. In: Giamo, B. and Grunberg, J. (eds) (1992), *Homelessness: Frames of Reference,* Iowa: University of Iowa Press.

Loader, I. and Sparks, R. (2011), *Public Criminology?* London: Routledge.

Luban, D. (2015), 'Human Dignity, Humiliation, and Torture'. In: Hiskes, R.P. (ed) (2015), *Human Dignity and the Promise of Human Rights,* New York: Open Society foundations.

Lukes, S. (2005), *Power: A Radical View,* London: Routledge.

Lytton C. (1914), *Prisons and Prisoners: Some Personal Experiences of a Suffragette,* London: William Heinemann.

Malpas, J.E. (1999), *Place and Experience: A Philosophical Topography,* Cambridge: Cambridge University Press.

Malpas, J.E. (2012), 'Suffering, Compassion, and the Possibility of a Humane Politics'. In: Malpas, J. and Lickiss, N. (Eds.) (2012), *Perspectives on Human Suffering,* Netherlands: Springer.

Mathiesen, T. (1974), *The Politics of Abolition* Oxford: Martin Robertson.

Mathiesen, T. (1990), *Prison on Trial,* London: Sage. Third ed. Hook: Waterside Press, 2015.

Mathiesen, T. (2006), *Silently Silenced,* Winchester: Waterside Press.

Matthews, R. (1999), *Doing Time: An Introduction to the Sociology of Imprisonment,* London: MacMillan Press.

Mawer, E. (2006), *Inside the Wire,* London: Author House.

Maybrick, F.E.C. (1905), *Mrs Maybrick's Own Story,* Milton Keynes, UK: Ingrams/Lightning Source.

Mayerfeld, J. (1999), *Suffering and Moral Responsibility,* Oxford: Oxford University Press.

Mayo, P. (1999), *Gramsci, Freire and Adult Education: Possibilities for Transformative Action,* London: Zed books.

McCormack, D. (2014), *Queer Postcolonial Narratives and the Ethics of Witnessing,* London: Bloomsbury.

McVicar, J. (2002), *McVicar by Himself* (2nd Edn.), London: Artnick.

Medlicott, D. (2001), *Surviving the Prison Place,* Aldershot: Ashgate.

Meisenhelder, T. (1985), 'An Essay on Time and the Phenomenology of Imprisonment', *Deviant Behaviour,* 6, pp 39–56.

Merrow Smith, L.W. and Harris, J. (1962), *Prison Screw,* London: Herbert Jenkins.

Meyer, L.S. (2017), *Sentencing in Time,* Massachusetts: Amherst College Press.

Mills, C.W. (1940), 'Situated actions and vocabularies of motive', *American Sociological Review,* 5(6), pp 904–913.

Mills, C.W. (1959), *The sociological imagination,* Oxford: Oxford University Press.

Mills, L. (2003), *Insult to Injury,* Princeton: Princeton Press.

Minneapolis Police Department (MPD) (2020) 'What are we talking about when we talk about 'a police-free future?": https://www.mpd150.com/what-are-we-talking-about-when-we-talk about-a-police-free-future/ (accessed 30 June, 2020).

Moore, L. and Scraton, P. (2014), *The Incarceration of Women,* London: Palgrave Macmillan.

Morran, D. (2013) 'Desisting from Domestic Abuse: Influences, Patterns and Processes in the Lives of Formerly Abusive Men' in *Howard Journal of Criminal Justice,* Volume 52, No 3. pp. 306–320 July 2013.

Morran, D. (2019) 'An Exploration of Neglected Themes in the Development of Domestic Violence Perpetrator Programmes in the UK, Unpublished PhD Thesis, University of Stirling.

Neild, J. (1812/2012), *State of the Prisons in England, Scotland and Wales,* Memphis: General Books.

Newcomen, N. (2017), *Independent Investigation into the Death of Mr John Ahmed a Prisoner at HMP Manchester on 29 July, 2015,* London: Prison and Probation Ombudsman: http://www.ppo.gov.uk/app/uploads/2017/07/L104-15-Death-of-Mr-John-Ahmed-in-hospital-Manchester-29-07-2015-ONN-41-50.pdf. (accessed 1 May 2020).

Nihill, D. (1839), *Prison Discipline in its relations to society and individuals as deterring from crime, and as conducive to personal reformation,* London: J. Hatchard and Son.

O'Brien, M. (2012), *Prisons Exposed,* London: Y Lolfa.

O'Donnell, I. (2014), *Prisoners, Solitude and Time,* Oxford: Oxford University Press.

Olson, M. (2010), 'Politics and the philosophy of life: towards a normative framework'. In: Yorke, J. (ed) (2010), *The right to life and the value of life: orientations in law politics and ethics,* London: Routledge.

Open University (2018), *Grenfell Tower and Social Murder,* Milton Keynes: The Open University.

Open University (2019), *Why we should abolish imprisonment for children and young people* (short OU documentary by Amoah, S., Trofa, C. and Scott, D.), Buckingham: Open Learn, Open University: https://www.youtube.com/watch?v=5SygFXPP6ck (accessed 20 February 2020).

Opotow, S. (1990), 'Moral Exclusion and Injustice', *Journal of Social Issues,* 46(1), pp. 1–20.

Parenti, C. (1999), *Lockdown America,* London: Verso.

Parker, N. (1998), *A Murderer's Life in Britain's Toughest Jail, Parkhurst Tales,* London: Blake.

Paterson, A. (1951), *Paterson on Prisons: Being the collected papers of Sir Alexander Paterson (edited by Ruck, S.K.),* Plymouth: Frederick Muller.

Patterson, O. (1982), *Slavery and Social Death: A Comparative Study*, London: Harvard University Press.

Patterson, O. (1991), *Freedom: Freedom in the Making of Western Culture*, New York: Basic Books.

Peckham, S. (1985), A *Woman in Custody*, London: Fontana Paperbacks.

Pee, H.W. (1917), '112 Days Hard Labour'. In Brock, P. (ed.) (2004), *These Strange Criminals: An Anthology of Prison Memoirs by Conscientious Objectors from The Great War to the Cold War*, Toronto Buffalo London: University of Toronto Press.

Phelan, J. (1940), *Jail Journey*, London: Secker and Warburg.

Polletta, F., Chen, P.C.B., Gardner, B.G. and Motes, A. (2011), 'The Sociology of Storytelling', *Annual Review of Sociology*, 37(1), pp 109–130.

Porowski, M. (1991), 'Human Rights of Prisoners'. In: Lasocik, Z., Platek, M. and Rzeplinska, I. (eds) (1991), *Abolitionism in History*, Warsaw: University of Warsaw.

Pratt, J. (2002), *Punishment and Civilisation: Penal Tolerance and Intolerance in Modern Society*, London: Sage.

Presser, L. (2004), 'Violent Offenders, Moral Selves: Constructing Identities and Accounts in the Research Interview', *Social Problems*, 51, pp 82–101.

Price, J.M. (2015), *Prison and Social Death*, London: Rutgers University Press.

Price, P., Rajagopalan, V., Langeland, G., and Donaghy, P. (2008). 'Domestic Violence Intervention Project Improving Women and Children's Safety: Report and Evaluation of the East London Domestic Violence Service January 2007-September 2008', London: DViP.

Prison Service Journal (2015), 'Reducing Prison Violence' (Special Issue), No 221: https://www.crimeandjustice.org.uk/sites/crimeandjustice.org.uk/files/PSJ%20221%20September%202015.pdf (accessed 11 September 2020)

Prison Reform Trust (1991), *The Identikit Prisoner*, London: Prison Reform Trust.

Prison Reform Trust (2019), *Bromley Briefing*, London: Prison Reform Trust.

Probyn, W. (1977), *Angel Face: The Making of a Criminal*, London: George Allen and Unwin.

Radzinowicz, L. and Hood, R. (1986), *History of English Criminal Law and its Administration From 1750: The Emergence of Penal Policy*, London: Stevens.

Rape Crisis Centre (2020), 'About Sexual Violence': https://rapecrisis.org.uk/get-informed/about-sexual-violence/statistics-sexual-violence/ (accessed 19 May, 2020).

Reade, C. (1856), *It Is Never Too Late To Mend*, London and Glasgow: Collins' Clear-Type Press.

Red Collar Man (1937), *Chokey,* London: Victor Gollancz.

Relph, E. (2008), *Place and Placelessness,* London: Pion limited.

Renvoize, J. (1993), *Innocence Destroyed,* London: Routledge.

Roberts, B. (2002), *Biographical Research,* Buckingham: Open University Press.

Rose, G. (1961), *The Struggle for Penal Reform,* London: Stevens & Sons Limited.

Ruggerio, V. (2012), 'How Public is Public Criminology?', *Crime, Media, Culture: An International Journal,* 8(2).

Rusche, G. and Kirchheimer, O. (2003), *Punishment and Social Structure,* New York: Transaction Press.

Said, E. (1994), *Representations of the intellectual,* New York: Vintage Books.

Salerno, R. (2003), *Landscapes of Abandonment,* New York: State University of New York.

Salmi, J. (1993), *Violence and Democratic Society: New Approaches to Human Rights,* London: Zed books.

Samworth, N. (2018), *Strangeways: A Prison Officer's Story,* London: Sidgwick and Jackson.

Scarry, E. (1985), *The Body in Pain,* Oxford: Oxford University Press.

Schinkel, M. (2014), *Being Imprisoned.* London: Palgrave.

Schmidt, H. (2016), '(In)justice in Prison — A Biographical Perspective'. In: Reeves, C. (ed.) (2016), *Experiencing Imprisonment,* London: Routledge.

Scott, D. (1996*), Heavenly Confinement?* London: LA Press.

Scott, D. (2006a), *Ghosts Beyond Our Realm,* Preston: VDM.

Scott, D. (2006b), 'The Caretakers of Punishment: Prison Officer Personal Authority and the Rule of Law', *Prison Service Journal,* 168, pp 14–19.

Scott, D. (2006c), 'Official Reports'. In: Bennett, J. and Jewkes, Y. (eds) (2006), *Dictionary of Prisons and Punishment,* Devon: Willan.

Scott, D. (2008a), *Penology,* London: Sage.

Scott, D. (2008b), 'Creating Ghosts in the Penal Machine'. In: Bennett, J. and Crewe, B. (eds.) (2008), *Understanding Prison Staff,* London: Routledge.

Scott, D. (2011), '"That's Not My Name": Prisoner Deference and Disciplinarian Prison Officers', *Criminal Justice Matters,* 84(1), pp. 8–9: https://www.tandfonline.com/doi/abs/10.1080/09627251.2011.576015 (accessed 20 May, 2020).

Scott, D. (2012), 'Sympathy for the Devil: Human Rights and the Empathetic Construction of Sufferers', *Criminal Justice Matters,* 88(1).

Scott, D. (2013a), 'The Politics of Prisoner Legal Rights', *Howard Journal of Criminal Justice,* 52(3), pp. 233–250.

Scott, D. (2013b), 'Visualizing an Abolitionist Real Utopia: Principles, Policy and Praxis'. In: Malloch, M. and Munro, W. (eds) (2013), *Crime, Critique and Utopia*, London: Palgrave.

Scott, D. (2014), 'Self Inflicted Deaths'. Official Submission to the Harris Review on Child Deaths in Custody, November 2014: http://iapdeathsincustody.independent.gov.uk/wp-content/uploads/2015/08/Submission-to-Harris-Review-from-Dr-David-Scott.pdf (accessed: 20 February 2020).

Scott, D. (2015a), 'Eating Your Insides Out: Physical, Cultural and Institutionally-Structured Violence in the Prison Place', *Prison Service Journal*, September 2015, 221, pp. 58–62.

Scott, D. (2015b), 'Walking Among the Graves of the Living: Reflections About Doing Prison Research from an Abolitionist Perspective'. In: Drake, D., Earle, R. and Sloan, J. (eds.) (2015), *The Palgrave Handbook of Prison Ethnography*, London: Palgrave.

Scott, D. (2015c), 'Critical Research Values and C. Wright Mills Sociological Imagination'. In: Frauley, J. (ed) (2015), *C. Wright Mills and the Sociological Imagination*, Aldershot: Ashgate.

Scott, D. (2016a), 'Regarding Rights for the Other: Abolitionism and Human Rights From Below'. In: Weber, L., Fishwick, E. and Marmo, M. (eds.) (2017), *Routledge International Handbook of Criminology and Human Rights*, London: Routledge.

Scott, D. (2016b), *Emancipatory Politics and Praxis*, London: EG Press.

Scott, D. (2016c), 'Hearing the Voice of the Estranged Other: Abolitionist Ethical Hermeneutics', *Kriminologisches Journal*, 48(3), pp. 184–202.

Scott, D. (2017), 'When Prison Means Life: Abolishing Child Life Sentences', Keynote address delivered to House of Commons, Houses of Parliament, London, November 15, 2017 (alongside politicians including Rt Hon Sir Keir Starmer, Rt Hon Lucy Powell, Rt Hon Yvette Cooper and Rt Hon David Lammy).

Scott, D. (2018a), *Against Imprisonment: An Anthology of Abolitionist Essays*, Hook: Waterside Press.

Scott, D. (2018b), 'The Ethics of Estrangement'. In: Pavarini, M. and Ferrari, L. (eds) (2018), *No Prison*, London: EG Press.

Scott, D. (2018c), 'How to Reduce the Prison Population: First Steps'. Report submitted to Minister for Prisons (Rt Hon Rory Stewart), May 25, 2018: https://www.academia.edu/38147952/How_To_Reduce_the_Prisons_Population_Starting_Points_Report_for_Prison_Minister (accessed 20 February 2020).

Scott, D. (2018d), 'Taking VAW Seriously and the Promotion of An Anti-violence Alliance', *European Group for the Study of Deviance and Social Control, Newsletter*, 2018: https://www.linkedin.com/pulse/taking-vaw-seriously-promotion-anti-violence-alliance-david-scott/ (accessed 20 May 2020).

Scott, D. (2019a), 'Ordinary Rebels, Everyone: Resisting the Mega Prison'. In: Hart, E., et al *(*ed) (2019), *Resisting the Punitive State,* London: Pluto Press.

Scott, D. (2019b), 'Abolishing Child Imprisonment'. Submission of briefing report to Rt. Hon James Frith for Westminster Hall (Led by Rt. Hon Emma Lewell-Buck), on June 25, 2019: https://publications.parliament.uk/pa/cm201719/cmagenda/fb190620.htm (accessed 19 November 2019).

Scott, D. (2019c) 'Abolitionism as a Philosophy of Hope' in Henne, K. and Shah, R. (eds.), *Routledge Handbook of Public Criminologies*, London: Routledge.

Scott, D. (2020a*)*, *No place like home*, Milton Keynes: Open Learn, Open University: https://www.open.edu/openlearn/society-politics-law/criminology/no-place-home-prisons-and-homelessness?in_menu=1574974 (accessed 9 October 2020).

Scott, D. (2020b), 'Abolitionism Must Come from Below: A Critique of British Anti-Slavery Abolition', *HERC*, June 23, 2020: https://oucriminology.wordpress.com/2020/06/23/abolitionism-must-come-from-below-a-critique-of-british-anti-slavery-abolition/ (accessed 30 June, 2020).

Scott, D. and Codd, H. (2010), *Controversial Issues in Prisons*, Maidenhead: Open University Press.

Scott, D. and Gosling, H. (2016), 'Before Prison, Instead of Prison, Better than Prison: Therapeutic Communities as an Abolitionist Real Utopia', *International Journal for Crime, Justice and Social Democracy,* 5(1), pp. 52–66.

Scott, D. and Sim, J. (2020a), 'Coronavirus and Prisons', *New Socialist,* April 2020.

Scott, D. and Sim, J. (2020b), Legal petition (affidavit), to the High Court on the dangers of the coronavirus (COVID19) to the prison population of England and Wales, official submission of evidence, on request of Kushal Sood, Nottingham Law Centre, March 22, 2020, in preparation for *Davis v Secretary of State for Justice.*

Scott, D. and Sim, J. (2020c), Report for the High Court of Justice (Queens Bench Division) Administrative Court for the case of *R v Secretary of State (ex parte Davis)* official submission of evidence to High Court, on request of Kushal Sood, Nottingham Law Centre, April 12, 2020.

Scott, D. and Sim, J. (2020d), Claim CO/1389/2020–Supplementary Report for the High Court (Queens Bench Division) Administrative Court, official submission of evidence, on request of Kushal Sood, Nottingham Law Centre, April 23, 2020.

Scott, D. and Sim, J. (2020e), 'The Coronavirus Pandemic and Prison policy', Open Learn: Research in time of Covid-19, May 12, 2020: http://fass.open.ac.uk/schools/school-social-sciences-global-studies/blogs/covid-19 (accessed 20 May 2020).

Scraton, P. and McCulloch, J. (2009), *The Violence of Incarceration*, London: Routledge.

Scraton, P., Sim, J. and Skidmore, P. (1991), *Prisons Under Protest*, Milton Keynes: Open University Press.

Sellin, J.T. (1976), *Slavery and the Penal System*, Oxford: Elsevier.

Serge, V. (1929/1970), *Men in Prison*, London: Victor Gollancz.

Shildrick, M. (2002), *Embodying the Monster*, London: Sage.

Sim, J. (1990), *Medical Power in Prisons*, Milton Keynes: Open University Press.

Sim, J. (1994), 'Reforming the Penal Wasteland? A Critical Review of the Wolf Report', pp 31–45. In: Player, E. and Jenkins, M. (eds) (1994), *Prisons After Woolf: Reform Through Riot*, London: Routledge.

Sim, J. (2003), 'Whose Side We are Not On'. In: Tombs, S. and Whyte, D. (eds.) (2003), *Unmasking the Crimes of the Powerful*, Bern: Peter Lang Publishing.

Sim, J. (2008), 'An Inconvenient Penal Truth'. In: Bennett, J., Crewe, B. and Wahidin, A. (eds.) (2008), *Understanding Prison Staff*, Devon, Willan.

Sim, J., Scraton, P. and Gordon, P. (1987), 'Introduction'. In: Scraton, P. (ed.) (1987), *Law, Order and the Authoritarian State*, Milton Keynes: Open University Press.

Smallman, E. (2013), 'Can Group Therapy Cure Domestic Violence', *The Independent*, December 7, 2013: https://www.independent.co.uk/life-style/health-and-families/features/can-group-therapy-cure-domestic-violence-8985289.html (accessed 20 May 2020).

Smart, C. (1989), *Feminism and the Power of Law*, London: Routledge.

Smith, C. (2009), *The Prison the American Imagination*, New Haven: Yale University Press.

Smith, N. ('Razor') (2005), *A Few Kind Words and a Loaded Gun*, London: Penguin.

Smith, S. and Watson, J. (2010), *Reading Autobiography* (2nd edn.), London: University of Minnesota Press.

Sofsky, W. (1993), *The Order of Terror*, Princeton, New Jersey: Princeton University Press.

Sparks, R., Bottoms, A. and Hay, W. (1996), *Prisons and the Problem of Order*, Oxford: Clarendon Press.

Spivak, G.C. (1988), 'Can the Subaltern Speak?'. In: Nelson, C. and Grossberg, L. (eds.) (1988), *Marxism and the Interpretation of Culture,* Illinois: University of Illinois Press.

Stanko, E. (1985), *Intimate Intrusions,* London: Routledge and Kegan Paul.

Stauffer, J. (2015), *Ethical Loneliness: The Injustice of Not Being Heard,* New York: Columbia University Press.

Stratton, B. (1970), *Who Guards the Guards?* London: PROP.

Sudbury, J. (2009), 'Challenging Penal Dependency: Activist Scholars and the Antiprison Movement'. In: Sudbury, J. and Okazawa-Rey, M. (eds.) (2009), *Activist Scholarship: Antiracism, Feminism, and Social Change,* London: Paradigms.

Sudbury, J. and Okazawa-Rey, M. (2009), 'Actavis Scholarship and the Neoliberal University after 9/11'. In: Sudbury, J. and Okazawa-Rey, M. (eds.) (2009), *Activist Scholarship: Antiracism, Feminism, and Social Change,* London: Paradigms.

Svendsen, L. (2014), *A Philosophy of Freedom,* London: Reaktion Books.

Swaaningen, R. van (1997), *Critical Criminology,* London: Sage.

Switzer, A. (2015), 'The Violence of the Super Max: Towards a Phenomenological Aesthetics of Prison Space'. In: Adelsberg, G., Guenther, L. and Zemon, S. (eds.) (2015), *Death and Other Penalties: Philosophy in a Time of Mass Incarceration,* New York: Fordham University Press.

Sykes, G. (1958), *Society of Captives,* New Jersey: Princeton University Press.

The National Audit Office (2020), *Improving the Prison Estate,* London: NAO: https://www.nao.org.uk/report/improving-the-prison-estate/ (accessed 30 April 2020).

Thompson, R. (Pseudonym) (2008), *Screwed: The Truth About Life as a Prison Officer,* London: Headline Publishing Group.

Tombs, S. and Whyte, D. (2017), *The Corporate Criminal,* London: Routledge.

Travis, A. (1999), 'Evidence Mounts of Jail's Brutal Regime "Amounting to Torture",' *The Guardian,* June 16, 1999: https://www.theguardian.com/uk/1999/jun/16/alantravis (accessed 1 May 2020).

Travis, A. (2017a), 'Four "Supersized" Prisons to be Built in England and Wales', *The Guardian,* March 22, 2017: https://www.theguardian.com/society/2017/mar/22/four-supersized-prisons-to-be-built-england-and-wales-elizabeth-truss-plan (accessed 19 November 2019).

Travis, A. (2017b), 'Closures of Ageing Jails on Hold for Five Years as Prison Numbers Soar', *The Guardian,* October 12, 2017: https://www.theguardian.com/society/2017/

oct/12/closures-of-ageing-jails-on-hold-for-five-years-as-prison-numbers-soar (accessed 19 November 2019).

Triston, H.U. (1938), *Men in Cages*, London: John Gifford Limited.

Tuan, Y. (1977), *Space and Place*, London: University of Minnesota Press.

Vick, G. R. (1958), *Inquiry into Allegations of Cruelty by Prison Officers at Walton Jail, Liverpool (Parts One and Two)*, London: House of Commons.

Vitale, A. (2017), *The End of Policing*, London: Verso.

Walker, A. (2019), 'Two-thirds of Homeless Ex-prisoners Reoffend Within a Year'. In: *The Guardian*, Aug 12, 2019: https://www.theguardian.com/society/2019/aug/12/two-thirds-of-homeless-ex-prisoners-reoffend-within-a-year (accessed 1 May 2020).

Walters, R. (2003), *Deviant Knowledge*, London: Routledge.

Wang, J. (2018), *Carceral Capitalism*, California: Semiotext(e).

Ward, J. (1993), *Ambushed*, London: Vermilion.

Warden (Pseudonym) (1929), *'His Majesty's Guests' Secrets of the Cells*, London: Jarrolds.

Warren, D. (1982), *The Key to My Cell*, London: New Park Publications.

Watkins, J., Wulaningsih, W., Zhou, C., Marshall, D.C., Sylianteng, G.D.C., Dela Rosa, P., Miguel, V., Raine, R., King, L.P. and Maruthappu, M.P. (2017), 'Effects of Health and Social Care Spending Constraints on Mortality in England: A Time Trend Analysis', *British Medical Journal*, 7(11) (November 2017): https://bmjopen.bmj.com/content/7/11/e017722 (accessed: 20 May 2020).

Watson, S. and Austerberry, H. (1986), *Housing and Homelessness*, London: Routledge and Kegan Paul.

Welsby, W.N.; Williams, W.J. and Baly, W. (1854), *Royal Commission on Birmingham Borough Prison (1853–4)* (25 January 1854), London: HMSO.

Wildeblood, P. (1957), *Against the Law*, Harmondsworth: Penguin Books.

Wood, S. (1932), *Shades of the Prison House. A Personal Memoir*, London: Williams & Norgate.

Woolf, L.J. (1991), *Prison Disturbances (Part One)*, London: TSO.

Wyner, R. (2003), *From the Inside*, London: Aurum Press.

Zeno (1970), *Life*, London: Pan Books.

Index

A

abandonment *121–138*
Abbott, Jack *147*
abolition *33*
   abolitionism *161–184*
   abolitionist imagination *30, 205, 207*
      'disimagination machine' *166*
   abolitionist scholarship *185*
   of child custody *178*
abuse *30, 113, 207*
   sexual abuse *125*
accountability *172, 178, 191, 222*
activism *48, 161, 172*
   political activism *187*
affirmativity *34*
against the grain *192*
agents of change *182*
agora *171, 179, 192*
Ahmed, John *91*
Alcoff, Linda *72*
alienation *30, 37, 52, 121*
alliances *192*
Andrews, Edward *80*
answerability *212, 228*
antagonism *107*
anxiety *122*
apathy *109*
apprenticeship *182*
'pedagogic apprenticeship' *65, 71, 74*
attachments *123*
austerity *192, 225*
Austin, William *81*
authoritarianism *49*
autobiography *52, 79, 92*
automatons *115, 150*

B

'bad person' *54*
banishment *130*
Bauman, Zygmunt *171, 214*
beating *83*
befriending *222*
behaviour *37*
   cognitive behavioural therapy *221*
   problem behaviour *216, 229*
belonging *123*
Bickershaw *186–206*
Birmingham Prison *80–82*
blame *35, 161, 233*
   'criminal blame' *208*
Blanchot, Maurice *137*
blind eye *92*
boredom *150*
Boyle, Jimmy *89, 121*
Braddock, Bessie MP *87*
Bristol Prison *90*

Brocklehurst, Frederick *114*
Broxson, Tony *195, 201*
brutality *80, 86, 98*
   animal brutality *109*
bullying *75, 85*
Bumiller, Kirstin *220*
'buried alive' *151*
Burney, Christopher *110, 146*
Burnham, Andy *201*

C

Caird, Rod *118, 150*
capacity-building *191, 202, 204*
Carasov, Victor *128*
Cardiff Prison *90*
care *30, 176, 215, 225*
   care homes *125*
cat o' nine tails *85*
CCTV *75, 94, 98*
cell *232*
   cell inspection/spin *38, 133*
   punishment cells *83*
   toilet/lavatory like *54, 128*
Chain Report *127*
chaplain *55, 106*
Chartists *225*
children
   child detention/custody *178, 179*
claustrophobia *151*
coercion *40, 77, 98, 161, 210*
cohesion *215*
Coldingley Prison *232*
Cole, George D H *227–228*
common sense *62, 163, 169–170, 192*
compassion *99, 215*

concentration camp *147*
conflict handling *228*
consciousness-raising *192, 204*
'consent' *77*
control *108*
   control and restraint *91, 128*
coping *156*
COVID-19 *40, 176, 231*
crime
   crime control *235*
   'invisible crime' *217*
Critchley, Simon *210*
Croft-Cooke, Rupert *148, 151*
Cronin, Harley *111*
cruelty *116*
culture
   cultural mediation *54*
   'cultural scripts' *54*

D

Dartmoor Prison *81, 83, 90, 103*
Davis, A Y *231*
Davitt, Michael *83*
Dawkins, Jim *93, 111, 135*
death *29*
   avoidable and premature deaths *224*
   death-bound subject *139*
   death consciousness *30, 139, 156–160*
   deaths in custody *91, 234*
   'living death' *228*
   self-inflicted death *64*
   'symbolic death' *44*
   various forms *33*
deference *95*
degradation *41, 55, 112, 216*

democracy *161*
   democratic accountability *172*
   reclaiming democracy *171–184*
Dempsey, Michelle *218*
Dendrickson, George *103*
desistance *37*
desolation *130*
despair *57*
despotism *112*
detachment *37, 114*
dialogue *72, 198*
   'dialogical transformation' *192*
difference *59, 204*
Diggers Festival *195*
dignity *33, 51, 54, 90, 99, 120, 207, 212, 216–229*
   human dignity *29*
   indignities of prison *109*
disability *125*
disadvantage *125*
discipline *234*
discretion *77*
discriminatory treatment *95*
disease *40*
dissent *167*
distancing
   COVID-19 issues *176*
   psychic distancing *107*
diversity *59*
dividing practices *110*
domination *49, 74, 235*
Doncaster Prison *75*
Dorling, Dany *224*
Douglas, Robert *93, 111, 119*
Drake, Deborah *108*

'dream space' *171, 213*
drugs *154*
due process *59*
Durham Prison *134*
Dussel, Enrique *26, 33, 34, 45, 47, 100, 101, 161, 189, 207*

E

Ede, Chuter *87*
education *37, 165, 189, 235*
eligibility *44, 77*
   less eligible *39, 66, 106*
elitism *173, 189, 235*
empathy *29, 46, 66, 99, 120, 207, 213–229*
employment *125, 235*
'enemy within' *130*
engagement *66*
enmity *110*
equity *212, 227*
estrangement *34, 48, 52, 67, 121–138, 154, 159*
ethics *29, 207*
   affirmative ethics *45*
   discourse ethics *58*
   ethical encounters *204*
   'ethical loneliness' *70*
   'ethical openness' *50*
   feminist ethics *222*
   liberation, etc. ethics *63*
   negative ethics *41*
   socialist ethics *27, 33–50, 212*
   virtue ethics *61*
Europe *75, 97*
example *190*
exclusion *177*

expert witness reports *175*
exploitation *36, 207, 235*

F

face *100*
   phantom faces *99–120*
fairness *59*
fear *122*
   climate of fear *75*
feminism *222*
Fergusson, Harvie *150*
flashbacks *157*
flogging *81*
Floyd, George *234*
force *91*
Forest Bank Prison *94*
Foucault, Michel *52*
Fovargue, Yvonne MP *201*
Frankl, Victor *147*
freedom *27, 47, 120, 176*
   positive freedoms *227*
Freire, Paulo *169*
Fricker, Miranda *61*

G

G4S *179*
'ghosting' *134*
Giroux, Henry *166*
Gladstone Report *40, 83–86*
Glen Parva *90*
Gouldner, Alvin *108*
Gramsci, Antonio *168, 188, 208*

H

hanging *81*

harm *35, 58, 99*
   criminal harms *207*
   harms of the powerful *211*
   hidden harms *229*
   self-harm *64, 118, 179*
   state-corporate harms *226*
   zero harm *179*
hazards *175*
   Hazards Campaign *226*
healing *222*
health *39, 234*
Hercules, Trevor *109, 115, 131, 151, 155*
hermeneutics *51–74, 212*
hierarchy *48, 99, 165, 190, 227*
   sexist hierarchies *222*
Hignett, Norman Howarth *104, 115, 133*
Hindley Prison *186, 195*
HIV *40*
home *123–138*
   homelessness *122, 125, 129*
Home Office *40*
homicide *224*
hope *161, 162, 182–184*
   loss of hope *141*
hostility *36, 82, 107*
housing *235*
Hudson, Barbara *46, 59*
Hull *221*
   Hull Prison *175*
humanity *51*
   common humanity *47, 120, 182*
   dehumanisation *112*
   human connectedness *33*
   human flourishing *223*
   human needs *129*

human rights *34, 49*
human vitality *182*
Universal Declaration of Human Rights *49*
humiliation *34, 57, 109*
hunger strike *154*
hurt *99*

I

identity *70, 124*
idleness *36, 150*
Illich, Ivan *166, 181*
impotence *89*
Independent Monitoring Board *98, 232*
indifference *109, 114*
Ingarden, Roman *143*
inmate. See *prison: prisoners*
inspection *98*
intellectuals *167*
  intellectual capital *181*
interpretation *71, 73*
intimacy *54*
invisibility *122*
isolation *38*

J

JanMohamed, Abdul *159*
Jewkes, Yvonne *154*
Jones, John *81*
judicial review *176*
justice *51, 105*
  justice for all *35, 68, 74*
  procedural justice *59*
  Reclaim Justice Network *178*
  social justice *183, 191*
  transformative justice *222*
  Justice, Power and Resistance *180*
justification *92, 229*

K

Kane, Paddy *133*
kindness *103, 137*
knowledge *181*
  counter-carceral knowledge *181*
  local knowledge *191*
Kropotkin, Peter *33, 120, 139, 189, 208*

L

labelling *54, 69, 109, 219*
Labour Party *200*
language *171*
law *176*
  law and order *211, 231*
  repressive penal law *228*
leadership *204*
learning
  collective learning *168*
  learning communities *181*
  learning to learn *73*
  self-motivated learning *181*
  unlearning *191*
Leech, Mark *89, 113*
Lefebvre, Henri *141, 142*
legitimacy *46, 76, 120, 173, 177*
  cloak of penal legitimacy *56*
lethargy *150*
Lewin, Kurt *158*
liberty *101, 106*
  deprivation of liberty *121*
life *34, 207*

'bare life' *121, 129*
life-world *70, 73, 123, 139, 222*
paradigm of life *29, 46, 63, 120, 171, 223*
right to life *120*
listening *51, 182, 191*
unprejudiced listening *61*
literacy
criminological literacy *73*
emotional literacy *102*
penological literacy *62, 171, 192*
Liverpool *195*
Liverpool Prison *75, 87*
Long Lartin Prison *232*
Lushington, Sir Geoffrey *40*
Lytton, Lady Constance *115*

M

Manchester
Manchester Prison *90, 195*
marginalisation *173*
masculinist bias *235*
mask *115*
Matthews, Roger *141, 143*
Mawer, Elizabeth *95, 118, 134*
Maybrick, Florence *151*
Mayerfeld, James *57*
McVicar, John *134*
media *98, 179, 203*
mediation *210, 227*
non-coercive mediator state *228*
Medlicott, Diana *146*
Meisenhelder, Thomas *154*
melancholy *150, 158*
mental health *62, 71, 126, 235*
Merrow Smith, L W *111*

Millbank Penitentiary *106*
Minneapolis *234*
monotony *103, 150, 155*
morality *34*
flawed moral character *77*
moral conversations *59*
moral deficit *210*
moral exclusion *99*
moral inclusion *221*
moral leadership *204*
morally tainted individuals *97*
prison morality *54*
murder *210, 224*
social murder *225*
myths *183, 192*
punitive myths *163*

N

National Audit Office *232*
needs *157*
'necessary needs' *226*
negativity *34, 136*
negative consequentialism *56, 65*
neglect *157*
negotiation *194*
negotiating strategy *205*
NHS *196*
niggling *109*
nightmares *157*
Nihill, Reverend Daniel *106*
'Not in My Back Yard' *198*
Nottingham Prison *232*
numbness *116*

O

O'Brien, Michael *117*
Olson, Mark *223*
ombudman. See *Prison Ombudsmen*
omission
  acts of omission *225*
openness *66*
oppression *192*
ordinary rebels *185–206, 234*
Othering *44, 52, 67, 106, 212*
  psychic Othering *107*

P

pain *28, 70, 116, 233*
Parker, Norman *116*
Parkhurst Prison *82*
Paterson, Sir Alexander *185, 228*
patriarchal values *219*
Patterson, Orlando *44, 141*
payback *96*
peace officers *235*
Pee, Hubert *112*
penal. See *punishment*
Pentonville Prison *232*
Phelan, Jim *149*
Pies Not Prisons *195*
place *123, 136*
politics
  emancipatory politics *167*
  local politics *201*
Porowski, Michal *41*
Portland Borstal/Prison *84, 86*
positive imagery *219*
poverty *207*
power *44, 176, 227*

  contesting state, etc. power *178*
  power based on difference *192*
  power dynamics *107*
  powerlessness *38, 57, 101, 109*
praxis *28, 182, 195, 205*
prison
  architectural blandness *132*
  cesspools *185, 228, 232*
  costly environments *185*
  HM Chief Inspector *232*
  mega prisons *179, 186*
  pits of human misery *34*
  prison code *37*
  prisoners
    black prisoners *234*
    pathological prisoners *97*
    prisoner narratives *53*
    research with *174*
    testimonies *175*
    un-naming *111*
    'unproductive' people *125*
  prison officers
    deference to *77*
    Prison Officers Association *98, 200*
  Prison Ombudsmen *98*
  prison puzzle *33–50, 209*
  prisons within prisons *38*
  'prison works' *183*
  'schools for scoundrels' *37*
  warehouses for the unwanted *122*
  width of imprisonment *107*
privacy *54*
privilege *189*
Probyn, Walter *109*
profit *80, 212*

protest *167*
   dirty protests *117*
psychology *221*
   'psychic distancing' *106*
   psychological injury *130*
   psychological survival *141, 153*
public space. See *space*
Pucklechurch Prison *90, 94*
punishment *185*
   'caretakers of punishment' *108*
   moral legitimacy *228*
   non-punitiveness *171*
     non-punitive intervention *183*
   penal paralysis *158*
   penal rationale *74*
   penal stasis *150*
   punishment cells *83*
Pūras, Dainius *178*
purpose *158*

Q

quality
   quality of mind *215–216, 224*
   quality time *145*

R

racism *235*
rape crisis centres *220*
Red Collar Man *85*
redemption *106*
redress *162, 228*
reform *55*
   limitations *35*
rehabilitation *35*
   rehabilitative myths *55*

relationships *37, 100, 121, 123, 146, 222*
   'forced relationality' *128*
   Relationships Foundation *107*
Relph, Edward *132*
remedy *213*
repair *162, 209, 228*
repression *74, 98, 235*
resettlement *45*
resistance *135, 167*
respect *61, 78, 97, 100, 185*
responsibility *39*
retaliation *96*
rhetoric *233*
rootedness *123*
Royal Commission
   1879 *82*
Ruggiero, Vincenzo *163*

S

sadness *131*
safety *75, 221*
Said, Edward *163*
Samworth, Neil *94, 111*
sanitation *232*
Scarry, Elaine *70*
search *133*
security *234*
   insecurity *122*
segregation *38, 83, 94*
self *67, 139*
   collapse of self *70*
   self-esteem *169*
   self-harm. See *harm*
   sense of self *114, 122*
Serge, Victor *146, 152, 185*

shame *41*
Shaw, Lord Justice *175*
silencing *53, 66, 69, 72, 174*
  self-silencing *73*
Sim, Joe *21, 43, 52, 176*
slavery *27, 30, 159*
  'slave' labour *36*
slopping out *90*
Smart, Carole *175*
Smith, Caleb *142*
Smith, Razor *104*
socialist ethics *27*
solidarity *46, 182*
solitary confinement *71*
South Hindley *199*
space *80, 171, 193*
Spivak, Gayatri Chakravorty *72*
Stanford Prison Experiment *57*
status *227*
Stauffer, Gill *74*
stereotyping *107*
  discriminatory stereotyping *74*
sterility *132*
Stocken Prison *176*
storytelling *194*
straightjacket *81, 85*
strangers *46, 215*. See also *Othering*
Stratton, Brian *88*
Strength to Change *221*
strip search *91*
suffering *33, 70, 99*
suicide *34, 157*
support *225*
  intensive support *222*
surveillance *98*

survivalism *121, 126*
  psychological survival *141, 153*
Swaaningen, Rene van *59*
Switzer, Adrian *132*

T

technology *98*
therapy *221, 235*
  'Duluth model' *222*
Thompson, Ronnie *111, 117*
time
  empty/heavy/wasted, etc. time *145*
  'ghosts of time' *157*
  marking time *154*
  prison time *144*
  quality time *145*
  'space-time' *142*
  suspended animation *148*
  time consciousness *62, 139, 233*
tiredness *150*
torture *82, 91, 97*
trauma *183*
treatment
  degrading, etc treatment *30*
Triston, H U *117*
trust *182*
truth *61, 71, 163*
  knowledge as 'truth' *177*
  'regime of truth' *177*
  truth to power *170*
tuberculosis *40*
typhus *40*

U

university *165–166*

unwanted people *136*

V

Vick, Sir Godfrey Russell *87*
victimhood *47, 51, 99, 214*
'view from below' *235*
violence *30, 42*
   'cultural violence' *78*
   institutionally-structured violence *65, 129, 224*
   normalisation *95*
   preventive strike *76*
   prisoner violence *78*
   prison officer violence *50, 75*
   righteous violence *97*
   state violence *98*
   'symbolic violence' *55*
   violence against women. See *women*
   visibility *77*
voice *51, 79, 90, 191, 198*
   'co-authored' *70*
   diverse voices *172*
   marginalised voices *173*
   subjugated voices *177*
   'ventriloquized' *69*
vulnerability *57, 109*

W

Ward, Judith *113*
Warren, Des *114*
wealth *227*
welfare *183, 196, 227*
   welfare cuts *225*
wellbeing *39, 100*
whitewash *177*

Wigan *194*
Wildeblood, Peter *115*
wisdom
   received wisdom *192*
women
   'escape routes' *220*
   violence against women *217*
   women's shelters *220*
Woolf, Lord (Justice) *59, 90*
World Without Prisons *180*
Wormwood Scrubs *75, 91, 104, 112*
worth *158*
wounds *183*
Wright Mills, Charles *215*
writing *172*
Wyner, Ruth *105, 116, 130, 152*

Z

zero harm. See *harm*
zombies *116*

Against Imprisonment

An Anthology of Abolitionist Essays
by David Scott
With a Foreword by Emma Bell

A collection of writings by Dr David Scott which build on his work teaching criminology for over 20 years. *Against Imprisonment* includes topics such as 'The Changing Face of the Prison', justifications of punishment, prison violence and the shortcomings of prisons and mega prisons. Readers seeking further background and information concerning prison-related abolitionist issues may wish to note that *Against Imprisonment* is the book that carved out the foundations for the narrative, themes, argument and call to action now set out by the author in *For Abolition*.

Paperback and ebook | ISBN 978-1-909976-54-2 | 2018 | 272 pages

www.WatersidePress.co.uk